Y0-AGT-856

MUSIC IN AMERICAN LIFE

A list of books in the series appears at the end of this book.

The Never-Ending Revival

ROUNDER RECORDS
AND THE
FOLK ALLIANCE

Michael F. Scully

University of Illinois Press
Urbana and Chicago

© 2008 by the Board of Trustees
of the University of Illinois
All rights reserved
Manufactured in the United States of America
C 5 4 3 2 1
∞ This book is printed on acid-free paper.

Library of Congress Cataloging-in-Publication Data
Scully, Michael F.
The never-ending revival : Rounder Records and the
Folk Alliance / Michael F. Scully.
p.   cm. — (Music in American life)
Includes index.
ISBN 10 0-252-03333-7 (cloth : alk. paper)
ISBN 13 978-0-252-03333-9 (cloth : alk. paper)
1. Folk music—United States—History and criticism.
2. Sound recording industry—United States—Social aspects.
I. Rounder Records (Firm) II. North American Folk Music
and Dance Alliance. III. Title.
ML3551.S38   2008
781.62'13—dc22   2007030909

To Doreen, Colin, and Kara, with love,
and to the memory of Phil Ochs

Contents

Acknowledgments

Three people are so central to my work that I could not have completed this book without them. My wife, Doreen Lorenzo, provided unquestioning love and support through years of research and writing. Archie Green has been a friend, mentor, tutor, and inspiration. My good friend Randy Pitts not only provided steady encouragement but also shared his encyclopedic knowledge of vernacular music and the folk music industry over the course of countless discussions and music listening sessions. I could not imagine a better companion on our numerous musical road trips.

All of my interview subjects, whom I identify in "Note on Citations," gave selflessly of their time and knowledge. The Rounder founders—Ken Irwin, Bill Nowlin, and Marian Leighton—were particularly generous. They spent hours answering questions, provided access to certain company records, offered introductions to others, and reviewed early versions of the manuscript to help me correct factual errors. Although I suspect that I have made statements with which they disagree, they approached this project in a spirit of intellectual honesty, understanding that the recounting of history inevitably involves subjective interpretation. They never asked for textual control, and they did not review the final manuscript. Any errors that remain are mine.

Phyllis Barney, onetime Folk Alliance executive director, gave generously of her time and provided me with access to Alliance archival material. Margo Blevin and Mark Moss read portions of the manuscript in draft and helped me gain a fuller understanding of the Alliance. Sharon Sandomirsky offered insight into the old-time music scene. Jeffrey Meikle provided encouragement, wisdom, and textual advice. Mark C. Smith, Bill Stott, Richard Flores, Douglas Foley, Ronald D. Cohen, and Ed Cray all helped shape my thinking, and the project is better for their involvement. Lara Pellegrinelli generously allowed me to quote from her detailed interviews with the Rounders. Jennifer Cutting provided reference assistance at the Archive of Folk Culture at the U.S. Library of Congress. Writers Julie Ardery and Lynne Margolis offered useful advice regarding publication. My children, Colin and Kara, provided me with untold joy and a sense of purpose through the years of research and writing. To everyone mentioned, and to any of my able advisers whom I have omitted inadvertently, I offer my deepest thanks.

The Never-Ending Revival

Where Have All the Folkies Gone?

In the second week of February 2006, the Hilton Hotel in downtown Austin, Texas, is doing what it does throughout much of the year—hosting a large business conference with participants from across the United States and overseas. The talk inside is the stuff of many such conferences, revolving around manufacturing, marketing, sales, budgets, and continuing professional education. This week, however, conference participants also speak of such intangibles as the role of tradition in American life, the importance of racial and ethnic heritage, and the meaning of community. They discuss concerns about the mixture of art and commerce and, sometimes with an ironic nod to the sterile nature of their locale, the danger posed by the increasing standardization of American life. Paradoxically, these varied subjects are commingled as conference participants school themselves in more efficient methods of packaging and selling the tradition, heritage, and sense of community that most of them claim to value. A cynic could have a field day here, mocking the perceived hypocrisy of one more group of hucksters, drinking in a hotel bar while figuring out how to commodify and profit from that which they claim is sacred. A closer look, however, might give this cynic pause.

The first hint that something more than mere profiteering is afoot is the music. It is everywhere. For five days the conference takes place amid a backdrop of music—music in the lobbies, in the hallways and meeting rooms, and, throughout the night, in guestrooms that are open to any casual wanderer. This is not the mellow "musical wallpaper" so prevalent in commercial buildings. Nor is it the music of mainstream radio, whether top-40, urban contemporary, classic rock, or any other standard format driven by listener demographics and target markets. This music is live and of a type virtually never heard on commercial radio. Musical instruments abound. There is an abundance of acoustic guitars, but also banjos, fiddles, and dulcimers. There are harmonicas, accordions, and bagpipes. There is bluegrass and old-time Appalachian fiddling, acoustic blues and gospel, a cappella mountain ballads and polka. There are songs that recount historic events and a plethora of deeply personal, confessional tunes of the type made famous by Joni Mitchell and James Taylor, circa the early 1970s. There is neither hip-hop nor teen pop. There is no grunge, no metal, and none of the contemporary, vaguely discolike dance music that fills the airwaves. Conference attendees perform virtually all of the music that saturates the hotel, and the sheer magnitude and strangeness of it force one to dig beneath the surface to determine just what this gathering is about.

From February 10 through February 14, 2006, the Austin Hilton hosted the Eighteenth Annual International Conference of the North American Folk Music and Dance Alliance, referred to popularly as the Folk Alliance. Founded in 1989, the Alliance exists "to foster and promote traditional, contemporary and multicultural folk music and dance."[1] Once a year the organization holds the international conference that constitutes its primary activity. The gathering brings together record label executives, booking agents, concert promoters, instrument makers, recording engineers, and musicians. They assemble to discuss folk music, defined here loosely—and just for the moment—as music that is rooted in the long-held traditions of disparate indigenous groups, whether those groups are characterized by race, ethnicity, geography, occupation, or some other unifying trait. Viewed narrowly, it is the goal of Folk Alliance members to take this music, which many consider the noncommercial expression of core community identity, and sell it, while respecting the uniqueness and value of both the art and the groups from which it flows. It is a seemingly contradictory exercise, fraught with the possibility of oversimplification, misrepresentation, and exploitation. Many Alliance members are aware of these perils, which have accompanied the promotion of folk culture in America for more than one hundred years. How folk music aficionados confront these difficulties at the dawn of the twenty-first century is the subject of this book.

I discovered the Folk Alliance in early 1993 through a *Sing Out!* magazine notice promoting its upcoming conference, held that year in Tucson, Arizona.[2] At the time I was a commercial litigator in San Francisco, growing increasingly bored with the practice of law. I was also a baby boomer and consummate music fan who, like many of my contemporaries, had lost touch with the popular music of the day. Hip-hop hadn't touched me. As far as rock was concerned, it's not that I disliked REM or Pearl Jam or other then-contemporary bands that I might have worshiped fifteen years earlier but that I was unfamiliar with them. Preoccupied with burgeoning family and professional responsibilities, I had stopped listening. Hoping to stem my boredom, I embarked on a conscious effort to enjoy music once more, and I began by turning to the familiar. In my case that was not the so-called classic rock that blossomed between 1967 and 1975, with which I was fairly well versed, but the popular "folk music" that flourished commercially in the late fifties and early sixties.

During those years the American entertainment industry invested heavily in folk music—or something called folk music—as a popular and profitable commercial commodity. So-called folksingers sold millions of records and concert tickets. New folk music stars, such as Bob Dylan and Joan Baez, launched lucrative and long-running music industry careers. Book and magazine publishers, instrument makers, and manufacturers of such products as liquor and cigarettes all sought to capitalize commercially on the folk music craze.[3]

Strictly speaking, a "commercial folk song" is an oxymoron. As traditionally understood, a folk song is an ancient artifact of unknown origin, one that has survived through oral transmission within and among relatively insular indigenous communities. Folk music is functional and participatory. It is the naturally occurring, noncommercial music that forms a part of everyday life—music performed at weddings and funerals, in the workplace, and amid children at play. Historically, the term does not refer to music presented in ready-made form, for profit, to a mass audience seeking passive entertainment. Thus, the sixties folk song movement rested on a contradiction. Participants valorized folk music as organic, informal, and community based. They then took that music and, motivated by respect, nostalgia, or the possibility of profit, presented it to a distant public, altering radically the context that captivated adherents in the first place.

Many participants in the sixties folk phenomenon, though aware of the problem posed by decontextualization, cared deeply about the preservation and presentation of genuine, noncommercial, indigenous expression. Working through a nationwide circuit of music festivals, small clubs, and independent record labels, these activists sought, studied, and promoted songs, musical styles, and performers from nonmainstream American sub-cultures, with a particular emphasis on the music of the rural American South. Still, the vast majority who experienced folk music in the 1960s did not hear genuinely traditional folk expression. Instead, they enjoyed com-mercial arrangements of a repertoire derived from folk sources, and newly composed songs characterized, often for economic reasons, as folk songs. Millions loved "Tom Dooley," the Kingston Trio hit that ushered in the commercial folk craze. Recorded in a highly polished style and performed by clean-cut professional entertainers with a well-honed, easy-on-the-ears stage act, it was a perfect expression of the commodification of folk culture that proved so popular at that time. Those troubled by its success believed that, as presented, it communicated nothing about the history, present-day conditions, and musical style of its Appalachian source, subjects of tremen-dous importance to the romantic adventurers who roamed America's remote corners in search of truly local cultural expression.

Whether manifested through a polished concert performance, an old hillbilly record, or a staged re-creation of freedom marchers raising their voices in song, the collective activity surrounding folk music's presence in mass culture during the early sixties came to be known as the "folk song revival." The phrase is a contested one. Folklorist Neil Rosenberg, conscious of the extent to which folk music became a popular phenomenon, refers to the period more colloquially as the "great boom." Ralph Rinzler, who, from the 1950s to the 1990s, promoted indigenous culture as a musician, commercial entrepreneur, and government programmer, characterized the movement as one marked not by revival but by the "arrival" of a folk music awareness among an educated, urban, consumer society.[4] Rinzler's astute wordplay recognizes at least two truisms. First, in an unbroken line, up to and through the 1960s, Americans produced and disseminated noncom-mercial, community-based music as an unself-conscious part of their daily lives. Second, the conscious promotion of folk culture by those outside the culture in question—those promoting their own commercial, social, or po-litical agendas—predated the sixties by many decades.[5] The discovery and commodification of folk music by broad segments of 1960s society did not "revive" that which had never died.

In certain instances, however, the term *revival* is literally precise. For example, during the sixties, activists helped reinvigorate traditional Cajun music within its Louisiana home. Folklorist Archie Green acknowledges that true "revival" was part of the sixties phenomenon but adds that the movement also encompassed the "survival" of indigenous forms within enclaved communities and the "arrival" of such forms as they traveled "from special group to large society." Recognizing that language must strike a balance between communicative convenience and literal precision, Green concludes that *revival* was the best word to describe the "cultural explosion, sales boom, and expansion in consciousness about expressive matters" that characterized the early sixties.[6]

Born in 1954, I was too young to have experienced the revival as it occurred. I came to it in early 1968, in a moment that I recall with great clarity. Walking into the living room of my family's home in Queens, New York City, I saw a guitarist on television singing an explicit antiwar song, a type of song that I had never before heard. "Phil Ochs," said my older sister. At the time, I was a precocious thirteen-year-old with an incipient political consciousness and a developing fascination with the growing anti–Vietnam War movement. I fancied myself a fan of Bob Dylan and Peter, Paul and Mary, though I knew nothing of the context in which their careers developed, and I did not truly understand Dylan. I had never heard of Ochs but was immediately in awe of him. I quickly purchased his three albums on Elektra Records, which consisted almost entirely of topical songs drawn, as Ochs acknowledged proudly, from the day's headlines.[7]

The song I had heard on television was "I Ain't Marchin' Anymore," from the 1965 album of the same name. By the time I discovered it, the tune had become an antiwar anthem, though neither it nor Ochs had enjoyed anything approaching mainstream success. Like almost every song on those three records, its lyric was a straightforward expression of Ochs' leftist sociopolitical beliefs. As other albums revealed, Ochs' art was already moving beyond overt political commentary, but the topical explicitness of his earliest work was perfect, in my case, for educating a teenager ready to embrace the language of leftist "movement culture." I listened to those records virtually nonstop in that tumultuous year, 1968, leading my sister to joke that our neighbors, hearing the subversive sounds emanating from my bedroom window, would surely be calling the FBI. Now, whenever I hear someone pose the insoluble question of whether art can truly mold beliefs,

I remember that Ochs' lyrical commitment to humanism, pluralism, and genuine democracy shapes my political value system to this day.

I read everything I could find about Phil Ochs and quickly discovered the links between him and Bob Dylan and the coterie of New York performers who had been part of the folk song movement. I explored Dylan's early protest albums more thoroughly than I already had and purchased records—some recorded years earlier—by other Ochs contemporaries, such as Tom Paxton, Eric Andersen, Joan Baez, and Dave Van Ronk. Although I discovered North Carolina's Doc Watson during this period, I did not develop any broader interest in the older rural "source singers" whom, I learned later, many considered the more authentic folk performers. Nor, beyond Peter, Paul and Mary, was I interested in the numerous folk vocal groups that flourished in the wake of the Kingston Trio, such as the Brothers Four or the Limeliters. I considered such groups too smooth and corny for consideration. Cultivating my own absurdly romantic self-image—I was then an eighth grader at Sacred Heart Catholic Elementary School—I favored bohemians who, like Ochs, sang political songs or, like Baez, presented ballads free of stereotypical show-business adornment or, like Van Ronk, sang with some noncommercial grit in their voices. They were more accessible than someone like Clarence Ashley, the rediscovered Appalachian balladeer who first recorded in the 1920s, and, I knew intuitively, far cooler than those blatant show-business stylists the New Christy Minstrels and their vapid ilk.[8]

As I pursued this musical journey in the late 1960s, I was completely ignorant regarding the construct of the "folk," and I had no idea what it meant to be a folksinger or sing a folk song. I adopted an ad hoc definition that I shared with many, one that still thrives and continues to bedevil those who recognize *folk* as a term of art with a complex lineage. To me, a folksinger was someone who sang to the accompaniment of his or her own acoustic guitar. There might be other instruments in the mix, but they appeared sparingly and never interfered with the lyric, which was often political or historical and always demanded careful listening. For the most part, I believed, folksingers lived in New York's Greenwich Village or, at the very least, hung out there a lot, with other folksingers. I had never heard of the folk song revival. Nor did I know that this revival was purportedly over—extinguished, some claimed, a few years earlier at the Newport Folk Festival by Bob Dylan's electrified rock, in a "treasonous" yet overpowering rebuke to the acoustic protest movement that had brought him fame. I had never heard of the Newport Folk Festival.

Time passed, and during the 1970s I learned that these early musical heroes had played a major role in a cultural phenomenon that sought—imperfectly—to present and interpret disparate American cultures to a mass audience, an audience far removed in time and space from the varied cultures presented. Eventually, I did listen to Clarence Ashley and other "hillbilly" and "country blues" performers who had been so important to some revival activists. I dipped my toes into bluegrass and developed a strong appreciation for electric blues, which I understood, dimly, grew from indigenous African American expression. I enjoyed performers such as John Prine and Steve Forbert, two of the many singer-songwriters that the media trumpeted as "New Dylans." But I never pulled these varied strands together until the early 1990s. Clarence Ashley notwithstanding, I never analyzed my working definition of a folksinger as a Greenwich Village habitué with a guitar. I certainly never thought about what it meant to refer to something—such as music, or people—as "folk." To me, folk was an interesting, slightly subversive musical genre—a record store label that guided my consumer selections. There was classical music, jazz, rock, and folk.

All this changed as I listened again to my old records. With the enthusiasm of any newly committed hobbyist, I began a thorough exploration of precisely who these diverse folk artists were and why, during the sixties, they shared space on festival stages and recorded anthologies. I spent my free time at the library, poring through old newspapers and magazines in search of artist profiles or concert and record reviews, all circa 1960. I learned about John and Alan Lomax, the largely self-taught folklorists who, in the first half of the twentieth century, traveled the country recording artists and songs, providing much raw material for the sixties folk boom. Fancying myself something of a latter-day Lomax, I hoped to reconstruct artistic life in the Greenwich Village clubs and bars that possessed those fascinating names like the Gaslight, the Kettle of Fish, and Gerde's Folk City. Along with my wife, a filmmaker and then the owner of a small commercial production company, I set out to interview revival stalwarts such as Tom Paxton, Dave Van Ronk, and even the legendary Pete Seeger. To our astonishment, everyone whom we approached agreed, and—until faltering finances intervened—we built a small library of audiotaped or filmed interviews.

Very rapidly, I learned that the Village constituted only one of several cohesive geographic scenes and that similar "folk enclaves" had existed in Boston and Cambridge, in the San Francisco Bay Area, in Chicago, in Ann Arbor, and elsewhere. As I examined newspaper accounts of activity in those cities, I noted for the first time the breadth of performance styles that fell within the revival penumbra. Ochs, Baez, and Van Ronk were there, to be sure, as were the Appalachian and acoustic blues performers whom I had first heard as a teenager. But there was also Cajun music and Yiddish music and calypso and sometimes a smattering of miscellaneous European song that I could only characterize as "international." My confusion grew as I realized that I did not truly understand the forces that linked these disparate genres.

My ad hoc education also alerted me to the debate that raged in the sixties about whether specific performers and performances served as sufficiently authentic representatives of particular musical genres and the cultures from which they grew. Could Dave Van Ronk, a white man born in Brooklyn, New York, sing the blues? Did he exemplify an African American idiom, or a white man's honorable interpretation of that idiom, or was he a twentieth-century minstrel—a bad joke that undermined the civil rights revolution flowering around him? Did a twenty-minute presentation of Cajun music, transplanted from its community moorings to a northern festival stage, provide an elevating glimpse of Louisiana culture? Was it, instead, a freak-ish, commodified distortion that somehow trivialized Cajun life? Did the answer change if the music was or was not performed by native Cajuns? Did these issues need to be raised at all? Wasn't this simply entertainment? My effort to understand the importance of these questions—let alone answer them—forced me to formulate and confront those more basic questions that, I know now, are the subject of more than a century of inquiry—who are the folk, what is folk music, why do we study it, and what is the impact of such study?

These questions give rise to an important distinction, one that is central to my subject. Applying ancient—and admittedly changing—definitions, I am writing not about traditional folksingers as such but about folk revivalists. If the concept of an enclaved folk has meaning, then traditional performers are members of that folk and their singing is neither a commercial enterprise nor the dedicated pursuit of a hobby revolving around organizations and scheduled events. It is, instead, a more-or-less unself-conscious part of daily life. Folksinging, as I suggested at the outset, accompanies ordinary activity, whether that be work, worship, mourning, or nonprofessional community entertainment. Since people do not use academic terminology to label their own lives, many whom revivalists treasure as "true" folksingers do not consider themselves members of the folk—whatever that may be—and they do not think of their songs as folk songs.

Revivalists, by contrast, tend to be self-conscious folk song interpreters, not genuine, tradition-based folksingers. Finding personal meaning in some often highly idiosyncratic idea of the folk, they seek out songs or styles defined as folk and derive emotional satisfaction from the fact of that definition, apart from whatever satisfaction stems from the music itself. The best expression of this distinction known to me is that of I. Sheldon Posen, who is both a professional folklorist and a singer of songs. Posen, who grew up in Toronto as a member of the urban middle class, threw himself into the folk revival in the 1960s. A true devotee, he performed only material he could define as traditional—whether or not it had anything to do with any of his personal traditions. In 1970, seeking to further his devotion, he enrolled in a graduate program in folklore, an act that shattered the constructs that previously guided his performing career.[9]

Academic fieldwork led Posen to the home of a Newfoundland fisherman, where he discovered an entire community that reveled in informal singing and knew many old, indigenous regional songs. Watching these neighbors sitting together, grasping hands as they sang, for their own enjoyment, songs they learned from one another, sent Posen into an existential tailspin. "This," he decided, was "the real thing; this is how it should be done." The corollary to this striking discovery was that Posen's own activities as a so-called folksinger were entirely artificial or, to use the folklorist's vernacular, inauthentic. He was prone to getting onstage in front of a sea of strangers where he engaged in what suddenly seemed a ghastly charade, singing a diverse grab bag of songs to which neither he nor most of his audience had any family, community, or occupational connection. The realization was so disorienting that, for a time, he stopped singing in public. He had, he observes wryly, "authenticized myself out of the folksong business."[10]

It took Posen several years of study and reflection before he could reconcile his own singing with his new understanding of noncommercial community culture. Ultimately, he concluded that authenticity was relative and dependant wholly on context. No matter what songs he sang, no matter how well he mastered the appropriate musical idiom, he accepted that he could never be an "authentic" Newfoundland singer. Moreover, he realized that if he brought those Newfoundlanders to a revival stage, the resulting performance could never be a genuine representation of informal community expression. In each case, however, the performance might be artful, enjoyable, and educational, in addition to being an authentic reflection of the processes and values of one particular "folk group," that of the folk music revivalist. Able to perform publicly once more, Posen realized that he could sing whatever he pleased, in whatever style he pleased, without agonizing about the fact that he was neither a Newfoundlander nor a fisherman nor, for that matter, a Mississippi sharecropper. He was, he realized, an authentic revivalist, and, in singing songs from traditions not his own, he "was doing what an urban folkie was supposed to be doing as a properly functioning member of the folksong revival."[11]

Although Posen came to personal terms with the theoretical vagaries of revivalism, people still wrestle with the issues that troubled him. Through posing these seemingly eternal questions, scholars and music fans alike struggle to shape their own attitudes regarding the commodification of culture, the meaning and value of tradition, and the importance of heritage and community. With my own views still largely unformed, I attended the 1993 Folk Alliance conference in Tucson as little more than a curious, self-educated folk revival "scholar" in progress. I paid scant attention to the precise nature of the organization and gave no sustained thought to my own role. Without a professional agenda, it was sufficient for me that the conference was interesting and fun, and going seemed consistent with my informal exploration of "all things folk music." I attended varied panel discussions encompassing the quasi scholarly, such as "Beyond Copyright: Who Owns Traditional Music?" and the purely practical, such as "Newsletter Production for Folk Organizations." I enjoyed the formal evening "showcases" at which I heard a great deal of wonderful music, ranging from Mike Seeger's interpretation of U.S. southern mountain tunes to the "rural and urban folk songs" of Greece presented by Sophia Bilides, the contemporary Tex-Mex-influenced sounds of Tish Hinojosa, and the Japanese Taiko drumming of the all-percussion ensemble Uzume Taiko. By now, I was educated sufficiently that the latter's musical distance from Phil Ochs was no longer surprising.

I was, however, oblivious to the fact that I was attending a commercial trade show sponsored by a self-styled business organization. Having never attended a trade show of any kind, I had no understanding of its purpose. I did not know that showcasing artists were unpaid, but, had I thought about it, nonpayment would have seemed perfectly natural, since I assumed that we were all there to revel in four days of "folk fellowship." The conference program, had I read it carefully, would have brought me back to earth, by informing me that these artists had traveled and performed at their own considerable expense because they recognized that their fifteen minutes onstage could be "critical to their future."[12] They were there, after all, to display their talent to concert presenters, record labels, and booking agents, in the hopes of furthering careers as professional entertainers. These audience members were, in turn, looking to buy, provided the act was right for their venue, label, or agency. To a degree far greater than usual, these performances were all about business. I was similarly blasé about the exhibit areas, in which roughly one hundred businesses had paid to display services and products. This was an eclectic group ranging from management firms to instrument sellers and artists, who had all purchased fixed conference locations so interested buyers could find them. Dazzled by the posters, guitars, and the large number of complimentary CDs, I wandered through as if I were attending a somewhat unusual craft fair.

It was in Tucson that I met Ken Irwin, one of the founders of Rounder Records, the Massachusetts label that has greatly influenced my thinking about the nature of the folk revival in the postboom years. Though this "meeting" was nothing more than a quick introduction, I remember it because it accompanied one of the most spontaneous and magical nights of music I have ever experienced—an informal duet performance by Kate Brislin and Katy Moffatt, two singer-guitarists who recorded, separately, for Rounder. Beyond the memory of the music, the evening's significance lay in the unexpected opportunity to see Irwin at "work"—to watch him lose himself in a musical experience that served coincidentally as an informal audition for a professional combination still unexplored. The women knew of one another but had never met. Although Irwin has a label owner's interest in hearing new sounds, he is also an unabashed music addict whose life in the record industry grew from his love of a broad range of indigenous American song. In Tucson he grasped the opportunity to bring together two gorgeous voices, insisting that he was more interested in music than in potential commercial opportunity. He informed Randy Pitts, a mutual friend and then a California-based concert presenter, that Brislin and Moffatt intended to do some informal duet singing. Forewarned, Pitts and I kept Irwin in our sights until, around eleven that night, the women settled, with no announcement, into an empty meeting room.

To that point, Moffatt had tended to record her own country-inflected compositions, whereas Brislin focused on cover versions of songs from country music's earliest days. Each woman favored a direct, underproduced sound far removed from that of most modern Nashville recordings. For this evening's exploration of harmony singing, they leaned heavily on the repertoire of the "brother duets" that flourished in commercial country music from the 1930s through the 1950s. Identified with the Delmore Brothers, the Monroe Brothers, and the Louvin Brothers, this sound flows from voices matched with a perfection that seems possible only through years of sibling closeness. In addition to its sheer musical beauty, the repertoire's lyrics evoke in the modern romantic an earlier time and a "purer" music focused not on commerce but on family, community, and faith.[13]

To an astonishing degree, Brislin and Moffatt, though strangers, managed to re-create that sense of romance. Part of that stemmed from sheer technical skill—these women are simply great singers. Part stemmed from the excitement of the conference and part from the moment's seeming exclusivity. Though anyone could drop by, there were many other things going on, and relatively few wandered into this particular room. Though attendance shifted a bit through the evening, it never numbered more than ten at any given time. Moreover, the informal exchange between the singers rewarded those who stayed. Those merely passing through might witness a false start, or observe one of the women teaching a lyric to the other, or hear them fumble with forgotten chords. Only over time did the beauty emerge fully. Sitting inches apart, Brislin and Moffatt sang for hours, becoming more comfortable with one another as it grew later.

I stayed until about three in the morning, when fatigue overcame me. Pitts lasted until four, departing as the women still sang. Irwin remained. In an environment where some label executives might try to hear as much as possible—and there were many clamoring to be heard—he spent the entire night discerning the possibilities inherent in this particular collaboration. He stayed for love of the music and love of the romance, two impulses that helped shape the extensive Rounder catalog, which, in turn, helped shape the changing definition of folk music. Three years later Rounder released *Sleepless Nights*, a collection of duets by Brislin and Moffatt that captured the magic of their collaboration.[14]

I enjoyed my time in Tucson so much that I attended the Alliance conference the following year, this time in Boston. The 1994 conference was different in feel from the preceding year's event. Roughly six hundred registrants had journeyed to Tucson. The Ramada Inn Downtown, where all activities took place, had a warm and casual air, facilitated by a roomy courtyard and an outdoor swimming pool that guests managed to enjoy despite frequent torrential rains. In contrast, more than twelve hundred attended the Boston event, held at the 57 Park Plaza Hotel, an urban behemoth located just a few blocks from the city's crime-ridden, pornography-strewn "Combat Zone."[15] Early on, word got around that thieves had broken into a car belonging to Bob Franke, a popular Massachusetts-based performer, and stolen his guitar. This came as no surprise to those of us who spotted the frightening-looking prostitutes strolling the hotel corridors. The elevators were vastly inadequate to the task of shuttling attendees to the many conference events, and large, sometimes irritable crowds waited for conveyances that seldom arrived. This forced us into the stairwells, where a perverse sense of community coalesced around juvenile acts of civil disobedience, ranging from smoking in forbidden zones to propping open the fire doors.

Adding to the hectic, sometimes tense air of the Boston conference was a vastly increased sense of professional competition, apparent even to me despite my still limited awareness that I was attending a business event. The juried showcases I had enjoyed in Tucson were present, but this year unofficial "guerrilla" showcases, staged all over the hotel, accompanied them. In countless guestrooms, artists or their representatives turned beds on end, clearing floor space for audiences. Using flyers taped over virtually every available square inch of hotel wall space, they invited people to come, to listen, and to employ the many featured entertainers. The literally hundreds of unofficial performances—unannounced until the conference began—threatened to overwhelm the formal program. Many attendees loved the resulting anarchic, carnivalesque atmosphere with its opportunity to see far more musical attractions than anticipated. Others saw a darker side.

In both Tucson and Boston the official showcases presented a reasonably balanced mix of styles, similar to one another only in their departure from the commercial mainstream. To the contrary, the guerrilla showcases in Boston tended to feature acoustic guitar players singing their original compositions, with subject matter that often leaned toward the purely personal. To those who loved folk music because of its connection to indigenous tradition, these were nothing but "Joni Mitchell wannabes" dreaming of pop-crossover success and thus warranting nothing but contempt. What made matters worse was that some of these entertainers appeared to be manipulating the conference. Alliance management could control entry into the panel discussions, formal showcases, and exhibit hall, making certain that attendees were paid conference registrants. Anyone, however, could enter a hotel room if they had rented the room or received an invitation from the tenant. Some of those performing unofficially had not bothered to register but, in a naked, unseemly display of ambition, had merely shown up to take advantage of the conference. Many participants resented this as a breach of some unspoken community ethos.

Still, the business of the Folk Alliance went on, and it was during the Boston conference that I had an experience that altered forever my perspective on the contemporary folk scene. It grew out of a chance encounter in the exhibit hall, where I found myself in conversation with a young singer and songwriter whom I did not know. In a discussion that lasted perhaps three minutes, I explained my interest in the great folk boom and talked excitedly of the many interviews I had conducted. His expression suggested that he found my fascination with the sixties about as exciting as a discourse on nineteenth-century monetary policy. In a voice that seemed to dismiss my interests out-of-hand, he said simply, "You should make a film about what's going on now." Parting, I concluded that he was a pleasant, ambitious young man with an inadequate sense of his own history. The thought that "what's going on now" could rival in importance folk music's tremendous impact of thirty-five years earlier seemed ludicrous. Yet I never forgot his remark, and, over time, its wisdom grew inescapable.

In the early 1990s, little scholarship existed that analyzed the nature and impact of the sixties folk music revival. One exception was a 1985 article by folklorist Bruce Jackson that helped greatly in broadening my perspective. Jackson drew direct links between the folk boom and later government recognition of folk expression—as manifested in the annual Festival of American Folklife sponsored by the Smithsonian Institution, the Folk Arts Program of the National Endowment for the Arts, and the American Folklife Center, a division of the Library of Congress. In the realm of popular culture, he linked the revival directly to later folk music activism, concluding that the earlier phenomenon did not die, "so much as it became ordinary." Rock music, Jackson argued, would not have developed as it did without the influence of the folk boom. Moreover, he noted, there were more folk music festivals in the eighties than there had been a generation earlier. Academic folklorists, some of whom had themselves been fans during the great boom, directed many of these latter-day festivals, and their programming often displayed "real sensitivity and sophistication."[16]

Beginning in the mid-1990s, roughly ten years after Jackson wrote and several years after I began my own exploration, a spate of writing appeared that analyzed the revival's impact on American culture.[17] I read this material at a time when I was engaged in a great deal of reflection about the work of the Folk Alliance and the impact of those who attend its conferences. Ultimately, I grew to appreciate the extent to which the activists who formed the Alliance in 1989, though acting more than a generation after the commercial folk boom had supposedly crumbled, were part of an enormous network of people searching for new ways to promote folk music as an aspect of popular culture. Though linked collectively to a specific past, these "folk entrepreneurs"—people such as label owner Irwin and concert promoter Pitts—were focused on the present and the future. In joining the Folk Alliance they embraced an overarching infrastructure through which they could communicate, conduct business, and educate themselves. Once I realized this, I understood that there is still a broad-based commercial folk music movement afoot, albeit one that enjoys less public visibility than in the sixties.[18]

As during the boom, the present-day fascination with folk music owes much to a yearning for community and a desire to appreciate heritage. Some people, repelled by the coarser aspects of our fast-paced, mobile, and competitive society, use folk revivalism to connect themselves emotionally to idealized cultures that are removed from their own lives by time or physical distance. Rounder recording artist Christine Balfa, a member of a well-known family of musicians from southwestern Louisiana's Cajun country, maintains that people are particularly attracted to cultures that they perceive as more vibrant and close-knit than their own. "People hear about Cajun people," she says, "and they hear our music, and there is dancing, and there is food and there is the way that we live down here [in Louisiana], and I think a lot of them are very attracted to that because much of America has lost their sense of community."[19]

Balfa's husband, Dirk Powell, who performs both Cajun music and the southern mountain music played by his Kentucky grandfather, explains the modern conundrum that prompts his fellow revivalists to create participatory communities all their own. "With computers," he says, "you can find somebody around the world who thinks just like you do. In a way, this makes the world smaller, but it can also mean you can sit in your house and not know your own neighbor." Elaborating, Powell finds drawbacks in an American ideal that holds that a person can become anything through purely individual effort. "I think that a big problem in America today," he says, "is a lot of people are feeling like they don't belong to any given community." Although the lure of individual achievement is strong, "a generation or two down the line, you find people who are lacking those [community] roots. The opportunity to supposedly be anything you want," Powell continues, "doesn't mean that much if you don't know where you're coming from in some ways."[20]

During the boom, this search for community and heritage through music involved collection, preservation, adaptation, creation, presentation, and appreciation, in both the commercial and the nonprofit spheres. All of these activities continue, but their present environment differs from that of the sixties in important ways. Folk activists of today, for example, pursue their activities within an established context, one derived from the earlier phenomenon. The great boom not only created or nurtured many of the institutional structures of the present scene but also provides a reference point against which modern revivalists—including many still active sixties veterans—can assess their practices. Artists and businesspeople alike can evaluate ongoing discussion about the identity of the folk, the nature of a folk song, and the impact of commercial promotion against the experience of a relatively recent past, and thus bring to that discussion a useful measure of practical experience. Such a perspective is extraordinarily helpful when negotiating a multifaceted interest group that is extremely active, both intellectually and economically.

Another difference between the folk activism of yesterday and that of the present lies in the climate that surrounds that economic activity. Today, large, for-profit media interests no longer invest the word *folk* with meaningful commercial significance. There is no longer a regularly scheduled network television production that defines itself as a folk music showcase, such as ABC-TV's *Hootenanny*, which aired in 1963. Major record labels no longer market their releases as folk music, and mass-market magazines no longer provide regular coverage of folk music events and personalities. The major media do pay periodic attention to musical forms encompassed by the sixties revival, such as blues or bluegrass, but they no longer focus on the concept of folk music as such, and the term, along with even limited discussion of its often hazy meaning, has slipped from public discourse. This both frustrates today's revivalists and imbues them with a sense of exclusivity that can border on the cliquish—two sometimes-competing reactions that help shape their activities.

Despite the relative lack of interest by commercial giants, the ongoing folk revival encompasses a complex marketplace of interlocking commercial activity involving artists, agents, presenters, record labels, media, and audience. It remains true, as Bruce Jackson noted years ago, that there are more folk festivals today than at the great boom's commercial peak, and they are joined by countless specialty festivals devoted to bluegrass, blues, or "world" music, a catchall term that encompasses much of what folk boom commentators once referred to as international or ethnic music. Though mass-market magazines no longer pay regular attention to the folk scene, there now exist a multitude of small but nationally distributed periodicals devoted to both the art and the business of tradition-based indigenous music. Though major record labels no longer promote folk music per se, a new group of smaller record companies has arisen to replace the important, independent folk labels of the sixties that have either moved on to other styles or ceased operating. As the largest and most eclectic of these labels, Rounder Records best exemplifies the breadth of the modern folk scene and the problems inherent in commodifying that which some persist in considering noncommercial, community expression.

I will explore those problems more fully, but I note here that most of them stem from the romantic mist that has long surrounded the study of folk culture. At least as early as the mid-nineteenth century, scholars and aficionados alike have explored the identity of the "folk," the nature of their communities, the uniqueness of their artistic expression, and the supposed threat of their disappearance, with a tendency toward idealization that has submerged their subjects' complexity and thus their humanity. Only after the great boom had run its course did scholars in large numbers grapple explicitly with this tendency and begin to redefine both their terminology and their overall mission. Among the entrepreneurs who promote folk music within the broader world of mass culture, there exists that same tension between adherence to older romantic constructs and awareness of a more realistic complexity. It is a tension that serves a useful function, for although realistic complexity has much to offer the entrepreneur, the sense of romance that infuses the promotion of folk music is what gives the effort life and depth. It motivates the veritable army of adherents who help foster a broad awareness of indigenous artistry, despite the shifting nature of community identity and constant stylistic change.

Today's folk culture advocates, like those of the sixties and those of one hundred years ago, struggle against perceived loss in the face of social upheaval. In the nineteenth century advocates feared the impact of national expansion, urbanization, and industrialization. In the twenty-first century they fear the concentration of economic might and its tendency—based on a cold assessment of financial costs and benefits—to promote cultural forms that appeal to the greatest number, thereby squeezing out the idiosyncratic and the daring. In a world that seems—as always—obsessed with progress, these advocates ask us to recall and respect artifacts of the past and the community values that, they believe, fostered them. Despite folk music's leftist tinge, they are not political crusaders in the obvious sense. They do not, as a group, advocate the overthrow of existing governmental or economic structures—a stance that marks them as hopelessly naive to the few who cling to the Marxist inclinations of some earlier revivalists. Instead, they search those structures for space within which they can promote, through culture, an agenda of the local instead of the mass, the disfranchised instead of the powerful, and the unique instead of the broadly popular.

If the word *revival* served as an imperfect but adequate sobriquet for the multifaceted activities of the past, it continues to do so today. I use it as a term of art to signify the conscious promotion of traditionally based indigenous music and derivative musical forms. Though the phrase "folk music" has passionate adherents, some contemporary commentators trivialize or even disdain it. They see it, as I once did, as nothing more than a commercial label referring to solo singers accompanied by a lone acoustic guitar. Alternatively, it suggests those saccharine vocal groups that proliferated during the boom, which Christopher Guest satirizes skillfully in his film *A Mighty Wind.*

Those resistant to "folk" often embrace the term *roots music,* a useful phrase that encompasses much of what the music industry called folk music in the sixties. I prefer to speak of an ongoing folk revival because, properly understood, the phrase links contemporary activity to past practice. As they did during the great boom and as they have done for more than one hundred years, revivalists pursue the sometimes contradictory goals of preservation, creation, and commercial promotion. Still romantics for the most part, they nonetheless bring to their efforts the hardheaded skills of the modern businessperson. Diversified in approach as always, they advance their cause through methods as old as word of mouth and as new as digital sound and the Internet. Indeed, in many respects, today's folk activism is indistinguishable from that of the past, save for the present lack of interest by large commercial media. If the impact of that media rendered the sixties phenomenon a "great boom," today's devotees pursue a quieter revival, one that labors more in the commercial shadows and is more willing to seek its converts one person at a time. The study of this ongoing, never-ending revival reveals a great deal about Americans' eternal fascination with their past, their continuing desire for a sense of community, and their fierce—if sometimes hidden—resistance to cultural standardization.

This book does not examine every manifestation of postboom revival activity. My approach is thematic and focuses on ongoing intellectual and commercial issues common to revivalism as a whole. For the most part, I examine such issues through the vehicles of the Folk Alliance and Rounder Records. As an umbrella organization that annually brings together roughly two thousand folk entrepreneurs of varying stripes, the Alliance is a living laboratory that illustrates the revival's continuing concerns. Rounder, in the words of the *New York Times*, is "folk music's big small label."[21] Begun as an "antiprofit collective" by three left-leaning students who romanticized the folk, it has grown into one of the world's largest independent record companies. That growth helps illuminate commercial revivalism's development in the postboom years, a period that encompassed the countercultural movements of the late sixties, the music industry upheavals of the 1990s, and the digital revolution of the twenty-first century.

Rounder has engendered both admiration and anger. Some praise it for eclecticism and an "artist-friendly" approach. Others criticize it for alleged instances of sharp business practices. I do not offer a detailed business history, and I do not explore the countless encounters, spanning decades, that reflect positively or negatively on company personnel. This is, instead, a cultural history that examines the label's overall place within the never-ending revival. I look at Rounder's expanding catalog, which has reflected and contributed to a reassessment of the term *folk*. I examine the label's transition from a self-proclaimed antiprofit hobby to the proudly profitable roots/pop/rock hybrid it has become. I analyze how a company that once sold records from a van at folk festivals now manages to sell them competitively at Wal-Mart. I explore how a label that began by issuing "peoples" music survives in the age of media, label, and retail consolidation. I linger over particular company transition points—such as the unionization effort of the 1970s and the record retailing crisis of the 1990s—because these help illustrate the broader commercial transformation that has confronted revivalism as a whole.

This book concerns music, an aural and emotional phenomenon that is notoriously difficult to describe in words. The fact that I am not a musician only compounds this difficulty. I lack the easy, almost intuitive familiarity with a musical vocabulary that might allow me to describe adequately those features that make musical forms distinguishable from one another. It is a common problem, one that I share with many folk fans. In discussing old-time American fiddling, a revival staple, musician Jeff Davis notes that "most people—the vast majority of the public—can't distinguish one tune from another or one style from another."[22] In the present context I trust that this problem is mitigated by the fact that I am writing not about musical forms as such but about the social function of broad musical categories. Even the many folk fans who cannot discern one fiddler's bowing technique from another possess preferences that are both passionate and meaningful. A song's age and origin, the nature of its lyric, its instrumentation, the context of its performance, and even the identity of its performer at a given moment all contribute to its acceptance or rejection by one revivalist faction or another. Indeed, musicians complain often that nonmusicians revel in distinctions unimportant to the artists themselves, who are generally far more likely to tolerate artistic exploration than those drawn to folk music because of its implicit sociocultural significance.

As my reference to "factions" suggests, I structure some of my discussion around controversies that roil the folk music world. This does not mean that I consider revivalists more prone to disagreement than any other passionate interest group. I find that on the whole they are remarkably tolerant of one another and tremendously concerned about locating common ground. Within the "folk press" and at Folk Alliance conferences, references to the "folk community" are frequent and sincere.[23] Still, ardent folk fans tend to be intelligent true believers who participate in revivalism precisely because they believe deeply in its potential to offer meaning. In this quest for meaning they traverse constructs—such as heritage, tradition, authenticity, and the idea of the folk itself—that are inherently ambiguous and thus subject to diverse, even shifting, interpretations. Through their often-contentious disagreements, revivalists struggle to elucidate the multifaceted nature of their passion, clarify their beliefs, and highlight their often considerable commitment. In the end their ongoing debates enhance the value that music serves in their own lives and help strengthen the civic role of heritage, community, and art.

Ken Irwin, Marian Leighton, and Bill Nowlin in the apartment
that served as their home and an early Rounder Records office.
On the wall behind them are the jackets of Rounder's first five
releases. Somerville, Massachusetts, December 1971. (Photo by
Carl Fleischhauer)

Marian Leighton and Ken Irwin selling records at the Bluegrass Unlimited Bluegrass Festival, Indian Springs, Maryland, June 2, 1973. At right is musical activist Kathy Kaplan, who emceed bluegrass festivals, hosted a bluegrass radio show, and wrote album liner notes. (Photo by Carl Fleischhauer)

Bill Nowlin, Marian Leighton, and Ken Irwin at an academic Bluegrass Music Symposium, Bowling Green, Kentucky, September 9, 2005. (Photo by Carl Fleischhauer)

Producer Scott Billington, Rounder Records' longest-serving employee, in the studio with rhythm-and-blues legend Ruth Brown. UltraSonic Studios, New Orleans, July 29, 1998. (Photo by Barbara Roberds)

Sing Out! magazine receives the Folk Alliance's Lifetime Achievement Award. Editors from throughout the publication's history joined the ceremony, including *(from left)* Irwin Silber, Happy Traum, Bob Norman, and Mark Moss, joined by *Sing Out!* board member David Baskin. Nashville, Tennessee, February 8, 2003. (Photo by Peter W. Urbaitis II)

The Versiteers, consisting of Belinda Carter and original members Myrtle Barton and L. V. Starling, have been performing a capella gospel music since the 1940s. Here they perform in a workshop titled Jacksonville Gospel Traditions at the 2002 Folk Alliance conference, Jacksonville, Florida. (Photo by Michael Scully)

Performing songwriters entertain at an International Songwriter's Workshop at the 2006 Folk Alliance conference, Austin, Texas. (Photo by Neale Eckstein)

Multi-instrumentalist Annie Wenz on flute performs in a hotel-room showcase at the 2006 Folk Alliance Conference in Austin, Texas. (Photo by Neale Eckstein)

Randy Pitts, artist booking agent and onetime Folk Alliance board member who has also worked in record distribution, music retail, and as a concert presenter. Here he networks at the 2002 Folk Alliance conference, Jacksonville, Florida. (Photo by Michael Scully)

Folkies enjoy an informal jam session at the Northeast Regional Folk Alliance
Conference, in Pennsylvania's Pocono Mountains, 2000. (Photo by Alan Rowoth)

A round-robin performance at an informal showcase sponsored by Fox Run Concerts, at the 2006 Austin, Texas, Folk Alliance conference. *From left*, Kate McDonnell, Siobhan Quinn, Michael Bowers, and David LaMotte. (Photo by Neale Eckstein)

Phyllis Barney, a founding Folk Alliance member who served for ten years as the organization's executive director, at the first annual Southwest Regional Folk Alliance Conference, near Austin, Texas, 2000. (Photo by Alan Rowoth)

ONE

Folklore, Fakelore, and Poplore: From the Creation of the Folk to the Great Boom and Beyond

In a 1954 introduction of Elvis Presley, from the stage of the now-fabled country music show *Louisiana Hayride*, announcer Frank Page declared, "They've been looking for something new in the folk music field for a long time . . . and I think you've got it."[1] Decades later, no one thinks of Elvis as a folk musician, and when the great boom was at its peak he was in Hollywood starring in B movies, far from the nation's revival showrooms. Page's endorsement, however, illustrates both the confusion surrounding the nature of folk music and the concept's ongoing interaction with the mass-culture industry. Speaking in 1980 after both Elvis and the boom had passed from the scene, quintessential revivalist Pete Seeger noted that the term *folk song* lacked any consistent meaning. "I really try not to use the (phrase)," he said. "I'd call it 'old songs' or 'people's songs.'" Seeger is one of many who have stopped attempting to define both folk music and the broader concept of folklore, recognizing that such efforts run headlong into a quagmire of differing purposes and values. Meanings held by academics, musicians, businesspeople, and the listening public converge and diverge in an atmosphere of interdependence, respect, mistrust, disdain, and utter indifference.[2]

Though the elasticity of the term limits its descriptive value, *folk music*—notwithstanding definitional uncertainty—remains widely used by fervent revivalists. At a minimum it serves as convenient shorthand, alerting acolytes to the presence of artistic, cultural, and sometimes political sympathizers. Thus, *Sing Out!* magazine, a mainstay of the revival since 1950, carries the subtitle "Folk Music–Folk Songs," connecting it instantaneously to a long-standing heritage. The cover of *Dirty Linen*, a periodical founded in the 1980s, trumpets its devotion to "Folk and World Music," a linkage that joins often older revivalists to a younger audience, one less attached to the word *folk* but drawn to new musical hybrids born of increasing globalism.

So long as there exists a self-styled folk music scene, adherents ponder what falls within and what without. Among those who book folk clubs and host folk radio shows there is no rush to program either urban gangsta rappers or suburban grunge rockers. No matter how homegrown their sound, no matter how closely it is tied to specific communities, no matter how topical or antiestablishment their lyrics, there is no hue and cry to invite such performers inside the folk fold. Nor do the rappers and rockers seem to care. The Folk Alliance has hosted discussion on the folkloric nature of early hip-hop, but the hip-hoppers themselves are not among the hundreds of musicians plying their trade at the organization's annual conferences.[3]

This largely pragmatic need for classification fuels seemingly never-ending discussion of "what is folk," which in turn prompts continued debate about the meaning and value of heritage, tradition, authenticity, and commerce. Many activists revel in this occasionally contentious discourse, using it to identify, refine, and advocate their own values. Not surprisingly, the Internet serves as the locus of much of this discussion. Electronic discussion groups devoted to folk music abound, and the question of definition surfaces often. The Mudcat Café, an electronic bulletin board that specializes in "blues and folk music," hosts so many such debates that its manager has tried to archive them collectively under the omnibus title "Threads on the Meaning of Folk." The simply named "FolkMusic," a discussion list devoted to the contemporary, acoustic-based professional singer-songwriter, takes a different approach. Though such performers have been ubiquitous among revivalists for decades, many persist in excluding them from the category of "true" folk singers. Unwilling to see his list consumed by endless debate, wanting simply to get on with discussing the artistry he admires, the moderator of this list expressly prohibits argument on the point. The Folk Alliance, though devoted to folk music in all its myriad forms, maintains an official refusal to define the term that provides its name, fearful of discouraging potential members.[4]

When contemporary American revivalists do discuss the nature of folk music, someone notes inevitably that spontaneous, nonprofessional group performance is now exceedingly rare. Few of us know families who sing together, and, in the homes of all but our poorest citizens, multiple television sets and radios, joined now by MP3 players and electronic game consoles, divide family members, pulling each toward individual forms of packaged entertainment. Similarly, few among us have any direct exposure to occupational songs such as the mining tunes that avocational folklorist George Korson collected in the Pennsylvania coalfields as late as the 1960s. Our city streets do not ring with the songs of the urban sanitation worker; the tunes of the toll collector form no part of the cacophony at our highway interchanges. In the 1930s John and Alan Lomax explored southern prisons searching for long-isolated performers, free from the mass media's growing influence. Decades later, prisoners form rock and rap bands, covering popular songs they learned from the radio. In a world dominated by media and mobility, where scholars and entrepreneurs have seemingly cataloged every once unknown song and style, revivalists struggle to define that which they celebrate as folk music.

Recognizing that they are self-aware promoters of an ideal, very few revivalists cling to the early formulation of a folk song as an anonymous composition passed on orally through community tradition. Those who honor that early definition generally see it as a valued analytical starting point, while acknowledging the need for modification to allow for the existence of a contemporary, living folk music. A few continue to exalt only the most ancient of songs. Others accept new compositions but favor those that sound like older forms, with a preferential nod given to styles anchored in the heritage of marginalized communities. Still others, caught up in the revival's linkage of folk music and the Left, characterize a song as folk if it conveys some social message. A participant in an Internet discussion devoted to the question of whether the commercially successful performer Jewel is a folk or pop singer concluded that she is a folksinger when she sings songs that address social issues and, presumably, a pop singer the rest of the time.[5] For those who see electricity and volume as symbolic of the modern media and the star system, a folk song is a quiet song, performed on acoustic instruments. Whenever this discussion surfaces, it is almost certain that some relatively uninitiated participant will spark groans by offering the old bromide, attributed most often to bluesman Big Bill Broonzy, which holds, "I guess all songs are folk songs. I never heard a horse sing one."

Many revivalists revel in their own communities of folk song aficionados, which serve as a substitute for the idealized communities from which the construct of the folk emerged. For these seekers of fellowship, low volume and spare instrumentation serve as means to an old-fashioned end. A simple acoustic arrangement lends itself to audience participation, allowing the dedicated amateurs who populate the revival's song circles and jam sessions to perform it in a comfortably collective fashion. Mark Moss—longtime editor of *Sing Out!*—favors a definition that takes explicit account of such community-building ends, holding that "the true vein that defines folk music [is] participation." Though acknowledging the value of formal concerts and other "consumption type" events, he maintains that "continual informal singing and playing coupled with dances, family and kids' stuff, for me, comes the closest to the 'community' basis on which all folk arts are based."[6]

Moss speaks fondly of the annual Kerrville Folk Festival in Texas, a three-week, self-described singer-songwriters' festival that draws campers from around the nation. People stay for a few days or a few weeks, and many never watch the featured attractions onstage. Instead, they perform their own contemporary "semipop" songs with old and new friends in an atmosphere of "community sharing." "I defy you," Moss says, "to make an argument that that is less folk music" than the old songs deified by early scholars. Unwedded to any particular stylistic approach, Moss also refuses to characterize electricity and amplification as a dividing line between folk and "not-folk." The only reason that early folklorists did not find informants who played electric Casio keyboards, he insists, is because the instrument did not yet exist. To Moss, such keyboards are the dulcimers of the modern age. Widely accessible, relatively inexpensive, and easy to carry, they are perfect for the informal music making that forms the essence of the folk song.[7]

To the dismay of some, this thoughtful discussion goes on within a popular environment that often dismisses anything labeled "folk" as either a quaint vestige of the sixties or an even more ancient artifact that survives only because of its historical interest to a few devotees. The *New York Times* has characterized a thriving musical coffeehouse in New York State's Hudson River valley as an anachronistic throwback to a faded era, complete with carrot cake and cider. "I guess we're a bunch of old lefties," concedes one participant. "We're all sort of refugees from the 60s," adds another. Aiming more broadly, journalist Don McLeese describes "folklife" as "stuff that couldn't survive a single afternoon if it had to depend on its own entertainment value." Casting his lot with those "entranced by the trash, dazzle and vitality of popular culture," he finds folk music more akin to macrobiotics and enemas—"bad experiences that are supposed to be good for you." New York's *Village Voice*, after a brief bow to the idea of community culture, pigeonholes the music that has "come to be known as 'folk' [as] generally soft, inoffensive acoustic guitar–based mush." Music critic Jon Pareles echoes this theme with his own comment on Jewel, whom he lumps with a cluster of unnamed songwriters who indulge in "folkie psychobabble."[8]

In discussing singer, songwriter, and fiddler Eliza Carthy, the daughter of two well-known pioneers in the revival of British traditional music, *Pulse* seems determined to cover all bases by taking positive advantage of her personal revival roots while avoiding folk's contemporary image, which the magazine—perhaps correctly—considers a commercial kiss of death. Stressing Carthy's nose ring, turquoise hair, and a sound that "ain't your father's folkie music," *Pulse* assures us that she is an "alterna-folk iconoclast" who "takes folk into a pop-friendly millennium for a new generation that didn't grow up with Dylan and hootenannies." "Think folk music is for old fogies; that fiddlers are fusty?" *Pulse* asks. "Think again."[9]

Devoted folk fans consider all of this nonsense and object to a press that did not understand revivalism in the sixties and does not understand it today. The *Boston Herald* summarizes much current sentiment in a headline that reads, "Clueless: Mainstream Media Gets Folk Wrong, Over and Over." The accompanying article bemoans both the failure to comprehend the diversity of the scene and the ongoing fascination with stars such as Dylan, whom few have considered a folk singer for 40 years. The Folk Alliance—with a philosophy that embraces Dylan, Carthy, and a whole lot more—hopes to counter these negative images by communicating the vibrancy and thoroughly pluralistic nature of contemporary folk music. Still, as part of a personal search for meaning, staunch preservationists dismiss ambitious musical innovators as pretenders, sometimes using the ostensibly neutral descriptor "revivalist" as a pejorative. Country fiddlers, blues guitarists, and others whose performing style seems linked to older musical roots complain about "singer-songwriters," itself a pejorative reserved for the James Taylor clones who purvey the "psychobabble" that seems unconnected to any past other than the composer's own. Those same singer-songwriters, resenting this derision, are among those complaining of fusty fiddlers and sixties throwbacks.[10]

Such discord is hardly new and is in no way limited to commercial popu-larizers. For more than a century scholars have struggled to define folklore within the context of their times. In 1949 the editors of a standard academic reference work eschewed a single definition in favor of allowing twenty-one contributors to offer twenty-one individual points of view.[11] Two decades further along, folklorist Jan Brunvand noted that the "basic definition of folklore has not yet been formulated to anyone's complete satisfaction," resulting in a discipline that seems to be "going in circles." Almost three de-cades beyond that, Brunvand acknowledged ongoing uncertainty, citing the article of academic faith that holds that any definition must take into account who is studying whom, "plus how, why, and for whose advantage."[12]

Indeed, in the more than 150 years since its first formal expression, the discipline of folklore has witnessed a theoretical upending so pervasive that in 1998 the *Journal of American Folklore* devoted an entire issue to the question of whether scholars should abandon the word *folklore*. "Is 'folklore,'" the journal asked, "still a useful and appropriate way of describing the work we do and the area of culture that intrigues us?" The underlying ambiguities have led folklorist Roger Abrahams to refer to his chosen field as "a complex cultural fiction." Echoing this theme, other commentators have noted the existence of a constructed "idea of the folk" or written sarcastically of "once upon a time [when] there was a place called traditional society."[13]

Looking back at generations of field collecting, indexing, and anthologiz-ing, close observers have come to understand that there never existed any pure, unmediated, unself-conscious folk music, springing organically from the collective consciousness of isolated American communities. The tunes and lyrics that constitute the American folk music canon stem from varied sources, foreign and domestic, and blend ancient songs of unknown origin; locally composed material created for purposes of entertainment, commen-tary, or ritual; and wholly commercial products disseminated through travel-ing shows and, later, radio and records. Those who compiled this canon pos-sessed personal agendas governing their often idiosyncratic decisions about what to include, rendering their efforts less an exercise in canon preservation than in canon construction. Consequently, contemporary scholars generally adopt the approach of Regina Bendix, who wrote—and I paraphrase—the crucial questions to be answered are not "What is folk music?" but "Who needs folk music and why?" and "How has folk music been used?"[14]

Despite these conceptual difficulties, the discipline of folklore does pos-sess a core terminology, subject matter, and set of values. While scholars ponder their professional identity, that core continues to exert a powerful hold on many drawn to indigenous musical expression. Thus, despite challenges posed by social change and unimagined technological innovation, the principles that motivated fledgling folklorists more than a century ago continue to influence the dissemination and reception of what the music industry calls folk music. In the opinion of folklorist Gene Bluestein, the revival's casual blend of scholarship and commerce has troubled some conservative academicians, who see revivalism as something akin to an overly intrusive in-law—they recognize that it bears some relationship to folklore, but they don't really want it in the house. Bluestein observes this conundrum in the scholarly reaction to revival giants Seeger and Woody Guthrie. "While academic critics may have grudgingly admired their work," he writes, "its alleged contamination by pop traditions has put them in a sort of limbo. They have obviously done something with folk material, but what they have done is difficult to evaluate within the obsolete definitions of folklore still in vogue."[15]

Bluestein overstates the case. Scholarly folklorists and revivalists have influenced one another for quite some time. Folklore's disciplinary core provides revivalists not only with a subject matter and a vocabulary but also with the intellectual and emotional framework that drives their activities. Revivalists, in turn, have pushed folklorists to broaden the "obsolete definitions" of which Bluestein complains. This reciprocal process, which has accelerated since the end of the boom, has enhanced our ability to understand the manner in which the media advance indigenous artistry and has encouraged the creation and commercial promotion of some wonderful and diverse music. Although a detailed history of folklore scholarship would overwhelm my present subject, a full understanding of the ongoing folk revival demands some appreciation of folklore's scholarly core and its shifting path, along which theory pursues such diverse strands as urbanization, industrialization, political activism, and the growth of the music industry. This, in turn, compels us to start at a point that is both germane to the task at hand and upon which there is reasonable agreement—if not a definitive beginning, then at least an accurate and utilitarian one.[16]

Englishman William John Thoms coined the word *folklore* in 1846 in a pseudonymous letter to the *Athenaeum*, a British periodical. A lifelong civil servant, Thoms was also an avocational antiquarian who compiled and published anthologies that collected the myths and legends of his native land. He offered the term—which he hyphenated as "folk-lore"—as a more encompassing substitute for such then-conventional phrases as "popular antiquities" and "popular literature." Fearing the loss of the "lore of the people," he urged the *Athenaeum* to solicit examples of such lore, which he identified as the "manners, customs, observances, superstitions, ballads, proverbs, etc., of the olden time." His brief letter made clear that he derived his motivation from a perceived need to rescue such material from imminent disappearance. Reflecting on the amount of lore that was already "entirely lost," he encouraged the preservation of that which "may yet be rescued by timely exertion." In a retrospective account of his creation Thoms confirmed that advancing modernity spurred him on, noting that he acted "when the railroad mania was at its height, and the iron horse was trampling under foot all our ancient landmarks, and putting to flight all the relics of our earlier popular mythology."[17]

By 1888 Thoms' neologism and his purpose had taken firm hold in the United States. That year, the founders of the newly created American Folk-Lore Society (AFS) called for the preservation of "the fast-vanishing remains" of folklore in America. Bemoaning the perils of growth, urbanization, and homogenization, the maiden issue of the society's *Journal of American Folk-Lore* urged exploration of the "older and more retired towns" in search of the vanishing products of "the quiet past" before they were "absorbed into the uniformity of the written language."[18] Forecasting the folklorist's continuing fascination with those outside the mainstream, the journal displayed a strong interest in the cultural products of all those marginalized—politically, economically, and socially—by political consolidation and rapid industrialization. In doing so, it helped define "the folk" as a dispossessed and powerless peasantry, while contrasting them implicitly with the presumably more enlightened, more educated, and certainly more powerful would-be saviors of their legacy. Dillon Bustin links the antimodernism at the heart of the fascination with folk culture to the romantic transcendentalists of mid-nineteenth-century New England, who idealized rural, premodern life and extolled Henry David Thoreau's call to "simplify, simplify."[19] The line between idealization and derision, however, could be a fine one. In romantic terms the folk were unspoiled, pastoral, and close to nature. More pejoratively, those same folk were backward, superstitious, and illiterate. In the end, given the inevitability of change and the folklorists' self-definition as men of "science," even the ostensibly positive descriptors carried the whiff of paternalism.[20]

Though early folklore scholarship raised various themes that suffuse the discipline to this day—including antimodernism, romanticism, and co-lonialism—definitional uncertainty existed from the outset. Early on, the search for a clear, unifying principle centered on expression and behavior passed on through oral tradition. This focus on orality stemmed from two impulses. To a degree, it affirmed the primitive status of those studied, who did not necessarily avail themselves of modern means of communication or record keeping. More important, it helped define the concept of tradition itself, by emphasizing that which was so enmeshed within a culture that it did not warrant written codification. Tradition, this view suggests, reflects deep-seated community values, as opposed to an individual interest, a pass-ing group fancy, an entrepreneurial gambit, or a ruling-class dictate.

Thus, folklorist Kay L. Cothran characterizes tradition as the "context of context," the backdrop that gives form and meaning to individual activity and community discourse. More colloquially, she calls it simply "our way, our means, our category, our system."[21] Obsessed with preservation of the threatened, early folklorists also gave tradition a core meaning that situated the past and modernity as "polar opposites."[22] They consequently associ-ated tradition with "survivals," defined as customs "carried on by force of habit into a new state of society different from that in which they had their original homes," remaining "as proofs and examples of an older condition of culture out of which a newer has been evolved."[23]

In contemporary times, it is axiomatic that cultures are not static entities but living organisms that modify customs over time, in part due to ongoing cross-cultural interaction. None of the North American racial or ethnic groups that interested the AFS in 1888 lived in total isolation, and inter-group contact resulted inevitably in an alteration of customs and texts that revealed itself only gradually. Thus, by the time the society began its drive to preserve Native American "survivals," such supposedly indigenous customs already reflected two centuries of Anglo-Indian interaction. In recognition of this reality, the contemporary concept of tradition encompasses not only a body of customary expression but also a process that presumes change as an integral component of its nature, even if that change occurs through the crossing of perceived cultural boundaries.[24]

Incorporating both the idea of custom (that which is understood, ac-cepted, and repeated) and process (that which travels and varies through space and time), Henry Glassie calls tradition "the creation of the future out of the past." The corollary to this definition holds that change by itself is never antithetical to the existence of strong traditions. Tradition, Glassie explains, is the opposite of change only in those instances in which the "disruption is so complete that the new cannot be read as an innovative adaptation of the old," thus suggesting enormous, often abrupt, and sometimes violent social dislocation.[25] The more gradual, long-term change associated with tradition may proceed at times so slowly or quietly that it creates the illusion of stasis, whereas at other times it may display a momentarily dizzying fluidity. Often, it is only through a retrospective glance that an observer can determine the impact or existence of change. Though Glassie's analysis was unavailable to nineteenth-century folklorists, they feared that the heady rush to conquer and modernize that marked North American development constituted, in many instances, the complete disruption that served as tradition's enemy.

Tradition's companion is "authenticity," a multilayered construct that, in the words of Bendix, encompasses a broad-based modernist reaction to "urban manners, artifice in language, behavior, and art, and against aristocratic excess." Like Bustin, Bendix finds raw material for this intellectual stance in the work of the literary romantics, emphasizing the value they placed on unmediated experience, intuition, and unspoiled nature.[26] If one seeks preservation of the ingrained raw material of indigenous community life, one must locate that which is truly an innate part of community identity, avoiding that which is imposed or merely ephemeral. At its most simplistic, authenticity refers to the extent to which a text or behavior accurately replicates some ideal exemplar. Revivalists, who often fail to dig deeply in this regard, tend to evaluate authenticity by charting measurable attributes. They might, for example, examine an Appalachian ballad to determine whether its particular lyric, tune, or performance style was actually circulating within Appalachia at a chosen point in time, presumably before "outsiders" managed to alter purely indigenous culture. A fuller examination depends on a clear understanding of many variables, encompassing not only lyric, tune, and style but also the precise identity of the community in question, the performer's connection to that community, the community values examined, the setting and purpose of presentation, the determination of what constitutes an outside influence, and the extent to which the seeker of authenticity tolerates such influences.[27]

With their professed interest in authentic remnants of endangered, premodern, indigenous expression, early folklorists helped solidify the tone of their emerging discipline. Francis James Child, a Harvard literature professor who devoted his professional life to locating texts of Anglo-Saxon ballads, was paramount among these scholars. Possessed of a strong bias for the ancient, Child, born in 1825, exalted the earliest texts. He subjectively discerned some drastic qualitative decline once the printing press allowed a thriving business in commercial balladry. To ensure the value of his collection, he focused on texts created before 1475, the year the printing press arrived in Britain. Child avoided living informants, fearing that they might pass on a lyric corrupted by the entrepreneurial influences of the preceding 400 years. Instead, helped by a network of researchers in the British Isles, he scoured archival sources for handwritten texts that had survived for centuries, eventually publishing 1,300 variants of 305 separate titles. During the great boom, newly professional folksingers often exalted these "Child ballads," drawn by their beauty but also by the multiple attractions of preindustrial antiquity, unknown origin, and scholarly gloss. In a typically snide—but not altogether untrue—reference to the great boom, *Time* magazine reported that "Folkupmanship absolutely requires that a ballad be referred to as Child 12, Child 200, or Child 209," rather than by the actual name of the song.[28]

Scholar Cecil Sharp built on Child's accomplishment by documenting the prevalence of British ballads among the citizens of America's Appalachian Mountains. In fieldwork conducted between 1916 and 1918, Sharp—using oral informants of the type Child had spurned—collected more than 1,600 versions of 500 songs, almost all British-derived material. Sharp helped solidify the romantic image of the supposedly premodern Appalachian mountaineer, whom he considered "just exactly what the English peasant was one hundred or more years ago." He praised the mountain folk for their "elemental wisdom, abundant knowledge, and intuitive understanding" drawn from a life lived "in constant touch with Nature and face-to-face with reality." Ignoring the realities of hard work and hardship, Sharp, in Benjamin Filene's wry observation, "made the mountaineers' closeness to nature sound less like subsistence poverty than like an ascetic philosophy."[29] His idyllic picture of a pastoral wonderland populated by figurative noblemen, unscathed by the evils of modernity and ringing with the sound of Child ballads spontaneously sung, has exerted a powerful hold on the ongoing folk revival.

Of the early collectors whose work has endured to influence generations of revivalists, perhaps none is better known than John Avery Lomax. Born in Mississippi in 1867, Lomax grew up in Texas, where he developed an appreciation for the regional tunes sung by neighbors and traveling musicians. As a late-blooming Harvard graduate student, he began researching the songs that cowboys "made up" while they worked. His efforts resulted in the 1910 publication of his now classic *Cowboy Songs and Other Frontier Ballads*, a book arguably responsible for the preservation of many American standards, including "Buffalo Skinners," "Git Along, Little Dogies," and, most famously, "Home on the Range." Lomax's emotional connection to folklore's romantic, antimodernist tenets is plain, as is his fascination with the old England that appealed to both Child and Sharp. His book describes his geographic focal point as "the wild, far-away places of the big and still unpeopled west," where there "yet survives the Anglo-Saxon ballad spirit that was active in secluded districts in England and Scotland." Lomax saw the "unique and romantic" cowboys who roamed this land as authentic primitives, "illiterate . . . isolated and lonely" occupants of "the skirmish line of civilization." Like other primitives of the day, Lomax's cowboy was disappearing. "The changing and romantic West of the early days," he concluded, "lives mainly in story and in song."[30]

Lomax offered a description of cowboy life so vivid that one could believe that he collected songs while personally battling rustlers. He stated explicitly that the songs "as a rule have been taken down from oral recitation." Perhaps someone initially captured the songs in this manner, but it was not likely to have been Lomax. For the most part, the lyrics came from newspapers, library archives, and through the mail, provided by those responding to Lomax's several printed solicitations. He included songs that he knew had been published as well as some that had definite authorship. When it suited his aesthetic he altered texts and combined variants, seeking the subjectively "best" lyric narrative. In this regard he was similar to Child, who excised "tasteless" material from his collection and occasionally "improved" a lyric with his own additions. Each collector anthologized that which he liked and served his particular preservationist ethic; each omitted that which he disliked. The result in each case was the same—the preservation of valuable cultural artifacts that might otherwise have been lost. "Home on the Range" had an identifiable composer and a publication history that predated Lomax's book. Nonetheless, the song was obscure. Had Lomax recorded only texts that circulated solely within oral tradition, it might have disappeared forever. Unlike Child, Lomax acknowledged his editorial hand. "Frankly," he explained, "the volume is meant to be popular." Nonetheless, he was not always comfortable with his intervention. On occasion, when confronted with evidence that a song was less than an absolutely authentic product of the range—such as a lyric's erroneous description of cowboy gear—he defended himself by claiming textual purity.[31]

If Lomax, with his connection to Harvard and its heritage of Child's ballad collecting saw tension between the scholarly and the popular, other early-twentieth-century song collectors assuredly did not. Beginning around 1920, scouts seeking commercial opportunity on behalf of the fledgling record industry sought potential stars in disparate pockets of the United States. Scholars now recognize these industry pioneers as "unwitting folklorists" who played a seminal role in preserving the songs and song styles favored by rural Americans at the dawn of the twentieth century.[32] At the time, the repertoire of many rural musicians consisted necessarily of songs learned largely through oral tradition. This did not, however, mean that the songs themselves were the survivals of dying cultures. Even in the century's earliest decades people traveled into and out of relatively isolated regions, and tunes, whether written down or not, moved with them. Many rural residents learned songs from professional performers affiliated with traveling tent shows. Then, whether through wholly informal singing within families or through quasi-professional entertainment, they passed them on to others. Some songs were indeed old British ballads; some were hymns; still others were minstrel or vaudeville tunes. To the listeners and to many of the performers, they constituted a free-floating repertoire of unknown origin, available to all.[33]

Most early rural entertainers were farmers or laborers who played for their neighbors at social gatherings. Those with a more commercial orientation sometimes sought prizes at organized fiddle contests, drummed up crowds on behalf of retailers or politicians, or performed on street corners in return for loose change. With the rise of radio and recording in the 1920s, it was not long before all concerned recognized the new business opportunities—and the new modes of living—that technology placed within reach. The more ambitious performers realized that the new media could help them earn a living from their art. Correspondingly, media executives understood that these local musicians provided a relatively inexpensive talent pool through which they could build commercial opportunity. Seeking a successful marketing strategy, the fledgling country music industry, in the words of Richard A. Peterson, crafted an image "as a rustic alternative to urban modernity." Record company executives mined the South for capable musicians who could record the familiar tunes already performed informally among rural southerners. By the end of 1924, New York–based Okeh

Records, to take just one example, had released approximately forty tunes drawn from the long-circulating corpus of rural material, all recorded by and marketed to white southerners. Seeking an image of well-worn, comfortable rusticity, the record companies turned to depictions of stereotypical hillbilly mountaineers, coupled with the use of the phrase "old-time." In a pattern followed by other labels, Okeh devoted catalog space and advertising material specifically to "old time tunes" played "in the real old time way." By the end of the decade, the U.S. record industry had issued approximately thirty-five hundred distinct titles in the self-defined "old-time tune" category.[34]

Once the entertainment industry entered the world of rural folk song, the problem of copyright arose. In the course of the informal oral transmission that predated recording, performers altered lyrics, melodies, and even titles, sometimes consciously, sometimes not. They would, at times, claim to have composed these variants, but such "authorship" was a loose concept. As Gene Wiggins notes, "Sometimes when they say 'wrote' they mean 'crystallized a personally meaningful version.'" Bill Malone reports, "In a sense, virtually every hillbilly musician was an 'arranger,' but few bothered to copyright their arrangements" until the late twenties, when the country music industry began to take shape in earnest.[35] By then, the prospect of making money collided with the reality of a vast number of recorded old-time tunes originating from within a uniform body of informally circulating material. The threat of copyright litigation became a significant concern. To avoid it, industry executives needed new songs. They were not, however, willing to abandon the successful "old-time" marketing niche. To solve the problem posed by the apparent commercial exhaustion of well-known material, they arrived at an ingenious, thoroughly businesslike solution: they sought brand-new tunes that sounded like the old-fashioned, traditional ones—"music that connected with the past and extended the tradition," which Peterson aptly calls the "simulation of tradition." If record buyers believed that they were, in fact, hearing old, traditional tunes, so much the better. Thus, the phrase "old-time" came to describe not just a temporal category but an aesthetic and commercial one as well.[36]

During the 1930s folk revivalism took on its explicit and still lingering left-wing political coloration. Since so much of the folk song canon was broadly recognizable and easy to perform, leftist activists, hoping to advance the cause of what they considered an oppressed proletariat, turned to traditional American tunes for use as an organizing tool. In the words of communist cultural critic Mike Gold, use of those old, familiar tunes made "the revolution as easy and simple as 'Old Black Joe.'" Harking back to the theoretical idea of community composition, political workers viewed these songs as creations of "the people" themselves, thus positing them in opposition to the products of a presumably exploitative popular culture industry. As Richard Reuss put it, "The [folk song] form was not strongly identified with bourgeois music institutions such as Tin Pan Alley or Broadway, but instead was a product of the American cultural experience associated with the rural lower classes."[37] Often, leftist performers composed new, politicized lyrics for well-known traditional melodies, a technique that provided the foundation for the fame of Woody Guthrie and the later careers of Pete Seeger and Bob Dylan. Though such activism brought folk music to the attention of an entirely new audience, the specter of educated, urban, political workers organizing to the accompaniment of newly composed "folk songs" that condemned the capitalist system further muddied the question of what, if anything, was an "authentic" folk song.

Interest in folklore grew throughout the first half of the twentieth century, prompting scholars and entrepreneurs to produce countless collections of printed lore, consisting not only of songs but also of stories, riddles, and games.[38] It became increasingly difficult to separate supposedly pure products of oral tradition from new hybrids that changed with dizzying speed. In 1944 Benjamin A. Botkin, who had served as curator of the Library of Congress Archive of American Folk Song, published *A Treasury of American Folklore: Stories, Ballads, and the Traditions of the People.* More than nine hundred pages long, this collection ranged far beyond song in documenting arcane pockets of American popular expression. Under quaint chapter titles such as "Tall Talk" and "From the Liar's Bench," the book presented tales of legendary true-life figures such as the young Abe Lincoln and of mythical heroes and villains, such as John Henry, the famed "steel driving man," and "Stackalee," who sold his soul to the devil so he could "go round doin' things no other living man could do."[39]

In preparing his anthology, Botkin did no anthropological fieldwork. He drew his wildly varied material from published books, local newspapers, and magazines, both pulp and highbrow. He made little effort to situate any portion of this vast potpourri within particular indigenous communities. Nor did he track textual changes over time or place, or explore how any given group of people used the material in their daily lives. Instead, he merely provided readers with access to an enormous collection of colorful miscellany, allowing them to use it as they wished, often for no purpose other than an evening's entertainment. In a swipe at academe, he characterized the book as a corrective to the problem of those who considered folklore "the possession of the few who study it rather than of the many who make or use it."[40] Like Lomax, Botkin was a popularizer, selling the best possible story to the masses.

This approach infuriated Richard Dorson, then a young scholar destined to become one of America's most influential folklorists. Dorson detested the practices of popular anthologizers, which he considered devoid of scholarly standards. He was, at heart, a cultural anthropologist who hoped that his still developing discipline could bring scholarly illumination to the expressive life of groups. He saw Botkin as akin to the "dude fisherman who buys his catch at the market." Branding the result "fakelore," Dorson argued that "to get the full-bodied lore, someone, somewhere along the line, must talk to the folk."[41] Only through such talk could one gradually discern that which is truly traditional and acquire some sense of the vibrant life within the lore. Presaging the battles between "purists" and popularizers that raged during the great boom, Dorson also took aim at the commercial folksinging career of entertainer Burl Ives and the folk music radio broadcasts of Alan Lomax, John's son.[42] Superficially, much of this was a struggle over nomenclature. Dorson could ignore Botkin's literary endeavors and other "folksy" entertainment but for the fact that they dared carry the name "folklore." The misuse of that term, however, signaled the scholar's deeper concern—his belief that popularization severed lore from its cultural moorings, thus trivializing and demeaning vast numbers of richly expressive people spread across the American landscape.

Despite their differences, Botkin and Dorson each recognized that by the mid-twentieth century, folklore, however defined, was bound inextricably to the products of the mass-culture industry. Botkin saw popular culture as one source of the "folklore of the present." The "so-called lively arts," he wrote—referring to "jazz, vaudeville, burlesque, comic strips, animated cartoons, pulps—often have a folk basis or give rise to new folk creations, such as Mickey Mouse and Donald Duck." In offering his own theoretical perspective, Dorson continued to eschew reliance on third-hand, mediated accounts, but disclaimed any desire "to tilt at the windmills of our culture to restore pure, unpolluted folklore. Rather, I suggest that the American folklorist consider the relationship between mass culture and folklore patterns," suggesting that current streams of expression might reveal "motifs of unsuspected antiquity, clothed in new dress to suit modern times."[43] Even as he proposed searching for folklore within contemporary mass-mediated culture, Dorson still spoke in terms of survivals. His use of the words *pure* and *unpolluted*, along with his ongoing battle against "fakelore," conveyed a strong preference, both scholarly and emotional, for preindustrial oral expression.

As the great boom took shape in the late 1950s, entrepreneurs began blurring the boundary between folk and commercial music to a degree previously unimagined. For the first time it became possible to become both famous and extremely wealthy by appealing explicitly to a broad-based consumer appetite for folk music. Discussions about the true meaning of "folk culture" not only continued among scholars but also entered popular discourse. Sincere preservationists, commercially driven manipulators, and the many who lay in between recognized the power of such nebulous constructs as "the folk," "tradition," and "authenticity," through which songs, performers, and events could be brought within or excluded from the profitable machinery of the folk song revival. The stench of commerce gone wild in an arena that some considered sacred cultural ground fueled the long-running debate.

Until approximately 1958, despite growing commercial activity, fervent folk music revivalism remained the province of a relatively small, quasi-bohemian subculture populated largely by left-leaning true believers. Strictly speaking, they were popularizers themselves, but many knew something about the underpinnings of folklore and respected the importance of heritage. A few specialty record labels catered to these committed devotees. The most eclectic was Folkways Records, which Moses Asch founded in the late 1940s. Though Asch released albums by Guthrie, Seeger, and others who shared his leftist views, the bulk of his collection is not overtly political. For Asch, politics lay in giving voice to a broad array of racial and ethnic music. The resulting catalog is a wildly varied mix that encompasses Appalachian ballads, Mississippi blues, African war drums, and Afghani teahouse music, among many other things.[44]

Elektra Records, the revival institution that college student Jac Holzman started in 1952, occupied another part of the folk music spectrum. Whereas Folkways leaned toward the idealized authentic, producing many field recordings by nonprofessional musicians, Holzman's offerings generally featured professional revivalists such as Theodore Bikel, the actor and singer; cabaret songstress Cynthia Gooding; and Oscar Brand, the New York radio host and a polished performer. In the words of critic Nat Hentoff, Elektra was "known for its catalogue of 'entertainment' folk music—recordings that often do appeal to the specialist but basically are aimed at that wider market of listeners who like their folk songs programmed, performed and packaged so that they can enjoy the music immediately." As an opinionated young Turk in 1957, Village musician Dave Van Ronk plunged into revivalism's eternal cultural war—dismissing Elektra's catalog as a "sarcophagus" that contained "pallid" imitations from which the "guts have been deftly extracted."[45]

In New York City the 1950s scene was marked less by antagonism to commerce than by the sheer absence of meaningful commercial possibility. Devotees gathered for Sunday-afternoon jam sessions in Greenwich Village's Washington Square Park, participating in informal performances that musicians and observers alike viewed as little more than a chance to relish music and friendship. In the evenings or during inclement weather the party simply moved elsewhere. The local American Youth Hostel and the Labor Temple on Manhattan's Fourteenth Street each served as alternatives to the square. These were not concert halls but gymlike facilities that functioned as places to gather, pass a guitar around, and sing. Groups would split off from one another and perform in different styles, the competing sounds bouncing off the walls. A few promoters presented formal concerts, but New York at the time lacked sufficient professional venues for staged folk music performances. The musicians often promoted their own concerts in storefronts, churches, and small theaters, which were not available until around midnight, after the evening's theatrical presentation had ended. Happy Traum, a Bronx native who began taking regular subway rides to the Village around 1954 as a teenager, recalls it as thoroughly social scene, marked by a cohesiveness born of the participants' shared enthusiasm. Everywhere you went, he said, you saw someone you knew. "We felt like we were part of a real something happening. . . . In the forefront of something, sort of in the vanguard of some kind of a movement, but only we knew about it. It was something very special."[46]

In 1958 the Kingston Trio altered this subterranean scene irrevocably when it released its version of "Tom Dooley." Other than the label "folk music," the group seemed to have little in common with the more committed Greenwich Village folk devotees. Whereas the latter hovered on the edge of bohemia, the trio committed the unpardonable sin of dressing in uniform or at least matching creased, pinstriped shirts that might as well have been uniforms. Moreover, they seemed utterly unconcerned with the most basic measures of authenticity, shortening the song's story and delivering what was left in a polished, well-modulated vocal style that utterly effaced its Appalachian origins. Onstage they augmented their clean-cut appearance and relatively bland musical approach with glib patter that evoked the dreaded Tin Pan Alley. *Time* magazine summarized the overall effect as a "slick combination of near-perfect close harmony and light blue humor."[47]

It was particularly galling to the committed that this flagrantly inauthentic, apolitical, hopelessly uncool show-business "product" proved phenomenally successful. At a time when Pete Seeger's opposition to McCarthyism led to blacklisting and a felony conviction, the Kingston Trio took "Tom Dooley" to number 1 on the pop charts, selling almost four million singles, the first of a string of successes. In their wake came the imitators—the New Christy Minstrels, the Highwaymen, the Serendipity Singers, and others—all equipped with polished acts, polished clothes, polished repertoires, and lucrative contracts. The immediate reaction of the cognoscenti was to ignore these pretenders and, when that grew impossible, to mock them. Confronted with something far worse than the mildly mainstream offerings of Elektra Records, Dave Van Ronk recalls sneering references to "the New Crunchy Monsters" and describes the general reaction of his peers as, "These people wash too much." "We were," he went on, "needless to say, very, very critical. One thing, we had a grittier worldview than [the commercial groups]. For another thing, we either truly disliked, or affected to dislike, the audience that they were reaching for."[48]

Ultimately, the boom created a world of professional opportunity that reached far beyond urban bohemians and whitewashed folk superstars. By 1962 a well-defined circuit of folk clubs and coffeehouses had developed across the United States. Folk music festivals became commonplace, and some of them—Berkeley, Newport, Philadelphia, and Chicago, in particular—showed real zeal in presenting performers who drew their music from their own lived traditions. Committed activists—often young musicians, not trained folklorists—sought out long-ignored, rural southern recording artists and brought them to the attention of this expanding audience. To the utter astonishment of devotees, old-time hillbilly and blues artists such as Clarence Ashley, Dock Boggs, Gus Cannon, Sleepy John Estes, and Mississippi John Hurt, who had last recorded in the 1920s and '30s, demonstrated their sometimes still-stunning abilities on revival stages.

Throughout the boom, *Sing Out!* served as a forum for seemingly never-ending battles. Some contributors decried the influence of overly commercial popularizers, painting a devastating portrait of new folk aficionados who sang all songs "with the same beat" and lacked "any understanding of what the songs are talking about, how they developed, or why people sing them." Others insisted that "without the newer groups folk music would not be on everyone's lips today. It would still be lying dormant in its own clique."[49] *Sing Out!* had its own faults. Though it made a reasonable effort to present all facets of the boom, it proved quite capable of idealizing traditional artists to an absurd, dehumanizing, degree. A profile of elderly Virginia balladeer Horton Barker is typical. The piece reveals nothing of how Barker, blind since childhood, survived up to the point at which the Chicago Folk Festival introduced him to a large revival audience. Instead, it cast him as the embodiment of a romantic literary hero, explaining that he possessed the "unpretentious dignity" that, for reasons left unexplained, was "so often a characteristic of the traditional ballad singer." Visitors to the home of this "genuine mountain man" would "probably find [him] sitting on the porch of the little house he shares with his sister and her husband." There "he might sing a ballad for you. On the other hand, he might choose to quote some Shakespeare or some Homer for you, instead."[50]

Although such cardboard characterizations are regrettable, *Sing Out!*'s readership was minuscule compared to that of mainstream, mass-marketed media, which offered revival reportage varying widely in quality and depth. Some coverage was so simplistic and demeaning that it fuels continued concern about the intersection of commerce and revivalism. Among the worst offenders were *Time* and *Newsweek*, which collectively sold millions of copies each week. These magazines had a distressing tendency to emphasize the otherness of indigenous southern music, highlighting its supposed eccentricity while infantilizing musicians as backwoods bumpkins with funny accents. Illustrative is a 1961 *Time* piece on bluegrass, which characterized the genre as "a particularly corny style of country music" and preeminent practitioners Flatt and Scruggs as "a couple of hillbillies." *Newsweek* showed even less taste when it mimicked the accent of one well-known performer: "Mah name is Jean Ritchie, and Ahm from Kentucky. [I'll play] an old murder song come down through our family fur generations."[51]

Such disrespect was consistent with the newsmagazines' propensity to explain the boom in extraordinarily superficial terms, treating folk music as little more than the latest popular craze in an eternally ongoing cycle of popular crazes. Neither periodical did much to suggest that the music had any function beyond the selling of products, musical or otherwise. They did not merely report on the revival's more commercial aspects but encouraged them, to the exclusion of any deeper presentation of the movement's cultural or political importance. Both *Time* and *Newsweek* were obsessed with the earning power of the more popular revival stars, with the former repeating a widespread joke that characterized a traditional artist as any performer who earned less than one hundred thousand dollars per year.[52] De-emphasizing the revival's cultural complexity, the magazines focused on the movement's most middle-of-the-road aspects, demonstrating a near obsession with performers' supposed college experiences. Old-time-music revivalists the New Lost City Ramblers (NLCR) were "a trio of college men." Buffy St. Marie was "an honor student," and singer Biff Rose "looked like a joker who might have flunked out of Yale, but actually is a 1959 graduate of Loyola University in New Orleans." In a straight-faced article that could have passed for parody, *Time* stressed that the members of the Highwaymen were hardly "campus misfit[s] with a guitar." They were, instead, prelaw students, fraternity officers, charity workers, golfers, and pole vault champions.[53]

The newsmagazines may have overdone their coverage of money and mainstream values, but apart from their excesses unparalleled commercial popularity was altering the sense of community that had nurtured the revival's early years. Strangers—both new audiences clamoring to see the folksingers and new performers, some exceedingly ambitious—inundated a once close-knit world. "I don't think we knew it would get as big as it did," said Traum, who saw his Greenwich Village scene transformed. The once familial Monday-night hootenannies at Gerde's Folk City became "unbelievably competitive. It was great music," Traum recalls, "and it was exciting as hell, but every night there'd be managers and agents and record company people."[54] Gradually, the music began to change. Undoubtedly, some artists saw the scene as a springboard to success. Others were simply young explorers determined to pursue new artistic paths. Some felt worn down by battles over authenticity that seemed increasingly nonsensical within the burgeoning commercial sphere. Even those who continued to value traditional music wanted to do more than perfect styles pioneered in other times and places. Dylan's lyrical flights of fancy and his turn toward electricity helped lead the charge, but he succeeded only because so many were willing to follow.

By the midsixties, among many of the most avid revivalists, status no longer rested on the traditionality of their repertoire or the authenticity of their style. What mattered now was the depth and quality of the artistry with which one expressed one's individual viewpoint, political or otherwise.

"People are demanding more of a folk singer," said performer Carolyn Hester in 1964. "You must stand up and say what you believe. . . . It's no longer enough to sing someone else's songs. Writers, that's what's new in folk singing today." Now, to be "authentic" meant to be true to one's personal artistic vision, without regard to commercial considerations. In 1967, while serving on the board of the Newport Folk Festival, Judy Collins was instrumental in presenting a program titled "Songwriters and the Contemporary Scene." Years later, Collins recalled that she proposed the program with a cutting slap at the old hierarchy. "You've got to stop living in a very isolated mode, in Lomaxland," she argued. Among those the program featured were Joni Mitchell and Leonard Cohen, whose highly personal lyrics were largely devoid of either traditional elements or any explicit political slant.[55]

Collins' early recordings, like those of Hester, had leaned heavily toward the traditional Anglo-Saxon ballad repertoire. Now both performers helped demolish the historical definition of the folk song—at least in the context of popular revivalism—arguing that it encompassed the personal creations of contemporary songwriters. Following the path of talented artists such as Mitchell and Cohen, legions of thoughtful, guitar-strumming, ambitious singer-songwriters, who continued to perform in the acoustic style associated with the boom, became known as "folksingers." To the continuing irritation of the more hard-core purists, they remain "folksingers" to this day.

Inevitably, the pop-culture machinery moved on. Many people remained traditional music devotees, but the record industry, the media, and the broader public shifted their attention, creativity, and money away from folk music and toward the British Invasion and rock in general. Within the span of a few years, many revival temples closed their doors. Both the star system and the accompanying demise of community contributed to the disintegration of the Newport Folk Festival—the mother ship of the popular festivals that had blossomed during the boom. The first Newport festival, in July 1959, attracted roughly thirteen thousand fans who enjoyed the mix of traditional, political, and popular that came to characterize the revival as a whole. In addition to the headlining Kingston Trio, fans saw Pete Seeger and the still largely unknown Joan Baez, plus acoustic blues, gospel, bluegrass, Appalachian balladry, and Irish music.[56]

Following Dylan's infamous 1965 electric set, festival producer George Wein began to increase the number of electric acts on the bill. Although electricity attracted pop music fans, and some hailed it as nothing more than a normal stage in folk's evolutionary process, it alienated those whose attraction to folk revivalism stemmed from its idealized connection to pre-industrial times. Electricity was part of the music business, and revival stalwarts—at least those not yet taken with garage rock—did not believe that it had anything to do with homegrown, community music making. Moreover, the electric stars of the late sixties attained an iconic status far greater than anything experienced by the stars of the folk boom, with the exception of the wayward Dylan. The resulting celebrity was at odds with the "just us folks" communitarianism that previously had been a revival hallmark.

These tensions played themselves out on the festival grounds. A record seventy thousand people attended the penultimate 1968 festival, which the *New Yorker*'s Ellen Willis characterized as an event in search of a rationale. Headliner Janis Joplin contributed to the overall sense of "orgiastic hero worship" that festival organizers—who, of course, invited Joplin's appearance—claimed they wanted to avoid. Electricity presented difficulties in an open-air setting that tried to tolerate both urban blues and back-porch fiddling. At a crowded blues workshop featuring the then relatively unknown Junior Wells and Buddy Guy, promoter Wein urged a lowering of the volume, which was interfering with other workshops. "Kill the others!" shouted some of the less communitarian patrons. "Stop the other workshops." Wein surrendered, and Guy invited the crowd to come see him in Chicago, where he assured them he would play even louder.[57]

The following year, which proved to be the festival's last, disturbances at the Newport Jazz Festival earlier in the summer led a frightened community to impose onerous security measures, sapping the folk-festival treasury. The town also ordered all parks and beaches emptied by midnight, discouraging attendance by those who relied on impromptu camping in lieu of hotel reservations.[58] Overall, this produced a darkening of the mood, which festival historian Cheryl Brauner characterizes as "an aura of suspicion and fear." Pete Seeger, who had appeared at every Newport Folk Festival, marked the 1969 event with a free concert at a nearby dockside, performing on the deck of the sloop *Clearwater* from which he championed a cleanup of the Hudson River. He promised a series of such shows in the coming months, assuring everyone that they would be free "because the Folk Festival has priced itself out of the American people."[59] Low on cash and under siege by its friends, Newport expired after the 1969 presentation. It did not die because its fan base evaporated or because it could no longer attract the headlining acts needed to draw a crowd. It died because its efforts to accommodate the pop music world of the late 1960s were at odds with the romantic goals of preservation and egalitarianism that had served as its raison d'être.

A similar fate befell the legendary Club 47, the small Cambridge room that, following its opening in 1958, had become ground zero for the vibrant Boston-area revival scene. To outsiders the club's reputation may rest solely on its status as the primary launching pad for Joan Baez. Far more than that, it presented bluegrass, gospel, blues, Appalachian guitar picking, jug-band music, and more—what critic and musician Ted Drozdowski called "American folk music in all its incarnations." Like Newport, the club fell before the onslaught of changing attitudes, the rise of the rock-and-roll star system, and an increasingly sophisticated "youth industry" that marketed entertainment on a massive scale. In the midsixties, rock clubs started opening in Greater Boston, finding financial success while the communitarian Club 47 was, in the words of onetime club manager Jim Rooney, "still apologizing for charging $1.50 at the door."[60]

By the summer of 1967, with increased competition from new venues, and with audiences more interested in bands than in solo folk performers, the club could not afford the fees of artists who now saw themselves as stars. Members of the Paul Butterfield Blues Band had grown up professionally within the folk world and were friends to Rooney and the club. They now demanded two thousand dollars for a six-night engagement. Rooney paid it once out of pride, unwilling to let a competitor have an act he considered one of his club's own. Still, it "broke the bank [and] that obviously couldn't go on." Exhausted after years of seven-day workweeks, Rooney resigned. His successor, Byron Linardos, considered relocating to a larger space and transforming the club into a multifaceted arts center but ultimately surrendered. "It was over," he said of the once-dominant revival showroom. "I think it went as far as it could without becoming something else."[61]

In the wake of the great boom, in decidedly nonlinear fashion, a new generation of folklore scholars began to examine aggressively once-sacred disciplinary precepts, attempting to situate folklore within a world marked by mass media, a growing popular music industry, and rampant cultural exchange. Among them was Roger Abrahams, himself a Greenwich Village folkie who had once hosted periodic folksinging gatherings in his Lower Manhattan apartment. In 1963, Abrahams took direct aim at folklore's romantic gloss. "Too often," he argued, "the theoretical ideal of pure oral transmission" encouraged the folklorist to see himself as "dealing with sacrosanct matters, lore transmitted from the pure 'golden age' of the primitive past of Indo-European culture by word of mouth, and thus divorced from contemporary discourse, except as vestige." Arguing that folklore was "a very live cultural phenomenon," Abrahams urged analysts to study it in as full a cultural context as possible, the better to understand the competing forces that give communities, however defined, their identities.[62]

Alan Dundes distilled much developing thought in noting that folklorists needed to focus on present-day expression or they "would in time follow the folk itself into oblivion." Contemporary folk, Dundes said, consisted of "*any group of people whatsoever* who share at least one common factor." Given this "flexible definition," individual groups could overlap and might consist, for example, of surfers, motorcyclists, computer programmers, or, as Sheldon Posen realized, folk song revivalists.[63] Dundes took issue with Dorson's vitriolic condemnation of fakelore, recognizing that for most groups it had been a long time, centuries perhaps, since they had been insulated from either the intrusion of the marketplace or the conscious manipulation of their expressive traditions. Thus, rather than rail against fakelore, Dundes argued that the more productive course is to accept it for what it is—"an integral element of culture just as folklore is." "Let us study it," he wrote, "as folklorists."[64]

Expanding conceptions of the folk, recognition of the omnipresence of the mass media, and an explicit rapprochement with fakelore all represented a shift in the folklorist's perspective. The time was right for a reformulation of the field that distilled all of the socially driven changes in disciplinary scope. In the late sixties Dan Ben-Amos, a young scholar who had studied under Dorson, began formulating just such a restatement. In an essay that has proved to be one of the most influential in disciplinary history, he called for a redefinition of folklore as "artistic communication in small groups." After surveying the semantic swamp that had long plagued his field, Ben-Amos argued that, as an academic discipline, folklore's distinctive contribution lies in its ability to analyze the cultural dynamics of groups. Thus, the "folkloric text," whether in the form of a song, story, or custom, exists by definition within the confines of a structured group, and its role depends on that group's unique social context. Folklore, Ben-Amos thus maintained, is not an aggregate of things such as songs or stories but "a process—a communicative process, to be exact."[65]

In the contemporary world, where musicians perform "folk songs" on television before a diverse audience of millions, the singer is, at the moment of performance, divorced from any unique group function. It is legitimate, therefore, to ask if the song is a folk song as televised or merely a text that sometimes functions as a folk song. If the folklorist's underlying goal is to understand groups, then analysis of the time, mode, and manner of communication is as essential as the particular text or practice communicated. Thus, Ben-Amos argued, folklore, properly understood, consists of the totality of a given communication that unites presenter, text, and audience as part of a single face-to-face event. In provocative fashion, he called on his colleagues to jettison their historical insistence on the requirements of orality and tradition. In his view, these are artificial limiting factors that inhibit the valuable study of small-group artistic communication, a process that he considers culturally significant without regard to either mode of transmission or textual longevity.[66]

Notwithstanding Ben-Amos's well-received effort, the definition of folklore remains muddled, leading to continued calls for clarification, redefinition, or outright abandonment. In the 1990s Gene Bluestein added his voice to those arguing that the idea of the folk fails to reflect the reality of the American experience. In its place, he urged the embrace of "poplore," a word that Archie Green had coined. Green offered the term after attending the 1967 Berkeley Folk Festival, which joined so-called traditionalists such as Doc Watson with popular revivalists such as Pete Seeger and then-contemporary rock bands such as Red Krayola and Country Joe and the Fish. Poplore, Green maintained, encompasses "knowledge, actions, and manners which are conveyed by and accepted from such institutions as commercial entertainment and advertising." It comprises materials "which are disseminated by commercial entertainment and related media, but which function traditionally." An ardent believer in the value of small-group expression, Green proposed *poplore* not as an alternative to *folklore* but as a supplemental rubric.[67]

Bluestein expands the term into a de facto substitute. Traversing ground examined decades earlier by Botkin and Dorson, he bows briefly to the notion of a traditional folk culture but deems it largely irrelevant to "the characteristic American experience [that] involves a melding of folk and pop in the context of many diverse cultures." "The United States," he writes, "does not possess a body of anonymously created materials developed over long periods of time. What the nation has is poplore, an obvious mix of folk and pop elements that is associated with known artists, whose esthetic contributions often change the inherited materials before our eyes." Seeger, perhaps recognizing a theory that provides the imprimatur of scholarship to his own work, is impressed. The man who has ceased attempting to define "folk song" deems poplore a "very sensible new word." "Two centuries ago," he adds, "the word 'folklore' made sense, describing the traditional culture of the peasant class, 90% of the population. In these industrial-technology ridden times, it's better to use a new word than try to make an old one fit."[68]

Despite decades of conscious reformulation, both the academy and the popular revival continue to wrestle with the meaning and importance of tradition and authenticity. In the face of long-standing confusion and disagreement, and given the ongoing pitfalls of romantic paternalism, decontextualization, and racial and ethnic essentialism, it is hardly surprising that many present-day revivalists throw up their hands when confronted with the definitional fray. Understanding that their frequent involvement in concert production or record promotion places them firmly within the mass-mediated-culture industry, recognizing the often marginal commercial status of the musical styles they enjoy, and appreciating the substantial overlap among both cultures and musical genres, many simply hope to explore as wide an array of music as they can, as respectfully as they can.

My own effort to find an appropriate terminology has centered on the concept of vernacularity. Green has explored the term *vernacular* at length, concluding that, like *folk*, it is a "problematic tag." In a broad survey of the arts, he finds it applied most often to expression that is, in popular parlance, "native and home grown," as opposed to that which is the product of self-described or readily apparent elites, be they artistic or commercial. Avoiding any strict requirement of traditionality or orality, vernacularity suggests nonetheless a close connection between art and long-lived cultures in ways that transitory popular artifacts do not. Significantly, however, the concept is broad enough to encompass commercial forms, particularly those linked to specific grassroots subcultures, such as western swing, rhythm and blues, and early manifestations of rock and roll. Imperfect, but perhaps suitable, vernacularity encompasses a wide range of music derived, sometimes loosely, from the traditional folk forms of diverse ethnicities, races, regions, and occupations.[69]

As the boom ended, disparate styles of vernacular music still thrived throughout the United States. Much of it existed within local, thoroughly noncommercial scenes, such as the conjuntos played in the bars and community centers of San Antonio or the polkas popular at wedding and anniversary parties in Cleveland. Such innate community expression never had anything to do with the commercial revival, and the boom's passing did not affect it one bit. But large numbers of self-conscious revivalists kept at it as well, still relishing the old ballads and blues and banjo tunes that formed the movement's heart. Neil Rossi, who recorded one of Rounder Records' earliest releases as a member of the old-time revival band the Spark Gap Wonder Boys, recalls that, even as the boom withered, there remained in Boston "an active subculture of people who liked and listened to folk music. The Folk Song Society of Greater Boston," for example, "was always very active, and they could fill a hall if you wanted to listen to [tradition-based singers] Sara Grey or Gordon Bok or whoever was popular at that time." Reflecting his own experience as an old-time musician in the postboom years, he says, "You couldn't make a living at it but you could still go and pick up a few bucks and just have a good time."[70]

Many of these latter-day revivalists enjoyed—if only for an evening—a brief journey to a romanticized vision of the American past. Others simply liked the sound of a fiddle or the clarity of a story sung well. Some received satisfaction from music that exemplified an admired heritage. Others disliked the volume of rock or the clubs and dance halls in which it thrived. Still others loved dancing that involved actual steps and partners, as opposed to the free-form abandon that marked the rock-and-roll ballrooms. Reflecting one of the revival's central contradictions, some felt bound to folk music by the movement's leftist political coloration, whereas others reveled in tradition's rootedness and sense of conservatism.

In 1969 Happy Traum, by then the editor of *Sing Out!* magazine, published an article in *Rolling Stone* that discussed the passing of the "folk sound" from mass consciousness. An optimistic Traum saw promise, both in America's still thriving vernacular artistry and in a commercial world that the folk revival had transformed. Popular groups such as the Byrds and the Band, among others, now drew freely from a vast array of traditional Anglo and African American sources, accepting, in Traum's words, "what is good, without having to put self-conscious labels on it." As a result of the seeds planted by the revival, he concluded, "folk music and its influences have been incorporated into the total picture of American popular music." Recognizing, however, that more esoteric music—some of it deeply traditional—still struggled commercially, Traum criticized America's "all-or-nothing" approach to popularity, in which the mass acceptance of one type of music seemed always to come at the expense of other styles. He called for a circuit of venues catering to specialized tastes, whether for folk music, jazz, chamber orchestras, or performing poets.[71]

At least as far as folk music was concerned, the circuit Traum yearned for was taking shape as he wrote, comprising both new venues and surviving boom-era entities. Geographically dispersed, and consisting of venues and organizations that come and go with the economic tide and the strength of volunteer interest, that circuit survives. Though individual components vary in emphasis, the contemporary folk scene as a whole encompasses all of folklore and revivalism's disparate strands: an appreciation of tradition, enthusiasm for the vernacular heritage of many cultures, an often tight-knit sense of community and an affinity for artistic forms that those who wield commercial power tend to marginalize. Participants in amateur singing circles and instrumental jams have come to understand that their connection to folk music stems not merely from their repertoire but also from the nature of their informal artistic bond with one another. Following Ben-Amos, a group of friends gathered to sing Beatles songs, or to swap verses of their own compositions, are making folk music of the truest kind. In general, in the postboom era, the more localized a performing folk music scene, the more ties it has to ongoing community activism and the less it tries to compete within the larger pop music arena, the more likely it is to thrive. Among those revivalists who do try to work within the music industry, the tension that has always marked the intersection of the marketplace and the folk continues. However, though an excessive emphasis on commerce does prompt revivalist concern, there is also a pragmatic recognition that commercial success can bestow desirable respect and cultural power.

Whereas the original Newport Folk Festival died at the end of the sixties, the Philadelphia Folk Festival, which began in 1962, has continued. That festival grew out of the Philadelphia Folksong Society, a nonprofit, community-based organization that began in 1957, before the great boom seized public awareness. The society originated in the Gilded Cage, a coffeehouse where folk music aficionados of the late fifties gathered. Society members began the festival as a fund-raiser for their own organization. In time, the event grew sufficiently profitable that the society was able to engage in a variety of local philanthropic activities. Among other things, festival proceeds have supported music-therapy programs for emotionally disturbed children and have financed concerts by traditional performers in schools, nursing homes, and orphanages.[72] The Newport festival had also engaged in philanthropy, but its orientation was national, not local, and its managing board consisted of music-industry professionals who lacked routine contact with either their host community, which merely tolerated the festival at best, or with one another. In contrast, Philadelphia's festival is an adjunct to an ongoing community organization that offers social and entertainment opportunities, as well as an opportunity for civic involvement. It is not an end in itself but a means to an end. For that reason, it managed to survive when folk music was no longer a national preoccupation.

Other festivals survived by steering clear of music-industry excess. In 1966, one year after Dylan electrified Newport, Bob and Evelyne Beers started the Fox Hollow Family Festival of Traditional Music and Arts on the hilly parcel of land they owned in New York's Adirondack Mountains. Fox Hollow, which ran annually until 1980, embodied the promise of community and noncommercialism that had gone astray at Newport. In reviewing the 1967 gathering, *Sing Out!* concluded euphorically, "The one ingredient that sets this Festival apart from all the others is love," which was present "in such abundance and profusion that it is virtually inescapable." Putting this effusive romanticism in more tangible terms, and striking a stark contrast with the last days of a starstruck Newport, the reviewer's most lingering memory was of the "lack of fences." There was "no forbidden back-stage area, no special down-front section for the press . . . no police, no endless series of pass checkers and no need for them." Instead, one found at Fox Hollow "a wonderful spirit of cooperation, a close and friendly intermingling of audience, press and performers, a sense of belonging to and being part of the togetherness of the festival."[73]

Other surviving revival organizations have displayed a similar interest in community, at times accompanied by an utter lack of interest in the stars and machinations of the music industry. One such group is the Folklore Society of Greater Washington (FSGW), which a couple of dozen District of Columbia folk music fans founded in 1964, hoping to encourage local performances by traditional musicians. For its first concert the group booked Seamus Ennis, a forty-five-year-old Irish piper and storyteller whose career, at the risk of understatement, did not lend itself to pop stardom. When illness forced Ennis to cancel at the last moment, three society members performed in his place, a perfectly acceptable alternative among people whose primary goal was participation and friendship. More than forty years later, the FSGW still sponsors traditional music concerts and, of perhaps greater importance, regular participatory events for its members and guests, often held in members' homes. These are advertised in a monthly newsletter that contains reminders such as "Bring your favorite snack to share." Events include "English country dances," "open sings," semimonthly gospel sings, and "storyswaps," designed to foster the sharing of tales. Built on a foundation of community fellowship, while avoiding the need for sound systems, excessive performance fees, and large venues, the D.C. society has carried on long after the boom's demise.[74]

Across the country in 1968, Nancy Owens, a dissatisfied twenty-six-year-old Oakland, California, preschool teacher, was yearning for a new career. She enjoyed the bohemian atmosphere she had discovered on visits to New York's Greenwich Village and had found a bit of that at Jabberwock, a Berkeley folk music club that arose during the early sixties. Jabberwock did not survive the onslaught of rock, and by 1968 it had closed, along with the Cabale, described by one regular as a Club 47 spin-off that helped establish a "Cambridge-Berkeley link." Despite a complete absence of relevant experience, Owens decided that she would start a musical coffeehouse. She located a vacant storefront in Berkeley, retained the name of the used furniture store that had once occupied the space, and opened the Freight and Salvage in July 1968. With an 87–person capacity, mismatched tables and chairs, and a dressing room barely bigger than the tiny bathroom, Owens did not have to worry about attracting rock stars. Very quickly, the Freight drew a crowd of respectful music fans, developing a reputation as a quality listening room.[75]

The first act to take the stage was the Cleanliness and Godliness Skiffle Band, a Berkeley street aggregation that played whatever it liked, including Billie Holiday tunes, 1950s rock and roll, and early rhythm and blues—all without electric guitars. With music that was predominantly acoustic and decidedly nonmainstream, and a physical environment that was small and, politely phrased, unpretentious, the Freight, in the words of Cleanliness and Godliness member Annie Johnston, helped foster "a good, noncompetitive musical community." Unfortunately, it was never profitable. Owens claimed a salary of fifty dollars per week, "when we could afford it." Needing to move on, she sold the club in 1978. It passed through a couple of successors until 1983 when a coalition of musicians and patrons formed a nonprofit corporation to purchase and run the venue. The resulting influx of energy, along with the nonprofit's ability to solicit grant money and tax-deductible contributions, allowed the club to hang on but did not insulate it from financial pressure. Needing to sell more tickets, backers moved the Freight to a new 240–seat venue in 1988.[76]

Through it all, the Freight's musical fare has stayed remarkably constant. The corporate name—the Berkeley Society for the Preservation of Traditional Music—is convenient shorthand. Though somewhat consistent with the club's regular offerings of old-time music, bluegrass, and, to a lesser extent, blues and gospel, it fails to convey the full story. The room has never confined itself to vanishing traditions. It presents a steady stream of the contemporary singer-songwriters who have been a mainstay of folk venues since the midsixties. Additionally, it mixes music from a wide array of American regional traditions with small doses of acoustic jazz, music from other lands, a capella vocalizing, and oddball experimentation. The Freight's true essence is a noncommercial, mostly acoustic eclecticism in a setting that conveys intimacy. To varying degrees, depending on the evening and the performer, it embodies much of what passes for folklore in the twenty-first century: artistic communication in small groups, a connection to the past, respect for vernacular heritage, a sense of community, and an undercurrent of anticorporatism that constitutes an implicit link to the revival's leftist heritage and recalls those heady days before the music industry captured the great boom.

One of the more successful postboom folk music projects arose out of the one-time revival crucible of Greenwich Village. In the late seventies, when punk and new wave garnered the lion's share of attention from Manhattan tastemakers, "the Village" meant the East Village, launching pad of the Ramones, Blondie, the Talking Heads, and Patti Smith. Greenwich Village, to the west, had faded from the consciousness of all but a few musical cognoscenti. Still, Gerde's Folk City hung on and was a center of that performing folk scene that did exist, a scene then dominated by contemporary songwriters. Folk City, however, booked headliners. It was not a place that offered fledgling writers and performers the opportunity to test their skills in a nonthreatening, let alone supportive, environment. To create such a place, locals formed the Songwriter's Exchange in 1977, a loose assemblage of artists who performed in several different cafés and held weekly meetings in musician Jack Hardy's Village apartment.

Hardy, a prolific songwriter possessed of an intense focus and a propensity for hard work, was the catalyst for the Exchange. He had moved to the Village in 1973 and set himself to the task of rebuilding the neighborhood's dormant folk scene, in part to provide himself with an artistic home. Richard Mayer, an early Exchange participant, describes Hardy's role: "In the middle of everybody complaining that they had no place to play, no one booking them or recording them, he'd say, 'O.K., let's build a club, let's have a weekly meeting, let's make our own album.' He said he was Tom Sawyer whitewashing the fence."[77] With Hardy presiding, the group critiqued new songs, often harshly, with the common goal of artistic improvement. As Hardy put it, "Endless hours were spent discussing and debating the songs and the process of writing." Inevitably, friendships grew, and the musicians "hung out, played softball, ate, drank, traveled, and caroused together. What emerged was a sense of community."[78]

The group produced *Cornelia Street: The Songwriters Exchange*, a compilation album featuring songs by several of these writer-performers that garnered a positive review in the nationally distributed *Stereo Review*. "They *are* still out there," wrote critic Noel Coppage, "those troubadours with their simple acoustic backing, and Stash Records has made a beautiful little album with some of them." Eager to be heard, the group sought a stable performance venue from which to build an audience. In August 1981 they founded the SpeakEasy Café in the back room of a Middle Eastern restaurant, steps away from the legendary Greenwich Village intersection of Bleecker and McDougal Streets. Managed by a cooperative of more than fifty musicians and led by a steering committee, "the Speak" presented music six nights per week. Generally, after the scheduled performance, co-op members and guests took to the stage "just for the fun of it."[79]

Next, the restless Hardy spearheaded the creation of another all-volunteer effort—a monthly periodical with the awkward title *The Coop/The Fast Folk Musical Magazine*. Dedicated to the promotion of quality songs, *Fast Folk*, which debuted in February 1982, devoted itself to the promotion of emerging artists. The highlight of each issue, and the project's primary reason for being, was an accompanying record—later a CD—that usually featured songwriters performing original compositions. The name *Fast Folk* came from Hardy's insistence, at times over considerable dissent from craft-conscious performers, that the artistic process had to be accomplished swiftly. He wanted freshly written songs, and, when he could get his way, he did not allow multiple takes when recording. Striving for authenticity in the contemporary sense, he wanted inspiration, not the slightest hint of manipulation. "The whole idea was to do it fast," he said. "You could hear a song at an open mike or songwriters' meeting and two weeks later it was being played on the radio in Philadelphia or Chicago. It was urgent, exciting. It was in your face."[80]

In an account published in 1983, when the SpeakEasy and *Fast Folk* were going concerns, cooperative member Rod MacDonald discussed the personal meaning of the varied projects that had grown from the Songwriter's Exchange: "I'm sick of the attitude that folk music stopped being vital after the 1960's. That's before my time [and I think it's vital now]. . . . Folk music," he added, "is going public again here in the Village; and we're starting to hear from similar groups around the country, sharing information and good times. We're not trying to rehash the 60's though, it's the 80's and we want to move ahead, singing, writing, making the music we love."[81] These varied cooperative endeavors ended up having a national impact, succeeding beyond anyone's expectations. Starting in 1984 members presented annual Fast Folk Revues at the Bottom Line, then one of New York's premier music clubs. Songwriters from all regions sought recognition, leading to issues devoted specifically to local scenes stretching outward from New York to Boston, Maine, Toronto, Texas, and Los Angeles.

In 1985 Suzanne Vega, an early cooperative member and the magazine's first subscription manager, released her major label debut and soon had a national hit with her composition "Luka." Other prominent artists whose early work appeared in *Fast Folk* include Steve Forbert, Shawn Colvin, Tracy Chapman, and Nanci Griffith. Though shy of stardom, contributors such as John Gorka, Richard Shindell, Cliff Eberhardt, and Lucy Kaplansky became staples on the national folk circuit, recording and touring regularly. The entire enterprise was a testament to the belief that an audience still existed for folk music of some sort, and that with sufficient organization and initiative adherents could reach that audience.[82]

In southern California one more great-boom veteran sought to retain his connection to folk music amid a now more subdued local scene. Clark Weissman learned guitar in the late forties while a high school student in New York City. Following a well-trod path, he helped form his school's String and Frets Club, square-danced on Saturday nights, and enjoyed Sunday afternoons in Washington Square Park. While attending the Massachusetts Institute of Technology (MIT), he met Radcliff student Peggy Seeger, Pete's sister, and in 1955 he appeared as a guitar accompanist on her first album, *Folksongs of Courting and Complaint.* He relocated to Los Angeles after graduation in 1956, where he took a job in aeronautical engineering. In the early 1970s Weissman was working as a research and development specialist in the computer software field. Still a folk fan, he often bracketed his frequent business trips with weekend excursions to nearby folk festivals. He belonged to an informal folksinging club but wanted to do more than gather together and sing. He yearned to offer music lessons and host concerts.[83]

During a stint as club president Weissman discovered a cache of unopened letters from folk societies around the country, many of which offered to swap newsletters or inquired about Los Angeles–area performing opportunities. He began to answer these letters, and, as he traveled, he visited some of his newfound correspondents, discovering that many had common interests and concerns. One problem, troubling to both artists and fans, was the absence of suitable venues for relatively unknown but professional acoustic musicians, particularly those who favored more esoteric ethnic or regional styles. Weissman saw this problem in his own community. The Ash Grove, a once-successful boom-era club, had burned down in 1973. The strongest alternative was the 165–seat McCabe's Guitar Shop, a musical instrument store in Santa Monica that began a performance series in 1969. McCabe's, however, focused on performers with some degree of public or industry recognition.

Weissman and his wife, Elaine, realized they could fill a need. By moving the furniture in their home they could host almost as many patrons as McCabe's, without the overhead of an ongoing business enterprise. Aided by their growing library of folk society newsletters, they learned who was attempting to tour, discovering much new talent in the process. They began inviting people to play in their home, providing an audience as well as food and a place to stay. Musicians received a performance fee, raised through a modest cover charge, as well as the opportunity to sell cassettes and conduct fee-based workshops in songwriting or instrumental techniques. Although this provided one or two reasonable paydays, there remained the problem of prohibitive travel expenses for nonlocal performers. To justify the cost of a trip from, say, the East Coast, musicians needed more than the earnings from a single location. Thinking of Junípero Serra's chain of missions, Elaine envisioned a chain of locally supported folk venues stretching up the West coast, which collectively could provide economic support for relatively unknown performers. Soon she was working with or simply encouraging other local ventures, and ultimately she served as a booking agent, helping musicians organize tours along the California coast. The Weissmans continued presenting their own house concerts until 1994, when their home sustained significant earthquake damage.

In 1980 officials of the Beverly Hills Department of Parks and Recreation sought the Weissmans' assistance in creating an outdoor concert series. Clark and Elaine took this opportunity to produce a one-day folk festival in a city park, offering both performances and instruction. Invited back the following year, they expanded to two days. As the festival became an ongoing event the Weissmans organized the California Traditional Music Society (CTMS), a nonprofit corporation set up to handle the festival's increasingly complex funding and logistical needs. In 1999 CTMS won a competitive award from the Los Angeles Cultural Affairs Department, entitling it to lease an eleven hundred–square-foot former firehouse, which the society transformed into an administrative and performance space housing an ongoing series of concerts, dances, and participatory jam sessions. In 2005 the annual CTMS Summer Solstice Festival spanned three days and utilized multiple performance and teaching areas that featured music, dance, storytelling, and crafts from disparate traditions.[84]

Reflecting on his roughly forty years of postboom activity, Clark dismisses the idea that the end of the boom signaled the demise of a strong nationwide interest in folk music. It may have spelled the end of opportunities for large commercial success as a so-called folk musician, but wherever there were sufficient adherents, folk music hung on as a small-scale and participatory activity. Clark and Elaine successfully harnessed this residual energy in the late 1980s when they organized and hosted a conference of 130 folk music activists from across the United States and Canada—a gathering that became the founding meeting of the North American Folk Music and Dance Alliance.

Others also managed to turn their ongoing interests into national institutions, helping vernacular music survive as the media spotlight dimmed. Despite tremendous financial difficulties in the early 1980s, *Sing Out!* carried on, and its quarterly issues now exceed two hundred pages in length. Largely free of the overly precious romanticism that sometimes marred its reporting in the sixties, it provides coverage of indigenous sounds from all over the world. The great boom had helped revitalize bluegrass, a country music form that was fading by 1960, a mere fifteen or so years after its birth. When the boom ended, the music often received scant media attention. In 1966, frustrated at missing a nearby Stanley Brothers concert due to a lack of press, fans in the Washington, D.C., area began a newsletter designed to keep one another informed of local events. Dubbed *Bluegrass Unlimited*, that newsletter survives as a glossy monthly magazine that covers bluegrass around the world.[85] Two years later, Happy Traum and his wife, Jane, began

Homespun Tapes in Woodstock, New York, selling music lessons on audiocassettes. Still thriving, Homespun continues to satisfy the yearning for homemade music, offering lessons in many instruments and a wide range of vernacular styles via compact discs, videos, and DVDs. Instructors include acknowledged masters who either lived through the great boom or have benefited from its ongoing influence.

In 1970 a pair of young Chicago blues enthusiasts founded *Living Blues,* a magazine devoted to the African American vernacular form first recorded at the dawn of the music industry and itself a revival mainstay. Now published by the Center for the Study of Southern Culture at the University of Mississippi, *Living Blues* also carries on, documenting its obsession in loving and extraordinary detail.[86] That same year, three students in the Northeast released the first two albums on their new record label, Rounder Records. Rounder is an amalgam of its founders' multifaceted experiences, which encompass the early-sixties folk revival, southern fiddling conventions, the counterculture, the politics of the New Left, and the late-twentieth-century record industry. Through its extraordinary stylistic eclecticism, its casual mixture of the homegrown and the commercial, and its willingness to breach artistic and cultural boundaries, Rounder has helped strengthen the redefinition of folk music as a form that spans a wide continuum, linking poplore to the deeply traditional.

TWO

From Club 47 to Union Grove:
The Birth of Rounder Records

On February 23, 1983, members of the National Academy of Recording Arts and Sciences gathered in Los Angeles for the presentation of the twenty-fifth annual Grammy Awards. That year the proceedings highlighted Toto, a pop/rock band composed of onetime Los Angeles studio musicians that was then enjoying tremendous commercial success. The band's middle-of-the-road sound is well exemplified by "Rosanna," the multimillion selling paean to actress Rosanna Arquette that is etched permanently into the neurons of anyone who listened to pop music radio in 1982. As Toto reaped acclaim for Record of the Year, Album of the Year, and, collectively, Producer of the Year, few gave more than passing notice to the brand-new category of Best Traditional Blues Recording, won by *Alright Again!* Clarence "Gatemouth" Brown's maiden Rounder Records' release.[1]

Rounder, then twelve years old, had never before won a Grammy, and the album—a horn-laden, big-band amalgam of electric blues and jazz—was far removed from most of its other fare. Midwifed by the great boom, the label had historically emphasized the rural, acoustic sounds that dominated the more traditional side of that era. By 1983 it had ventured somewhat beyond that early defining sound, most successfully with the young white blues-rocker George Thorogood. Still, even when it journeyed from rec- ognizably rural fare it continued to favor a raw, underproduced, relatively homemade approach, one that Thorogood transferred figuratively from the back porch to the suburban garage.

Alright Again! was, at the time, an anomaly in the Rounder catalog. Producer Scott Billington, employed by Rounder in various capacities since 1976 and now in charge of his first studio session, had set out to capture the sound of a particular slice of urban nightlife. The resulting album sounded nothing like anything you would hear on a rural southern homestead. Instead, it echoed the sound of Los Angeles's Central Avenue, circa 1945, near where Brown had cut his first records. In the early forties clubs mushroomed along the avenue as blacks fled rural poverty to find work in wartime industry, providing eager audiences for ambitious entertainers and entrepreneurs. Central Avenue was, in the words of writer Mark Humphrey, "nearer to the fabled Hollywood and Pacific beaches than it was to sharecropper farms or cold northern tenements, so blues musicians freely broadened their palettes. . . . Bebop no less than blues could be heard on Central in the 1940s, and the close proximity produced some exciting hybrids."[2] This mix was the organic response of a dispossessed racial group searching for companionship in a new environment. As such, it should have had obvious intellectual appeal to those who appreciate indigenous art developed to serve the needs of community. Yet it was not—and to some degree still is not—viewed as a "folk form," given the long-standing revivalist prejudice favoring music that is acoustic, homemade in sound, and rural in origin.

Billington sought, unabashedly, a product that was simultaneously commercial and artistic, and he saw no conflict between the two. For this project, he disdained the revivalist's oft-stated desire to simply capture the sound of a performance unadorned. His goal was, as he puts it, to make a "record," not a "document." With this in mind he sought hook-laden songs, helped Brown assemble an experienced studio band, and led structured rehearsals in which the rhythm section perfected its parts in one room, while the horns practiced in another. All of this, Billington recalls, was "an uncomfortable concept for some at Rounder, given the idea that the visions of musicians should not be manipulated." Still, he moved forward, despite sensing some intracompany grumbling that his work was "too slick" for the label.[3] Ultimately, Rounder embraced the record, and this acceptance of a wide variety of vernacular forms has become a company hallmark.

Although *Alright Again!* differs from prior Rounder releases, its creator, Gatemouth Brown, could serve as the quintessential Rounder artist. Born in 1924 in Louisiana and raised in nearby southeast Texas, the African American

Brown grew up hearing his father, a railroad worker, perform a wide variety of styles on numerous instruments. "My daddy was a very great man," he recalled, "and he played music at house parties on Saturday nights. He played fiddle, guitar, banjo, mandolin, accordion, everything—played nothin' but country, bluegrass, and Cajun music." Brown set out early to become a professional musician. By the 1940s he was recording for Aladdin Records in Los Angeles and Houston's Peacock label, each of which fostered the then modern and decidedly urban blues and jazz hybrid dominated by horns and electric guitar. Due to his race and the sound of his earliest recordings, casual commentators generally characterize Brown as a bluesman, though he resisted such labeling with missionary fervor. "Look here," said Brown, "I refuse to be labeled as a blues player, jazz player, country player, bluegrass player, Cajun player, zydeco player, calypso player—I'm an American musician, and I'm going further than that. I play polkas—that's not American, that's German, and I laid that on them in Berlin."[4]

In many ways Brown was the epitome of the modern vernacular musician—a commercially savvy performer who roots his art in his own family traditions, which encompass the separate traditions of multiple, overlapping groups in an increasingly hybridized world. By these terms, Rounder is the epitome of the modern vernacular record label. Its vast catalog displays a deep reverence for music rooted in tradition, along with a recognition that tradition is a complex construct, encompassing constant change. Historically, most Rounder albums—even those as carefully constructed as Brown's Grammy winner—remain distant from the commercial mainstream. This has changed somewhat over time, but however virtuosic or polished some records may be, many remain rooted in specific ethnic, racial, or geographic communities. In addition to blues, the label's offerings include bluegrass and old-time tunes; Tejano and Cajun music; anthologies of union songs; traditional music from Mexico, eastern Europe, Asia, and Africa; and several hundred reggae albums. Rounder implicitly presents this "community music" as a genre of its own, one that transcends specific stylistic differences. Whereas ardent bluegrassers, for example, sometimes argue that their art is a historic part of the country music industry, Rounder situates it somewhat differently. Viewed as a whole, the company's extensive catalog presents bluegrass as an intrinsic part of the broader world of nonmainstream vernacular music. In Rounder's universe, bluegrass has far more in common with delta blues, Mexican conjuntos, and African tribal sounds than it does with Nashville's latest hat act or femme fatale.

Even before its founders aged, married, bought homes, and had children, corporate growth saw the end of Rounder's overt political stance, as well as the release of more contemporary pop than ever before. These things, along with an increasingly hierarchical structure, have fostered sometimes-vitriolic complaints that Rounder has "gone corporate."[5] Beyond any doubt, the label is today vastly different from the self-styled antiprofit collective of its youth. That may be due to political moderation, to reasoned pragmatism, to expanded tastes, or even to a yearning to make money. It may also reflect a desire to serve the legitimate needs of performers who want their records marketed in a manner that affords them an opportunity to reap the material benefits their society offers. Certainly, much of the company's catalog consists of records that seek merely, in Billington's words, to "document" a particular style. But the bulk of the collection features working musicians who hope that their efforts will earn them both money and recognition. Rounder has shown that the music of idiosyncratic vernacular artists can be as professionally recorded and as solidly entertaining as that of any mainstream major-label hit maker. In doing so, they have joined that eternal debate surrounding the juxtaposition of folk culture and commerce, which has energized and plagued folk music activism for decades.

Of the three individuals known colloquially as "the Rounders," Ken Irwin, Bill Nowlin, and Marian Leighton, only Irwin had a childhood that touched even remotely upon the possibility of a life immersed "in traditional folk music and its contemporary offshoots."[6] He was born in New York City in 1944 and, with his parents and older brother, moved north to suburban Westchester County at age four. Though not particularly active politically during Irwin's childhood, his parents possessed both leftist and intellectual leanings, those two staples of mid-twentieth-century urban revivalism. By the time of Irwin's adolescence, this leftism extended only far enough to make them ardent Adlai Stevenson supporters. Still, the political views of his father, Theodore, were sufficiently pronounced that Ken once asked if he had been a member of the Communist Party, which Theodore denied. Nonetheless, young Ken's earliest "political" memory is of sitting by the radio in 1953 awaiting confirmation that Joseph Stalin had died. Theodore was a freelance journalist who had changed his surname from Isaacs in an effort to avoid professional limitations imposed by anti-Semitism. Over a long career he published many articles in popular magazines, as well as several books ranging from detective fiction to practical health guides.[7]

By the 1950s Theodore may have been little more than a strong devotee of the Democratic Party, but his 1935 novel, *Strange Passage*, was a highly politicized attack on capitalism and American xenophobia. The book follows a group of undocumented immigrants facing deportation during a time of fervent U.S. antagonism toward all things foreign. Irwin summarizes what he sees as a prevailing American sentiment, as he condemns a government policy urging, "Go back where you came from, you dago, you hunky, you scoovy, you heine, you mick, you sheenie, you limey. Get out and stay out!" Throughout, Irwin's disdain for parochialism and bigotry is clear. He expresses his own cultural relativism succinctly in a scene set at a world's fair–like exhibition where his characters come upon an array of dried vegetables and "peasant pottery," used to decorate a simulated rural Italian household. Correcting a young girl who characterizes the decor as "crazy," a teacher explains, "In each country people have their own way of doing things. It's just different from ours, that's all." At the end, the protagonist convinces his beloved to seek refuge with him in Soviet Russia, which he extols as a land where "there is work for everyone . . . Where art is fostered for what it brings to the people—not for its cash value to exploiters . . . A new Promised Land."[8]

Marred at times by somewhat artless didacticism, *Strange Passage* is very much a product of the radical literary tradition of its day when, in the midst of a seemingly endless depression, many intellectuals saw in the Soviet experiment the romantic possibility of a better world. By the time Ken was growing up, Theodore may have moderated his political philosophy. However, his novel's themes of cultural pluralism, economic justice, antiauthoritarianism and the value of artistic expression found renewed voice in his son's effort to give disparate cultures pride of place in the realms of both art and commerce. To the considerable extent that the younger Irwin's own efforts are fueled by fervid romanticism, that too appears an inheritance from his father.

Rita Irwin, Ken's mother, also served as a source of progressive political and social values. Her response to the drive for nuclear shelters that gripped the country at midcentury was to obtain a rubber stamp or stickers containing the adage "Peace Is the Only Shelter," which she affixed to all of the family mail.[9] Though primarily a homemaker during Ken's youth, Rita had previously been a social worker and author. In the 1930s she coauthored a book titled *Practical Birth Control* at a time when such a project was still somewhat of an avant-garde, politicized endeavor. In doing so, she cast her lot with a crusade that, in the words of historian Christine Stansell, had previously given "political shape and purpose to a sexual revolution" and was thus "critical to feminist modernity." Rita Irwin advocated birth control for any reason that a couple deemed appropriate, which might include a woman's desire for sex despite the need for continued employment or nothing more than a couple's conclusion that they were unready for parenthood. In terms guaranteed to alarm old-fashioned moralists, she attacked the Catholic Church's contention that the so-called rhythm method of contraception is a "natural" one. "If the Church believes in the desirability of 'natural' methods," she wrote, "does it realize that making love by the calendar is an interference with the *natural desire* for sex relationship . . . ?" Demonstrating a deep understanding of the pervasiveness of politics in everyday life, Irwin's ostensibly "practical" manual confronts issues related to gender roles, economic class, and the civic function of organized religion.[10]

Theodore and Rita's record collection leaned heavily toward Broadway favorites. Ken discovered rock and roll in junior high school when a friend introduced him to the programming of Alan Freed, the popular disc jockey who promoted black rhythm and blues aggressively to white audiences, not only through radio but also through movies, television, and concert production. Riding the sound wave produced by such transitional pioneers as Bo Diddley and Chuck Berry, Freed helped launch the incipient rock-and-roll industry. Irwin, who developed a particular fondness for doo-wop, loved Freed's radio show, *Rock 'n' Roll Party*. He also listened to *Your Hits of the Week*, a competing broadcast, and watched Dick Clark's *American Bandstand* on television. Like virtually all pop music fans of the day, he heard white artists offer their versions of black-originated tunes, such as the Diamonds' rendition of "Little Darlin'" and Pat Boone's interpretation of "Blueberry Hill," which the Gladiolas and Fats Domino, respectively, had recorded initially. Though he considered many of these cover versions technically proficient, he preferred the allegorical "real thing," because the covers invariably "lacked the emotional feeling of the originals."[11]

Despite his parents' strong beliefs, Irwin describes himself as an apolitical high schooler in what he perceived as "a fairly apolitical time." In his senior year, however, Pete Seeger stirred some latent political consciousness, albeit in a fairly minor way. Irwin attended a Seeger concert at a neighboring school and enjoyed it enough to start listening to a friend's Seeger LPs. Following this baptism, he began delving into the world of commercial folk and topical music, enjoying the polished vocals of the Chad Mitchell Trio, the social satire of Tom Lehrer, and a Folkways LP titled *We Shall Overcome: Songs of the Freedom Riders and Sit-ins.* Trading a collection of *Mad* magazines for some old singles gave him his first unintended exposure to bluegrass, which he considered "hysterical . . . really laughable stuff."[12]

Family friends, however, knowing that Irwin liked folk music of some sort, decided that he needed to own at least one bluegrass album. As a high school graduation gift they gave him the self-titled debut by the Greenbriar Boys, a group of young, New York–based revivalists who were veterans of the Sunday-afternoon folksinging gatherings in Greenwich Village's Washington Square Park. Despite their northern and urban upbringing, the Greenbriar Boys had found some success within their idiom's southern base. They were the first band from the North to appear, in 1958, on the stage of the Old Time Fiddlers Convention in Union Grove, North Carolina, an annual event since 1924, and one that was later to mean a great deal to Irwin. In 1960 they won first place in the convention's old-time band contest. The significance of the Greenbriars' boundary crossing escaped Irwin entirely, and he hated their album. The "high nasal voices," he says, "were just not to my liking. Couldn't deal with it. Again, very laughable."[13]

His tastes broadened dramatically after he left home in the fall of 1962 to enter Tufts University in Massachusetts. The folk music boom was nearing a peak of commercial activity, and the nearby Boston and Cambridge area rivaled New York as a revivalist hub. With his relatively small folk album collection in hand, Irwin headed into this maelstrom to begin college life with Bill Nowlin, the stranger that Tufts had selected as his dormitory roommate.

Nowlin, the oldest of three children, was born in Boston in 1945, the son of an electronics salesman and a homemaker. While in the first grade he moved to nearby Lexington, where he developed his lifelong love of baseball in general and the Boston Red Sox in particular. Using a system of self-made stencils he produced a neighborhood newsletter with a sports page that compiled statistics drawn from local sandlot baseball games. He drew comics with war and space themes and humorous comics modeled on *Mad* magazine. He also displayed a penchant for organization that—with the benefit of considerable hindsight—he believes foreshadowed his interest in Rounder's business affairs. "I would just for some reason write down things like the longest rivers in the world and make a list of the top ten," he explains. "There was no point to it. But I think that had something to do with some kind of business aptitude later in terms of structure and organization." He was also a fledgling antiquarian of sorts. "I liked old books and magazines. I used to go downtown," he recalls, "to buy old comic books for three cents each and old books for a quarter, that type of thing. There were a lot of tattoo parlors and burlesque houses there at the time but that has all been renovated out to make a relatively boring place. It was kind of exciting as a kid."[14]

Nothing suggested that music would become a career path. Nowlin took piano and trumpet lessons as a child, but neither became an enduring interest. He enjoyed listening to music, but it was hardly a passion to rival baseball, and his record collection was not as esoteric as Irwin's. The first record he owned was "In the Middle of the House," sung by Rusty Draper, a bland country/pop crooner who had a number of hits in the fifties. The second was "Hound Dog" backed with "Don't Be Cruel," Elvis Presley's 1956 smash.[15] Nowlin's first album was *What'd I Say* by Ray Charles, a 1959 collection of singles on Atlantic Records. He also enjoyed Chuck Berry, Little Richard, and "quite a few one-hit wonders." He explored the burgeoning folk revival a bit, but, unlike Irwin with his collection of freedom songs, Nowlin ventured no further than its most commercial sounds. He recalls owning some Kingston Trio records, and his younger sisters owned at least one album by Peter, Paul and Mary.[16]

The adolescent Nowlin flowered in the field of politics. Though his household was less political than Irwin's, young Bill developed a precocious political awareness. Throughout his childhood his parents were passive Republican voters. One of Nowlin's earliest political memories is of watching the 1952 Republican Party convention on television, a somewhat different awakening than Irwin's Stalin deathwatch of one year later. The convention pageantry drew Nowlin in, and he decided, "What I really wanted to do when I grew up was go to these big conventions and wear buttons and have confetti and balloons come down and carry the sign that said Massachusetts, or something like that." His fascination with political theater took a stranger turn when the American Nazi Party staged a rally in downtown Boston. Nowlin went to observe the excitement, drawn by the show, not the message. An interest in political issues developed. "I remember listening to talk radio about when I was twelve and hearing people like Malcolm X . . . and getting interested in politics so to speak, in the way of political issues, and that's why I ended up majoring in politics, partly." He volunteered in local campaigns, where his enthusiasm served him well. "Even when I was sixteen, I had my own desk, my own office, and my own expense account on one of them. . . . I guess they were hard up for people, maybe, but I remember going out and having a steak lunch and charging it."[17]

Although Irwin and Nowlin each arrived at Tufts in 1962 with some degree of political consciousness, they had diametrically opposed ideologies. Irwin, though nowhere near the activist that Nowlin was, followed his parents' leftist leanings into a casual appreciation of Pete Seeger and Folkways Records. Nowlin, to the contrary, was a self-styled conservative Republican and an advocate of the incipient presidential campaign of the right wing's favorite, Barry Goldwater. Their divergent attitudes could easily have driven them apart. Instead, unpredictably, they began a mutual exploration of the Boston arts scene, an arena in which they found common ground. Reflecting his parents' interest in the Broadway stage, Irwin was a veteran theatergoer. Responding to a solicitation, he became a campus representative for the Charles Playhouse, which entailed posting promotional fliers around Tufts in return for free tickets. He enlisted Nowlin's assistance, and the pair then expanded these efforts to other theaters. Wanting to broaden the scope of their representation even further, they contacted Manny Greenhill, a leading promoter of folk music concerts in Boston and the booking agent for Joan Baez and other luminaries. Greenhill "retained" them as representatives, thus providing them with free access to concerts as well as the theater. Enterprising and diversified, they also posted fliers—for a fee—on behalf of evangelical "bishop" Homer Tomlinson, the 1964 presidential candidate of the Theocratic Party who, two years later, was to bypass the political process and declare himself "king of the world."[18]

Their bond sealed around music, a somewhat unpredictable occurrence since the politically conservative Nowlin hated Irwin's Pete Seeger records. Still, they were young, away from home, and music was a strong social lubricant. Irwin owned one of their dormitory's few record players, and it, along with their fairly small record collections, became a dorm focal point. The Greenbriar Boys' LP started getting a lot of play. They initially treated the record as a joke, singing its tunes out loud to deliberately annoy their friends. It grew on them gradually; as Nowlin put it, he "learned to like it." Later in their freshman year those selfsame Greenbriar Boys appeared in concert nearby, sharing a bill with Ramblin' Jack Elliott and Erik Von Schmidt, two other now legendary folk revival figures. The concert was a minifestival of interpretive revivalism, consisting of acts that fell in between the rural source singers and the commercial stylings of the pop/folk groups.

The Greenbriars represented all the city kids then finding freshness and purity in bluegrass. Elliott channeled the spirit and style of that already iconic outsider and rebel Woody Guthrie. Von Schmidt, a young white man, sang the blues in a roar that grasped at some unimaginable pain. Irwin loved the performance. Nowlin came along more slowly.[19]

Ultimately, the two became fans of *Hillbilly at Harvard*, a college radio program that broadcast bluegrass and early country music every Saturday. Begun in 1948, it was the Boston area's only major country radio outlet, and it routinely received listener calls from working-class suburbs far removed from the intellectual clime of Harvard Yard.[20] It was at Club 47, however, that the roommates succumbed to what became the religion of folk music. The Cambridge showroom offered "traditional music all the time," enthused Irwin. "They'd have Doc Watson coming in with Clarence Ashley and they'd have Muddy Waters and just about everybody that you could imagine. It was really, really incredible, a wonderful, wonderful place." Despite their devotion to the club, they were not part of the inner circle, and Nowlin recalls a distinct cliquishness that he found hard to penetrate. Though the sometimes-long lines of fans waiting for admittance contributed to the sense of separation between insider and outsider, they also exposed the duo to the expertise that resided within the audience. Nowlin recalls standing in line impressed by "really knowledgeable people" who "were very into records." They would overhear a fellow patron enthuse about "that third track on side B," and listen in amazement as "everybody else would say, 'Yeah, yeah, I really love the way they do that.' 'Cause people really knew."[21]

They embraced it all fairly rapidly and sometimes went to Club 47 even when they were unfamiliar with the featured performer, willing to trust the room and try anything. It did not take them long to recognize the difference between urban revivalists and the more "authentic" source singers, drawn straight from the idealized folk. They read album liner notes and saw, for example, that Ralph Rinzler of the Greenbriar Boys went to Swarthmore and seemed much like them. Seeking worlds unlike their own, they gravitated to the authentics, developing a real "romanticization about hillbilly music," which Nowlin believed represented "real folk musicians sitting on the back porch playing the banjo."[22] As he says, "They had an artistry to them." At least as significant as that artistry was the vast distance between the life experiences of this youthful resident of Greater Boston and those of the rural performers whom he admired. Whether from Appalachia or the Mississippi delta, the "genuine" folk singers lionized by Nowlin and Irwin, and by the revival as a whole, appeared as representatives of a foreign culture. "Maybe it was more interesting because it was a little exotic to some extent, because it was different from the background we had," says Nowlin. "It also seemed purer in some ways . . . coming from people who only learned from oral tradition, as opposed to the way that we learned from records and radio and so forth, and we knew that there weren't that many people like that going to be around too much longer."[23]

Their passion led them down roads both creative and amusing. When Clarence Ashley came to town to perform at Club 47 they devised their own path to involvement, despite the lack of any formal connection to the club. Recalling one of his childhood interests, Nowlin used a kit to create rubber stamps containing the image of an arrow and the words "Clarence Ashley Is Coming." The two stamped that phrase everywhere they went in the days before the concert and imprinted it on small cards that they handed to strangers. It was, Nowlin says, more akin to a "guerrilla art project" than a promotional effort. Not only was no promotion needed because the club's partisans knew the performer well, but the stamp contained absolutely no information useful to the uninitiated—neither an explanation of who Ashley was nor details of the performance. The entire exercise was nothing more than an outlet for their exuberant devotion to the rural old-time music and romanticized lifestyle that Ashley represented.[24]

This sense of romance was an almost inevitable byproduct of the rarefied confines of revival outposts such as Club 47. There, in the company of others utterly unfamiliar with rural working-class life, fans educated by *Sing Out!* stood in collective awe of these avatars of a purer, less corrupt world. To even attempt to pierce this veil one needed to journey beyond the safe confines of Harvard Square. For those willing, life in Greater Boston afforded at least one opportunity to experience live, southern, tradition-based music in a setting removed from the amber glow of revival preciousness. This opportunity came in the persons of the Lilly Brothers. Michael Lilly, known as "Bea," and his younger brother Everett were born into a musical West Virginia family in 1921 and 1923, respectively. They began performing professionally as children, singing old-time mountain songs on southern radio. They toured the south with various bands, sharing stages with Bill Monroe and other country music pioneers. In 1951 Everett joined Flatt and Scruggs on mandolin, while his brother settled down in West Virginia. Within two years Everett grew weary of the road. Tex Logan, a friend, fiddler, and MIT graduate student, invited the Lillys to form a band with him in Boston. They agreed, upon being assured that Logan could secure a single stable gig. With banjoist Don Stover, a friend from West Virginia then working as a coal miner, the brothers relocated to Boston in 1952.[25]

After a brief run at a fairly upscale lounge, the band began a six-night-per-week gig at the Hillbilly Ranch, a seedy bar in a seedy part of town near the Trailways Bus Depot. The Ranch featured steer horns on its exterior, scenes of mountain cabins on the interior walls, and a dance floor set off by fence posts. This decor stemmed from neither romance nor intellectualized irony. It simply reflected what the place was—a country music honky-tonk that served uniformed sailors on leave, shore-patrol personnel, and working-class locals. Many customers were themselves displaced southerners, and most liked to unwind to hard liquor and cigarettes with their music. The Lilly Brothers played mountain songs and bluegrass at the Hillbilly Ranch from 1953 until the late 1960s, and their presence inverts the oft-held assumption that urban folk revivalists were solely responsible for the movement of bluegrass from South to North. Although revivalists played a tremendous role in that process and in the overall commercial rejuvenation of bluegrass, the Lillys demonstrate that at least some of that transmission stems from natural migration and the innate ability of good music to find an audience.

Amid the hard-drinking, largely working-class crowd at the Hillbilly Ranch, Irwin and Nowlin got a taste of early country music as it might have been performed in rural roadhouses, unfiltered by interpreters, whether starry-eyed romantics, sober academics, or some blend of the two. Fred Pement, who discovered the Lillys while a student in the early fifties, recalls the Ranch as "no place for a callow youth" still attending college. Nonetheless, he ventured through its doors on more than one occasion, always alone because "I could never get anyone to go with me." Irwin began attending with Nowlin roughly a decade later, his mind filled with unconfirmed stories of "frequent knife fights [and] occasional shootings." It was "a pretty rough and rowdy place. But the Lilly Brothers played there, and we just loved the Lillys. They were," he adds, "real, real country, almost beyond description. But they were wonderful singers."[26]

By the sixties the folk revival crowd had begun to discover the Ranch, and Irwin's recollection—tinged as it is with the ever present possibility of flying bullets—may be touched by a romanticism of its own, albeit of a less pastoral sort than that which dominated Club 47. Nowlin recalls neither guns nor knives but confirms the grimy, rough-hewn feel of the bar. Their

devotion to the Lilly Brothers afforded the roommates a glimpse of southern musicians as flesh-and-blood working people, not merely as idealized
knights on the front lines of a revivalist crusade. Given what lay ahead, it
was perhaps an invaluable experience.

In still other respects, their willingness to explore brought them insights
beyond those afforded the casual fan. One summer Irwin took a course in
music appreciation, the only music course of his college career. Because it
required a great deal of listening, he became a frequent visitor to the campus
music library. Though the course fare was predominantly classical, he often
perused the holdings for other items of interest. Upon looking up bluegrass
in the catalog he came upon only one album, which he happened to have
heard on *Hillbilly at Harvard.* That record—*Folk Songs from the Bluegrass* by
Earl Taylor and the Stoney Mountain Boys—became his "daily companion
that summer." Roughly one year later, he was in a Sam Goody's record outlet
in New York. He located that Taylor album, as well as an additional album
by the same musicians. As he studied the jackets, contemplating which to
buy with his limited funds, a large man standing nearby said, "They're both
good." The man was Loy Beaver, a New York–area undertaker with some
interesting stories to tell.[27]

Music had fascinated Beaver since his childhood in northern Georgia, where he knew many local musicians. As a young man he worked as
a traveling salesman for an embalming-fluid company, crisscrossing the
states of Tennessee and Kentucky and steeping himself in regional styles.
Employed as an undertaker in 1945, he claimed to have embalmed Franklin
D. Roosevelt after the President passed away in Warm Springs, Georgia.
Sometime later he moved to New York where he raised a family and found
further work in the funeral industry. There he heard about Dave Freeman,
a New York mailman and rare-record collector who shared Beaver's interest in old-time southern string band music. Beaver tracked Freeman down
and introduced himself, and Freeman encouraged Beaver's own burgeoning
interest in collecting old 78-rpm discs, an avocation at which the undertaker
soon excelled. In Freeman's words, Beaver "was amazing [at collecting]. . . .
I don't know how he did it, but every trip he made he'd come back with
a ton of records. He could luck on to the right people—he had a nose for
it, or he had good luck, and mostly he'd be able to talk them out of their
records. He ended up in a very short time putting together a very, very
nice collection of records." Freeman's own strong interests soon led him to
found County Records, which began as a vehicle for reissuing early country

music recorded originally on 78s. Beaver assisted him with his first releases in 1964, collections titled *Mountain Fiddle Tunes* and *Mountain Ballads*.[28]

In talking people "out of their records" Beaver undoubtedly displayed the same gregariousness that enabled him to address Irwin. Beaver described his collection to Irwin, gave the fascinated young man his phone number, and invited him over to listen to music. Back at Tufts, Irwin and Nowlin checked the notes to some County releases and saw credits thanking Beaver for his assistance. "We had hit the jackpot," thought Irwin. On a future vacation they visited Beaver at home, bringing along Nowlin's tape recorder. There, they found "records, walls of them, all neatly filed." Beaver made selections. When the roommates heard something they liked, he pulled out still more by the same performer, allowing Nowlin to tape whatever he wished. They returned to Tufts believing, in Irwin's words, that "we probably had the best collection of old-time music in the entire Boston area. We also went back thinking about all the stories we heard from Loy about the artists and knew we wanted to hear and learn as much as we could about the artists and the music."[29]

In addition to their exposure to these relocated southerners, Irwin and Nowlin journeyed south themselves to hear their passion at its source. The genesis of these excursions lay in Folkways Records and Club 47. Each night as the audience entered, the club played albums over its sound system. One evening, intrigued by the sound of some recorded old-time fiddling, the duo examined the record jacket hanging near the entrance and discovered they were listening to a live Folkways' recording made at the Old Time Fiddlers Convention at Union Grove, North Carolina. Shortly thereafter, they located the LP at Briggs and Briggs, the record shop where they spent hours furthering their education through liner notes and listening. Taking the album into a listening booth, they played the entire collection while studying the notes, learning for the first time about an event that even then was a venerated institution, and one that had a tremendous impact on the future label owners. "Union Grove," wrote Irwin, describing his fascination with southern traditional music, "was what really did it for me."[30]

The southern fiddling convention, or contest, has historically been a forum that mixed professional and amateur musicians. Early commercial country artists worked the contest circuit in the twenties and thirties. Begun in 1924, the earliest Union Grove conventions attracted a mix of skilled amateurs, weekend professionals, faded hopefuls, and those with ongoing commercial ambition. H. P. Van Hoy, a teacher and amateur musician, began the convention as a fund-raiser for his local school district. Musicians paid an entry fee and competed for awards in the Best Old-Time Band category and, later, various individual categories. Approximately 150 people attended the first event, where they witnessed competition among six local string bands. In 1957 organizers augmented the competition with an additional category for "modern" performance, encompassing western swing, popular country music, and even some rock-and-roll tunes such as "Hound Dog" and "Blue Suede Shoes." Despite broadening the acceptable repertoire, organizers prohibited electric instruments, and the majority of bands performed traditional tunes. For thirty-five years the convention remained a predominantly local affair, until the burgeoning folk revival brought it to the attention of northern performers and fans. In 1958, the fifty-five entrants included fifty-one from North Carolina and one each from Virginia and Tennessee. The remaining two consisted of died-in-the-wool revivalists—Mike Seeger, who would soon coproduce the Folkways LP that introduced Irwin and Nowlin to the convention, and New York's Greenbriar Boys.[31]

Irwin and Nowlin first attended in 1966. "We learned that the festival took place each Easter weekend down in North Carolina," said Irwin, "and we vowed then to try and get there that year. The following spring, Bill and I, by then experienced hitchhikers, packed up . . . and headed for Union Grove."[32] Within a few years the glare of the national press would dramatically alter the complexion of the event, drawing an odd mix of bikers and college students, many of whom were more interested in alcohol than music. But in 1966, though attendance reached an estimated 8,500 people, the convention still struck the two outsiders from Boston as a southern and family-oriented affair. On that first visit they bedded down in their sleeping bags under a Tyson Foods' truck. Nowlin's most vivid recollection is of "old guys." Irwin was "particularly impressed by the egalitarian nature of the music." Not confined to the stage, musicians spread themselves throughout the audience, playing in a huge field where, Irwin recalls, "they were just normal people . . . the young and old and back-porch pickers and everybody just having such a good time. It made it so much more accessible than 'they' being onstage and 'we' being the audience. You'd just mix in and sing along." They had such a good time they returned the following year, when they saw a performance by George Pegram, a local singer and banjo player who had been performing at southern contests, fairs, and dances for roughly three decades. Within a few years Nowlin's photograph of Pegram would grace the cover of Rounder's first release, as the banjoist became the label's inaugural artist.[33]

In the summer of 1967, while Nowlin was in Europe, Irwin journeyed to Galax, Virginia, to attend still another fiddlers' convention. Hitching home, he and a friend received a ride from Ken Davidson, a West Virginia resident who ran Kanawha Records, a minuscule company devoted to documenting the indigenous music of the Appalachian hills. Driver and passengers discovered their common interests, and Davidson invited his guests to spend the night at his nearby home. The next day Davidson and Irwin visited several local musicians, including seventy-one-year-old Clark Kessinger, a sometime house painter and fiddle master whose professional career on the far edges of the country music industry encompassed local dances, radio broadcasts, the Grand Ole Opry, and almost one hundred tunes recorded for Brunswick Records between 1928 and 1930. He was also a fiddle-contest veteran, who counted among his prizes a world-champion trophy awarded at Union Grove in 1966. Kessinger promptly took that trophy to New York, where he displayed it to the millions who watched his appearance on NBC-TV's *Today Show*. In 1971, Kessinger would record again, for Rounder, in what turned out to be his final session.[34]

More than a source of entertainment, records, and interesting stories, the visits to Hillbilly Ranch, Union Grove, and Galax, as well as their friendship with Beaver, provided the two young folk fans with a perspective that they could never have found solely among their revivalist peers lined up outside Club 47. Folklorist Alan Jabbour recalls talking to the Rounders at fiddling conventions in the late sixties or early seventies. "They were just trying to plug into this world," he says. "Going to fiddlers' conventions is a great way to do that. It was even a greater way back then. [The conventions] were perhaps a little more local and a little less hothouse than they later became."[35] The two music lovers—who were later joined on these trips by Marian Leighton—met people who grew up with early country music and who saw it as something other than the antiqued residue of an imagined pastoral wonderland. To this larger circle, the enjoyment of southern rural sounds was not part of a political stance, nor an attempt—conscious or otherwise—at the construction of a currently fashionable identity. It was, to be sure, a vibrant and meaningful part of the lives of both musicians and fans but one understood intuitively as a commercial, as well as an artistic, endeavor. The music was an element of popular culture. It was entertainment enacted before and among crowds who saw no contradiction in being simultaneously appreciative and irreverent.

Moreover, those whom the Rounders encountered within this broader circle were of flesh and bone. They were working people, and, though possessed of often impassioned artistic impulses, they were not the disembodied knights and saints that floated through the pages of *Sing Out!* Jabbour contrasts the Rounders' experience with that of Moses Asch of Folkways Records, whose aesthetic, broad as it was, developed solely within the urban revival. Asch's many releases included old-time and bluegrass LPs, but, says Jabbour, "that really wasn't his world. He certainly never showed up at Union Grove or Galax or the other fiddling conventions. He was from an urban world, and everything that came to him, however rural and marginal, came to him because it was filtered through people in that urban world and they brought it to him."[36] The Rounders, on the other hand, made some attempt to meet the rural world on its own ground. However abbreviated and imperfect, such efforts mingled with their admitted romanticism, and their full impact lay undeveloped for years until the Rounders befriended, recorded, and marketed countless members of the once-imagined folk.

In 1966 Irwin and Nowlin graduated from Tufts, with degrees in psychology and political science, respectively. Neither contemplated a career in the music business. Nowlin entered the graduate program in political science at the University of Chicago. At the outset of his undergraduate years he had attended several meetings of the Young Americans for Freedom, the right-wing youth group that supported Republican presidential hopeful Barry Goldwater. His admiration for Goldwater crumbled, however, after the senator opposed the landmark Civil Rights Act of 1964. This opposition rested ostensibly on the mainstream conservative position that the proposed law interfered with states' rights, a view that the law's proponents considered a smokescreen for segregation. Nowlin had respected Goldwater in part because he believed that the senator was a fair-minded, racially accepting conservative. As the civil rights struggle gained national attention, Nowlin hoped that the senator would use his position to demonstrate that conservatives believed in racial inclusiveness. Instead, he concluded that Goldwater had sold out his own tolerant beliefs—or what Nowlin presumed were his beliefs—to advance his presidential aspirations, an approach that the young idealist deemed unacceptable. Whereas Goldwater's civil rights stance helped break the Democrats' electoral stranglehold on the southern states, it pushed Nowlin into a state of relative political apathy. Looking backward, his disillusionment with Goldwater stands as the first concrete political position of the adult Nowlin, who would ultimately advance his belief in cultural equity through music.[37]

In Chicago Nowlin's political interests returned, in part due to the over-powering presence of the city itself. Although some considered Tufts an urban school, it had seemed thoroughly suburban to local boy Nowlin. A mere seven miles from where he grew up, it allowed limitless access to the nest, to which he returned regularly to do his laundry, eat a meal, or borrow his parents' car. The urban problems of Greater Boston were largely invisible to this relatively privileged youth, absorbed in school and music and still warm in his family's embrace. The south side of Chicago, by contrast, was a ghetto, worlds away from anything Nowlin had ever experienced. With quick trips back home no longer possible, he became more attuned to his urban surroundings and the palpable black/white divide experienced with every trip to the market or Laundromat.[38]

He underwent a far more dramatic change after that first year of gradu-ate school when, during the summer of 1967, with some financial assistance from his father, he undertook a ten-week solo tour of Europe. Extremely homesick at first, he stuck it out and now considers the trip "a seminal event in my life." Throughout Western Europe he saw graffiti that read "US=SS," comparing his country's role in Vietnam to the fascist takeover of Europe just a quarter century earlier. Until then he had paid little attention to the Southeast Asian conflict, but young Europeans asked him about it regularly. Though he explained dutifully that the United States needed to keep the region out of Communist hands, he had no real confidence in this position. Many also asked him about U.S. race relations, and he had no easy answer for why ongoing racial disharmony kept his country in turmoil.[39]

He entered Yugoslavia with an apprehension borne of his long-standing anti-Communist fervor. He was surprised to find no overt oppression, no gun-toting soldiers on the streets, and even a lack of interest by the border guards in examining his passport. He realizes now that Yugoslavia was an atypical Eastern-bloc state and that his experience might have differed had he tried, for example, to pass into East Berlin. Still, the incident challenged his perceptions. He was blissfully ignorant of the reality of more deep-seated, hidden oppression, and he was unaware of the many ethnic divisions that embroiled Eastern Europeans. He was caught up in the easy tolerance and unencumbered questioning of youth during a year in which the scent of political and cultural change was palpable. Alone, far from home, constantly hitchhiking and conversing regularly with people from another world, he felt freer than ever before. Everything he saw and heard broadened his perceptions and ended any remaining possibility that he would come home merely to immerse himself in some Republican campaign. "To see that there were these other people that lived in other parts of the world that got along fine, that you could joke with them even if you didn't know a word of their language . . . that Charlie Chaplin could make everybody laugh 'cause what he does is funny. It just kind of came together."[40]

On the island of Crete he met Bill Kornrich, a politically left-leaning American about to begin the University of Chicago's graduate sociology program. They decided to room together in the States, and in the fall of 1967 they traveled to Washington, D.C., to attend one of the growing number of demonstrations protesting U.S. involvement in Vietnam. Nowlin did not yet consider himself either a political leftist or a committed opponent of the war. But Abbie Hoffman and the yippies, then the clown princes of the American Left, had announced their intention to levitate the Pentagon and exorcise the evil spirits within. To Nowlin this was simply great political theater of the type that had intrigued him since he was a boy. He went to the rally less to protest the war than because he thought it would be "fun." The march radicalized him. He saw U.S. marshals wade into the crowd starting fights. They "would just go club somebody," he recalls. They looked to him like "thugs" who contrasted sharply with the more benign border guards he had encountered behind the iron curtain.[41]

Looking back at his self-described "instant conversion" to left-wing radicalism, Nowlin mentions neither political theorists, admired professors, nor influential books. He eventually did develop a theoretical perspective, but the earliest phase of his leftward shift is characterized more by a fascination with direct action as opposed to any strongly held ideology. He was swept up in the theatrical aspects of the political and cultural ferment that marked the sixties. "I never went through a nonviolent pacifist phase or something. I just started throwing stuff at 'em." The marshals "made themselves the enemy. I just soaked up all this stuff immediately from the movement people around, and I was instantly converted to the cause." After a few photos he took of the rally appeared in a University of Chicago student newspaper, he started attending every demonstration that came along, taking pictures. He attended a few meetings of the Students for a Democratic Society (SDS), the group that came to symbolize the New Left of the 1960s, but their endless talk bored him. He wanted action. In May 1968 he returned to Washington,

D.C., and spent time at Resurrection City, the poor people's encampment on the national Mall, which federal authorities razed after approximately six weeks of existence.[42]

Amid these trips to the nation's capital Nowlin pursued his course work. He had never struggled academically at Tufts but found himself unprepared for the commitment demanded by graduate work at the University of Chicago. He managed to do well in his first year but then began to lose his bearings. He wanted to pursue photography, his newest passion. Inspired by a girlfriend, he hoped to study Italian. His university adviser told him that he was free to pursue these interests on his own time but that his formal course work had to advance his studies in political science. Eventually, his department rejected his proposal for a doctoral dissertation built around his photographs of Resurrection City. Instead, following his adviser's advice, he turned that project into a master's thesis and left the program. Later, in the fall of 1968, he returned to Tufts to complete a doctorate in political science, finally receiving that degree in 1980, ten years after he helped found Rounder.[43]

Irwin spent the summer after graduation teaching in a Headstart program. He then enrolled in Boston's Wheelock College to pursue graduate work in special education, which, in part, involved working with emotionally disabled children. In the summer of 1967 he relocated temporarily to Portland, Maine, where he worked at the Spurwink School, a facility devoted to children with psychological or neurological impairments. There, while he was reading in a coffee shop, Marian Leighton approached and asked if he was "talkable." Leighton, who had just completed her freshman year at Northeastern University, was back in her native state for the summer, working as an intern for the Portland Urban Redevelopment Authority. Irwin invited her to join him.[44]

Marian Leighton was born in 1948 and raised near the town of Cherryfield in rural Washington County, Maine, the easternmost county in the United States. Her childhood, like that of many bright kids raised in parochial surroundings, reflected a tension between the need to adapt and the desire to move forward. She was the oldest of four children in a family that occupied a rung on the economic ladder somewhat below that of the Irwins and the Nowlins. Her parents did what they needed to do to support their family. At various times her father worked in the lumber industry, served as a hunting and fishing guide, and raked blueberries for commercial sale. Though primarily a homemaker, her mother sometimes worked as a motel maid and also joined in the berry gathering, as did Marian. "It sounds so nineteenth century, [but] a main form of employment was either to work in the blueberry factory or to work in the fields, which is what I did every summer when I was growing up, because that's what practically every kid that I knew did as their summer employment to earn their money for their school clothes for the next year." The family kept a root cellar and a subsistence garden. "We raised all of our own potatoes," Leighton recalls. "We raised a lot of our vegetables. My mother would can vegetables for the winter, green beans and carrots and peas and all of that kind of stuff, and you'd use them through the wintertime and never have to buy canned goods."[45]

Despite characterizing her parents as members of the "rural poor," Leighton never felt deprivation. Her family had food, plenty of books, and, once Leighton reached junior high school, a television set. The community was close-knit in the sense that everyone knew everyone else, an inevitability when virtually everyone attended the same school, patronized the same small number of stores, and worshiped at the same few Congregational or Baptist churches. Leighton embraced her own Baptist congregation, where her involvement encompassed Bible workshops and a leadership role in the church's youth group. She also sang in the choir and, though not the best of singers, could solo when needed. Leighton, who converted to Judaism upon her marriage in the 1980s, never saw an African American or, knowingly, a Jew until college. Her community's only obvious diversity stemmed from the annual migration of the Mi'kmaq, a Native American tribe from the Canadian Maritimes that traveled down the coast every summer to work on the blueberry harvest. Outside the fields there was little mingling with the tribe, whom the townspeople tended to disdain. On payday, after one too many drinks, bored Mi'kmaq might entertain themselves by jumping off the bridge that spanned the Narraguagus River. One of Leighton's more negative recollections is of her neighbors gathering along the river "to see what the Indians were going to do this Saturday night," a diversion she attributes to the sad need of those who had little to look down on those who had even less.[46]

Pop music played no significant role in her childhood, evoking only a few memories. Her dad turned the radio on at about five thirty almost every morning, but it served primarily as a tool that provided local news and weather reports. She had a female cousin who "was a mad Elvis fan," but Leighton "loathed" the early rocker—"he reminded me of local guys

I couldn't stand."[47] Some hits filtered through. She has a distinct recollection of Ray Charles' 1961 smash, "Hit the Road, Jack" and Roger Miller's trademark, "King of the Road," a similarly huge hit in 1965. Her mother liked country music, as did many of her neighbors, and Leighton recalls hearing Hank Williams on her family's wind-up phonograph. In high school she turned against country music as part of a broader rebellion against what she considered her narrow surroundings. In a self-described highbrow mood, she ordered a classical piano album through a record club and was surprised when it seemed to trouble her parents, who perhaps sensed their daughter's restiveness. The British Invasion escaped her notice entirely, though its initial wave occurred while she was in high school. Unlike most of the country, she didn't watch the Beatles' February 1964 appearance on *The Ed Sullivan Show*.[48]

Leighton's strongest effort to transcend her surroundings involved her absolute immersion in books, which presented both an immediate alternative reality and a vehicle capable of delivering her from rural Maine. Her parents encouraged reading and on occasion would read the encyclopedia aloud. Though he lacked a high school diploma, her father enjoyed enhancing his and his children's vocabulary by picking words out of the dictionary for study. Leighton read through much of her town's small library, with the Bible a particular favorite. *None Dare Call It Treason*, John Stormer's 1964 anti-Communist polemic, also left a huge impression. Published to coincide with Goldwater's presidential campaign and promoted heavily by the Far Right's John Birch Society, it argued that the United States was not only in extreme danger from internal subversion but itself complicit in the spread of worldwide communism. Patriotic and Christian, Leighton accepted its thesis wholeheartedly, and in her role as an active high school debater argued the case for a Goldwater victory.[49]

While still in junior high, she began ordering Bible college catalogs, determined to become a missionary and "save the heathens of Africa and China"—a dream that reflected the downside of her close-knit community, "where you're interpreting the rest of the world in your own very limited black-and-white worldview." An ardent social Darwinist in her teens, she "really believed that . . . if [people] are underprivileged and economically deprived . . . it's their own doing." She adds, "I'd never met a black person, but I believed that probably black people in the South were discriminated against in part because they created that [situation for themselves]." Thus, she was determined not only to move beyond her relatively limited world but also to offer assistance to others, provided they were willing to do the heavy lifting needed to better themselves.[50]

She remembers vividly the incident that first suggested to her that inequality and oppression could shape people's lives to a degree they could not necessarily control. One of her high school teachers showed her a story in the *New York Times* about Goodman, Schwerner, and Chaney, the three civil rights workers whom Mississippi racists had brutally murdered. "I remember to this day sitting there in disbelief. This can't be. I can't understand how this could happen. This must be Communist propaganda, but . . . there's no way that the Communists so completely controlled the *New York Times* that they could get all of these facts and this entire story to be created out of nothing, that there had to be truth to this." Compounding her difficulty was trust in her teacher, who had always recommended provocative reading. This was "my best teacher bringing that in, who I respected a lot and I knew she was no flaming liberal who was supporting Communists. She was simply a normal, very intelligent, and halfway well-read person for our part of the world, and that sort of started my doubting."[51]

This teacher's openness contrasted sharply with the closed minds of others she had trusted. When she tried to discuss her love of books with her minister, to whom her church activity had brought her especially close, his reaction stunned her. He mumbled something about Shakespeare being "very important secular literature," his tone suggesting that the bard occupied a realm so inferior to that of the Bible that her predilection might lead straight to hell. Grasping that this was a part of her life that she could not share with the church, and knowing that it was a pleasure she would not surrender, Leighton chose sides decisively. "I remember thinking to myself, 'I love these books and I won't give them up. So, if I won't give them up, I guess I'll have to stop being a Baptist,' which I did by the time I was a freshman in college. I considered that I was an atheist." As her faith waned, her interest in Bible colleges transformed itself into curiosity about higher education in general. She grew focused on leaving Washington County, resulting in conflict with her strong-willed and vocal mother, who saw rejection in her daughter's increasingly palpable desire for escape.[52]

Looking back, Leighton credits her Maine youth with helping her achieve adult success in the male-dominated record industry. Middle- and upper-class girls, she believes, particularly in the 1960s and 1970s, were victimized by "the tyranny of nice and good," which demanded that they comply with certain stereotypical expectations regarding feminine demeanor and ambitions. In poor communities such as Washington County, however, everyone, whether male or female, learned to do what was necessary. Leighton's parents taught her that she could do anything a boy could do because life's exigencies demanded a resourceful child. This gender equality, however, was never black and white and was not without conflict. It did not, for example, mean that girls necessarily should do everything boys could do, if circumstances did not so demand. Moreover, if an empowered young woman decided to leave the community to pursue larger dreams, anxious parents sometimes saw this as a rejection of their way of life, which compounded any latent shame at being poor and uneducated. Leighton sensed this quandary in her own parents, but decided that pursuit of her dreams was, for her, the only viable option.[53]

Buttressed by financial aid, and supported by parents who were simultaneously loving, concerned, puzzled, and resentful, Leighton entered Boston's Northeastern University in the fall of 1966. There she discovered the promise of the rich, culturally vibrant life that she had dreamed of for years. Enthralled by opportunity, she spent a great deal of time in bookstores and at the theater. Given what she believed was an inadequate high school education, she assumed she would have to struggle for grades but found her course work relatively easy.[54] She did not, however, enjoy Northeastern's large lecture halls. By the time she met Irwin in the summer of 1967, she had arranged a sophomore transfer to Clark University, roughly thirty-five miles from Boston, where the smaller seminar-rich format was more to her liking.

She and Irwin began a romance that lasted through the birth of Rounder and into the early 1970s, after which they continued their relationship as business partners and friends. In the fall of 1967 Irwin shifted his studies to Cornell University in Ithaca, New York. He hoped to earn a doctorate in family counseling, an ambition he says he abandoned when he could not find academic support for a proposed dissertation analyzing the role of women in country song lyrics. During the 1967–1968 academic year, Irwin and Leighton regularly hitchhiked between Boston and Ithaca, as she replaced the absent Nowlin as his steady companion at concerts and the theater. Over the next few years, by combining independent-study courses with academic leaves of absence, they managed to live together in both Massachusetts and New York State.[55]

Leighton's musical interests expanded dramatically, in part due to Irwin's influence, in part due to her own desire to sample absolutely everything.

As early as their first summer together Irwin introduced her to *Hillbilly at Harvard*, through tape recordings he had made of the Cambridge radio program. She later experienced live bluegrass for the first time at Club 47, and it was there that she met Nowlin, in Boston for a visit, when the three attended a show by Chicago bluesmen Junior Wells and Buddy Guy. In the spring of 1969 she joined Irwin and Nowlin on a sojourn to Union Grove.[56] By this time folk music was not the only offering at the table. Rock had gained in gravitas and assumed many of the functions of popular folk revivalism. Though it lacked folk's more explicit connection to vernacular heritage, it created at least the illusion of a single unified culture among its listeners and at times offered overt political commentary of a type that had been the hallmark of much contemporary folk. They were all fans of Bob Dylan, now identified more as a rock artist than a folk star. To varying degrees they also admired the bluesier groups, such as the Rolling Stones, the Animals, Cream, the Doors, and the Jimi Hendrix Experience.[57]

It was through rock and roll that Leighton first experienced the full force of music's cultural power when, with Irwin, she attended a Little Richard concert that left her with an indelible image of personal freedom embodied. Though appreciated now as a rock-and-roll pioneer, Little Richard was not, in the late sixties, widely understood as a seminal figure. As rock grew in self-importance and ranged stylistically through psychedelia and early metal, many fans saw Richard, and other first-generation rockers such as Chuck Berry and Bo Diddley, largely as novelty acts—purveyors of "golden oldies" focused on dating, school days, and other teenage ephemera. But watching Richard Penniman in concert around 1969, Leighton and Irwin saw freedom in the form of a dancing, shrieking, gender-bending African American libertine.

Leighton recalls him performing in a fairly small room—one appropriate to his then diminished star power—while wearing red silk bell-bottom pants and a red top studded with diamond-shaped mirrors. Penniman worked himself into a fury until, sweating profusely, he stood atop his piano, removed his shirt, and, after twirling it overhead repeatedly, flung it into the crowd. With song, movement, dress, cosmetics, and the color of his skin, Little Richard had seemingly thrown off the strictures that oppressed not just blacks and gays but everyone. Recognizing the power of the politics of culture, Leighton saw him as "more radical than a lot of the people who were so-called radicals"—the embodiment of "true personal liberation" that flew "in the face of everything that establishment culture looks like, talks like, walks like. Here's Little Richard," she recalls, "and to me it was like the freeing of your soul." For Leighton, a lover of both music and politics, there is "a transcendent moment" at the instant when the two intersect, "and Little Richard—man, oh, man—at that point he personified the transcendent moment in all its glory."[58]

Captivated by that transcendent sense of freedom, Leighton and Irwin, like Nowlin, were swept up by the increasingly ubiquitous politics of the street. Irwin attended his first anti–Vietnam War rally in New York City in the late sixties, in the company of his older brother. He recalls a motorcycle officer who rode along the line of protestors, kicking Irwin and others as he went. In a parallel to Nowlin's experience at the Pentagon, what politicized him most was not the war but this violent, abusive suppression of speech by a policeman who seemed to hate the demonstrators with a passion entirely personal.[59] He and Leighton sometimes hitchhiked from the Clark campus to rallies in downtown Boston carrying football helmets, in the event the police began swinging their clubs. In April 1969 they were among the throngs on the Cornell campus voicing support for a contingent of armed African American students who occupied the Student Union building. Beyond demonstrating, Leighton immersed herself in political discussion, participating in campus "consciousness-raising" sessions that focused on sexism, racism, and the war. Her political conversion was only marginally less instantaneous than that of Nowlin. From her anti-Communist, Christian, conservative beginnings, she became a self-styled moderate Republican by the end of her freshman year and a leftist SDS sympathizer by the time she was a junior.[60]

Her parents grew increasingly distraught as their daughter moved further away from the observant Baptist of just a few years earlier. The March 1967 issue of *Ramparts*, the leftist periodical devoted to politics and culture, provoked a particularly angry row with her mother. That issue contained a story on the long-running official mistreatment of the Native American Passamaquoddy tribe, which resided on a reservation in eastern Maine. Quoting tribal claims that "no one will prosecute you in the state of Maine for robbing Indians," the article provided a great deal of ammunition for a college student ready to find fault with a hometown she had concluded was insular and racist. A second article offered a prescription for a better life, one far removed from the typical Washington County mind-set. "Hippies," it asserted, "have a clear vision of the ideal community—a psychedelic community" that "necessarily embodies a radical political philosophy: communal life, drastic restriction of private property, rejection of violence, creativity before consumption, freedom before authority, de-emphasis of government and traditional forms of leadership." Leighton's devotion to these "truths" proved too much for her mother, who deemed her an unfit influence on her younger siblings, prompting a "several month estrangement when it was made clear that my presence would be unwelcome during college vacations."[61]

It was through politics that Leighton and Nowlin formed a friendship somewhat independent of her relationship with Irwin. For Irwin, participation in the protest movements of the sixties was a more or less natural extension of the times and the leftist climate within which he had grown up. Leighton and Nowlin, however, not only possessed a more innate interest in matters political but also, as former right-wing Republicans, had the fervor of converts. Far more than Irwin, they identified themselves as political beings and began to throw themselves into political analysis. However, though they debated theory, joined countless demonstrations, and wrote occasional articles for the newsletter of the Black Rose Collective, a Boston anarchist organization, they never engaged in the time-consuming task of systematic, long-term organization. Their political involvement was always more intellectual and experiential than programmatic. They admired Emma Goldman and Alexander Berkman, well-known American anarchists during the early twentieth century. Nowlin eventually wrote his doctoral dissertation on Berkman, who believed strongly in the growth of personal consciousness as an essential precursor to social transformation. In Nowlin's words, Berkman maintained that America "rested on a social myth, [which held] that the United States was a special country, uniquely free and selflessly benevolent, welcoming the unfortunates of other lands and offering true liberty and justice for all." Nowlin and Leighton saw themselves in the vanguard of those who would demolish this myth. Toward that end, they embraced Berkman's call for "an inquisitive spirit, an empirical approach testing for verification, a love of freedom and a willingness to be different—to rebel if necessary."[62]

In the summer of 1968 Irwin and Leighton traveled to San Francisco through a combination of hitchhiking, trains, and a "drive-away" car, which they delivered to a distant state on behalf of its owner. Almost forty years later, Irwin still teases Leighton about the weight of the books she insisted they carry on their backs, which represented a small library of countercultural self-discovery. "I do remember as we were hitchhiking across country reading out loud to Ken from Thomas Mann's *Magic Mountain*," says Leighton. "I read *Buddenbrooks* that summer. I read Herman Hesse, who was very in vogue at that time. So I read all of *Steppenwolf* and *Siddhartha* and *Magister Ludi* and *Demian*. Oh, *Demian* was very big back then, although I did think that they were a little bit lightweight, but Thomas Mann was more my kind of thing and Brecht and people like that." On what was fundamentally a pleasure trip, countercultural style, they soaked in the rich Bay Area environment through panhandling, living in "crash pads," a bit of shoplifting, and attending musical and political events. They held a brief reunion with Nowlin, who was traveling separately and had been participating in political rallies in nearby Berkeley. They recognized that their adventure contained a large element of slumming. They knew they would be returning to school in the fall, where Irwin held a position as a teaching assistant and Leighton anticipated the renewal of her financial-aid package. "Ken was, I think, more interested in entertaining the notion of himself as more of a hippie," says Leighton, "whereas I was simply more into entertaining the notion of this as a good thing to do to sort of see some more of the country." Their ultimate motivation arose from the fact that they, like Nowlin, possessed an intense desire to participate fully in their times.[63]

Music remained a touchstone. They each received free albums by contributing record reviews to small periodicals. Irwin and Leighton helped establish the Ithaca Friends of Bluegrass and Old Time Country Music, and they produced concerts around the Cornell campus. Some of the musicians they met during their time in upstate New York, such as Walt Koken, later of the influential Highwoods String Band, and banjo innovator Tony Trischka, went on to long careers in music and spent years as Rounder artists. Others added to their close exposure to native southerners who, like the Lilly Brothers and Loy Beaver, came to rural string band music as a natural outgrowth of their own heritage. In one particularly exciting endeavor, Irwin and Leighton arranged an Ithaca performance by Red Allen, a native Kentuckian and a marvelous bluegrass singer who had recorded with the influential Osborne Brothers in the fifties. Upon his arrival Allen proved to be neither noble nor romantic but extraordinarily unpleasant, leading Leighton to characterize the experience as a "worst nightmare." Completely naive, the fledgling promoters had no written contract with Allen, who insisted on a payment that his hosts believed exceeded their oral commitment. He made long-distance phone calls from Irwin and Leighton's home without asking and, in a real clash of sensibilities, "smoked up a storm." It was sobering, Leighton recalls, to realize that someone you "idolized . . . had very big feet of lots of clay."[64]

In retrospect, a record company seems like an almost inevitable next step for these devoted fans who had moved from listening to music to marketing it, reviewing it, and producing it in concert. The start of Rounder Records is best understood if viewed, like all of the founders' other musical activities, as nothing more than a hobby, albeit one that, in Nowlin's words, "got out of control."[65] By 1970, with the great boom a thing of the past, there were relatively few outlets for original recordings of the rural string band sounds that the Rounders favored. "Records that we were collecting ourselves became unavailable," said Nowlin.[66] Folkways Records, though still grounded in eclectic, vernacular music, was noticeably less productive than just five years earlier. Elektra had moved on to more profitable styles. Though its roster still included boom-era folk "stars" such as Tom Paxton and Tom Rush, the label had attained huge success with the Doors and the soft pop of Bread, in addition to experimenting with the early punk and metal offered by the Stooges and the MC-5.

There remained a number of specialized independents interested in noncommercial, tradition-based music, but their distribution was limited and their output depended heavily on the idiosyncratic tastes of their owners. Sandy and Caroline Paton's Folk-Legacy emphasized ballad singing. Chris Strachwitz, founder of California's Arhoolie Records, was interested predominantly in blues, zydeco, and the music of Mexico. Strachwitz started a companion label, Old Timey, to release the music that the Rounders loved, but it was not where his heart lay. In any event, the short-lived Old Timey, like Dave Freeman's County Records at the time, emphasized the reissue of older recordings. Rebel Records, located in the Washington, D.C., area, focused on contemporary bluegrass and had had some success with the Country Gentlemen, a now widely respected band but one formerly charged with smoothing the rough edges of genuine mountain music. All of these labels were small and could offer only a few releases each year. Their founders often performed most chores themselves. With time and money in perpetually short supply and without significant sales potential, many worthy possibilities went unreleased.[67]

The Rounders wished, particularly, for a new release from the Lilly Brothers, still playing around Boston though the Hillbilly Ranch was gone. The Lillys had last recorded in 1964 for Prestige, a New York–based jazz label that made a relatively brief excursion into folk during the boom. By the end of the sixties its folk days were over, and it had become a subsidiary of California-based Fantasy Records, another one-time jazz label that had attained rock-and-roll success with Creedence Clearwater Revival. Determined to see the Lillys back on record, the fledgling label owners decided they would do the job themselves. Around 1970 the band scheduled a concert at Boston's John Hancock Hall, and the Rounders arranged to record it. Unfortunately, tragedy disrupted their plans. Shortly before the concert Everett Lilly's son died in a motorcycle accident. Though the Lillys took the stage as scheduled, their performance had the feel of an intensely personal memorial service, and the Rounders considered it unreleasable. "It was just so heavy," says Irwin. The repertoire "was 'We Shall Meet Again in Heaven' and, you know, all those kinds of songs, and it was so personal, and so that never happened." Still, they "had gotten the bug," and "we had decided that we wanted to start a company. No," Irwin corrects himself, "we really didn't decide to start a company. We decided that we wanted to put out some records."[68]

THREE

Surrealistic Banjos and Zydeco Rhythms: Rounder's Broad Aesthetic

In the early 1970s Seymour Posen struggled to reconcile his seemingly competing roles as an academic folklorist and a musician who performed songs from diverse cultural traditions. In 1993, looking back on a genera-tion in which musicians routinely adopted a broad array of regional, ethnic, and racial styles, he wondered why he had ever fretted so much about his lack of cultural authenticity. By that time, he had come to realize, most contemporary folk performers offered "a personalized collage of material, executed with reference to all manner of past styles and sources." Typically, performers blended these elements into an "overall sound," such as Celtic, or country, or even "traditional," which Posen characterized aptly as "another can of worms." "If anything," he concluded, the concept of authenticity had simply "become a 'flavor' within that performance sound."[1]

Although Posen offers an accurate assessment of evolving musical prac-tice, it is a practice that continues to distress those cultural partisans who cherish specific traditions and the groups from which they derive. In the twenty-first century vernacular music—folk music—continues to thrive in a perpetual state of tension, caught between those who pull it back toward an idealized past and context and those who push it forward toward a ka-leidoscopic blend of diffuse sounds and cultural referents. Watching the fray are the many music lovers—perhaps the overwhelming majority—who take no stand amid the intellectual wars but strive to hear as much music as possible, wanting simply to enjoy, learn from, and honor whatever styles they favor. I include among this presumed majority the Rounder founders, who have managed to float resolutely above the cultural battleground for decades. Avoiding any overarching theoretical posture, the Rounders have consistently released records that illustrate all of the varied approaches to the preservation, performance, and marketing of musical heritage.

The Rounders' decision to "put out some records" led to the creation of a label that merged Folkways' vernacular eclecticism with Elektra's early commitment to contemporary revivalists. The founders' aesthetic combines their idealized romance with rural traditions with the anarchic sense of freedom that they drew from the counterculture. They add to this their recognition that even the oldest, most hidebound definitions of folk music always described a form of popular culture. Long before Henry Glassie characterized tradition as "the creation of the future out of the past," Irwin, Nowlin, and Leighton understood intuitively that people could simultaneously treasure their cultural traditions, enjoy the best that the commercial music world had to offer, and sometimes merge the two in a hybrid of modern, yet tradition-oriented, music that is entertaining, contemporary in feel, and culturally specific. Drawn to the music of worlds other than their own, they accept instinctively the cultural borrowing on which the revival thrives. The resulting label catalog, viewed as a whole, reveals this full spectrum of experiences and attitudes. In this chapter I sample that catalog, demonstrating how Rounder's broad aesthetic manifested itself in sounds that helped shape an expanding definition of folk music in the contemporary world.[2]

Long before their catalog took form, the Rounders condensed this aesthetic into their new label name.[3] Derived in part from the whimsical observation that records are round, the name also reflects the outlaw self-image of three romantics who positioned themselves in opposition to capitalism, the programmatic rigidity of the old Left, and the more doctrinaire cultural rules of the folk revival itself. The image of the rounder in American culture is that of an eternal misfit—a recalcitrant ne'er-do-well who, literally and psychologically, traverses society's outer edges. An extended representation of a romanticized rounder appears in the lyric to "Rising Sun Blues" as recorded by Clarence Ashley in the early sixties. The song is also known as "The House of the Rising Sun," and, with variant lyrics, countless heroes of the great boom recorded it, including Woody Guthrie, Lead Belly, Bob Dylan, and British blues rockers the Animals. Ashley's rendition, recorded a few years before Irwin and Nowlin stamped his name around the Tufts' campus, offers a sympathetic toast to the "rounder, poor boy; who goes from town to town." "All in this world does a rounder want," Ashley sings, "is a suitcase and a trunk; the only time he's satisfied, is when he's on the drunk."[4]

The label name also honors the Holy Modal Rounders, the musical partnership that provided Irwin and Nowlin with their initial glimpse of old-time music when, in the early sixties, they heard the duo performing on a Cambridge street. Peter Stampfel, the Holy Modal's fiddler and banjoist, began performing with guitarist Steve Weber in 1963 when they were in their midtwenties. Initially a self-described purist, Stampfel loved the sounds he discovered on the *Anthology of American Folk Music*, the six-album Folkways Records collection of country music, blues, and spirituals that compiler Harry Smith drew from commercial recordings of the 1920s and 1930s. Eventually, however, Stampfel grew to hate the more-traditional-than-thou posturing he found in some revival circles. "There was a sense of pompous preening," he recalls, "not to mention the sanctimoniousness of the social stuff—'Sing what must be sung.' These people drove me nuts."[5] He is equally dismissive of the sectarian old Left, which he believes stripped music of its joy in the service of a doctrinaire political agenda. One of his earliest ensembles—the Berkeley, California–based Lower Telegraph Avenue Freedom Fighters String Band—changed its name after Stampfel grew tired of explaining that it was not one more aggregation of dour propagandists. The group advocated freedom in the artistic sense, focusing more on modes of expression than on political dogma and spurning any identification with what Stampfel called "freedom bullshit." Marking some distance from Pete Seeger, an early idol, he declares, "We weren't doing any 'If I Had A Hammer' shit."[6]

By 1964, when he and Weber released their debut album on Prestige, Stampfel was a self-described advocate of "progressive old-timey," an approach that stemmed from his perception of changing social conditions. Given modern mass communication, he realized that virtually everyone in the 1960s could hear "more music than almost anyone 60 years ago."[7] With the music of the world at his disposal, Stampfel found it impossible to honor the musicians on Smith's anthology by something as limited as sober replication. He wanted to present old-time music as he believed the artists of the 1920s would have themselves presented it had conditions been just a bit different. "What if Charlie Poole and Uncle Dave Macon and all those guys on the *Anthology* could be magically transported to the Sixties without aging at all," he wondered, "and then they heard rock 'n' roll? And that's been the basis of everything I've done since."[8]

A live recording from 1965 illustrates the musicians' penchant for wicked irreverence and demonstrates why Dave Van Ronk declared them leaders of the revival's "surrealist wing." Introducing Dave Macon's "Hold the Woodpile Down," Stampfel mocks the overwrought seriousness with which some revivalists plumbed their repertoire's history, often losing sight of a song's function as entertainment. Denouncing the original lyric as "dumb," Stampfel explains that he jettisoned all but the "great" chorus, added some words written by his girlfriend, and then "swiped a little splinter fragment from William Blake, noted English madman of yore. So this is me, my girl, Blake and Uncle Dave Macon in a daisy chain of arcane influence." Before striking the first notes of "Sugar in the Gourd," a staple of the old-time fiddle repertoire, Stampfel constructs a fanciful lyrical backstory drawn from popular folklore and American history. "Once upon a time," he says, "Johnny Appleseed and George Washington and Benedict Arnold were walking along hand in hand picking violets one day and they said, 'Behold that gourd, full of sugar. Let's write a song about it.' And they did."[9] Irwin and Nowlin, who would later transform their personal reverence for Clarence Ashley into a bit of absurdist street theater, had embraced an old-time revival band that brought that same sense of avant-garde theatricality to the very idea of old-time revivalism.

In 1970, however, the founders' expansive cultural stance was still inchoate. Their two simultaneous debut albums explored relatively mainstream revival territory that reflected both their northern and their southern experiences. The immediate seeds of *George Pegram*, released as Rounder #0001, lay in a trip Irwin and Leighton took to Mardi Gras. Before heading home they visited Ken Davidson, the Kanawha Records owner who had introduced Irwin to fiddler Clark Kessinger a few years earlier. Davidson played them a tape recorded by his occasional collaborator Charles Faurot, consisting of Pegram singing old-time tunes and hymns and playing banjo, along with fiddle, mandolin, and guitar accompaniment. The near financial collapse of his label had dashed Davidson's own hopes of releasing the recording. With Leighton and Nowlin's support, Irwin bought the tape from Faurot for $125, and the trio decided to release it themselves.[10]

Pegram, born in 1911, was no mere back-porch musician. His peripheral but lengthy career in the music industry encompassed performances at local

dances, in old-time music contests, and on the radio. Folk song collector
Bascom Lamar Lunsford "discovered" Pegram in the late 1940s, and began
promoting him at southern folk festivals. A 1948 review describes the musician as "a natural clown, with an excellent repertory of banjo songs and
solo dance numbers, and with an inexhaustible fund of showmanship."[11] In
1957, with the boom on the horizon, Pegram and harmonica player Red
Parham appeared on *Pickin' and Blowin'*, an album released by Riverside
Records. By the late sixties Pegram had, in Nowlin's recollection, several
missing teeth and a crazy laugh. Used to playing without amplification, he
sang with incredible volume. With a look and sound that appeared eccentric
to the young northerners and a repertoire of old songs, Pegram seemed a
"weird character" who "fit all the stereotypes," which combined to make
him "exciting" and "romantic."[12]

In 1969 the Union Grove judges named Pegram the world champion
banjoist. Shortly thereafter, journalist Carson Taylor reviewed a Pegram
performance, illustrating the artist in the era when the Rounders found
him. Describing Pegram opening with the old ballad "John Henry," Taylor
depicts a showman who rivaled Little Richard in emotional intensity. "He
closed his eyes and sang," the reviewer said, "bending to an almost kneeling
position. He wrung from the ballad all the emotion it is capable of exciting.
You could almost see John Henry swing the hammer; almost hear the hammer strike steel." In an instant Pegram transformed himself into a comic,
nodding "like a Tennessee walking horse while playing. Stretching to tiptoe,
he held the banjo's staff vertically, his fingers flying only inches from the
microphone." The audience, Taylor reports, went "wild."[13]

Though the Rounders now owned the Pegram tape, they needed a contract with the musician to release a commercial recording. Decades later,
Nowlin still does not know if Pegram saw them as the hobbyists they were
or considered them somewhat akin to RCA. Pegram seemed pleased by
the interest, since it had been so long since anyone had recorded him commercially. The Rounders retained an attorney who drew up a one-half-page
agreement in return for two copies each of the label's first two recordings.
The contract, which Pegram signed on August 14, 1970, promised a royalty
of twenty-five cents per record for the first five hundred records sold and
fifty cents per record for each additional copy sold. Royalties were payable
at increments of one hundred copies sold. Irwin, through Rounder Records,
was entitled to market the Pegram release for "as long as he desires."[14]

The three friends also pursued their label dreams with the Spark Gap

Wonder Boys, a youthful old-time revival trio based in Boston consisting of George Nelson on vocals and guitar plus Dave Doubilet and Neil Rossi who both sang and, collectively, played banjo, guitar, fiddle, mandolin, harmonica, and Autoharp. Rossi had previously performed folk music in the style of the Kingston Trio until a chance teenage encounter with country music radio left him a diehard bluegrass and old-time fan. While Stampfel and Weber explored their surrealist approach, Spark Gap sought stricter fidelity to the sound of early country records. The group formed in 1966 and dubbed itself Dr. Doubilet and the Park Street Undertakers, a jocular reference to "Park Street Under," then a Boston subway stop. Formed too late to benefit fully from the folk boom, it was a part-time affair, performing two to three times per month at campus coffeehouses in the Boston area.[15]

In 1968 the band made the pilgrimage to Union Grove. They became the Spark Gap Wonder Boys on a whim just before registering for the competition, after deciding that their morbid pun would not go over well outside Boston. Nelson was an automobile mechanic, hence the term *spark gap*. Rossi still chuckles over the elderly woman who took their application while saying something like, "Oh, Spark Gap! I've got relatives who live up there." The group was third-runner-up that year in the old-time band category, and Nelson's guitar playing earned several individual ribbons. Perhaps the biggest prize of all was a one-sentence mention in *Newsweek* that highlighted the distinctiveness of their northern origin. In 1970, their third consecutive year at Union Grove, judges named them the world champion old-time band.[16]

That victory led to an overture from Irwin and Nowlin. Demonstrating both initiative and naïveté, they approached timidly, worried that more established labels would be competing for the services of this world-beating aggregation. Rossi laughs, "We knew we weren't going to get recorded by anybody else. There wasn't anybody else. People like Elektra and Vanguard and all of the other folk labels had gone on to do other things, and they were really only interested in making money, and I can't blame them for that. So they weren't going to be pushing a part-time group from Boston." Irwin and Nowlin "were quite up front," says Rossi. "They had no money. They had no experience. All they had was an interest in the music and a love for it. We had talked at some length about what they wanted to do and how they wanted to approach the music. It was clear that they had a great deal of respect [for] and knowledge about the music." Pegram excited the Rounders because of the aura of authenticity created by his southern origins and long musical history. Spark Gap excited them for a different reason. "'We want to record somebody new,'" Rossi recalls them saying, "'because we want to preserve the music. This is a good place to start.'"[17]

They recorded the album, ultimately titled *Cluck Old Hen*, during several sessions at the Harvard and MIT radio stations, where friends had access to free equipment during off-hours. The Rounders had little involvement in the studio. Spark Gap arranged the tunes and made all technical decisions. The band requested no advance, nor did those who helped out in the studio or worked on graphics request any payment.[18] The three Rounders did front the entire recording budget of approximately seven dollars for two reels of tape. After also paying for disc pressing and packaging, funded in part by fifteen hundred dollars that Irwin had saved, the "label" took delivery of five hundred copies each of its first two albums. Its three owners had no distribution arrangement in place and no understanding of how record distribution worked. They had neither ads nor an ad budget. All they had was a belief in their music, a willingness to work, and two LPs of archaic old-time tunes performed by musicians who, for all practical purposes, were total unknowns. It was October 20, 1970, and Rounder Records was born.[19]

Utilizing one of the few outlets available to them for free publicity, the Rounders submitted their debut albums to *Bluegrass Unlimited* for review. The reviewer was Richard Spottswood, a Washington, D.C., radio host and avid collector of rare 78-rpm discs who later worked with Rounder as an outside producer and anthologizer. He liked both albums but understood the fundamental distinction at their core. Pegram, he noted, was "an older North Carolina pre-Scruggs banjo man . . . [and] a great artist in the primitive style." Applauding the instrumental virtuosity, Spottswood called this "an especially good album for anyone wishing to trace historical banjo styles [though] its appeal will be limited for others." He judged the Spark Gap Wonder Boys by a standard that took explicit account of their role as urban revivalists. "Here's another group of city folks," he wrote, "trying to play old-time pre-grass music." Spottswood, a known "proselytizer for ethnic and traditional music," confessed that he usually found such "imitations" wanting, but he recommended the record, finding it a welcome exception to the usual revival fare. "They are very good," he wrote of Spark Gap, "and know how to play effectively in a number of styles. Their singing is not so good—but then city singers in this genre rarely are and they seem well aware of their shortcomings."[20]

Rounder debuted within a month of the drug-related deaths of both

Jimi Hendrix and Janis Joplin, tragic events that symbolized the dangers of the star system and rock-and-roll excess. *Rolling Stone* placed these deceased icons on two successive covers, but in unrelated articles appearing that month it also looked fondly at the remnants of the great boom. One piece detailed a recent Hollywood concert celebrating Woody Guthrie, which served to raise funds to combat Huntington's chorea, the disease that had ended the performer's life. It was a star-studded event that drew eighteen thousand fans to the Hollywood Bowl to hear Guthrie's son Arlo, as well as Pete Seeger, Joan Baez, Country Joe McDonald, Richie Havens, Odetta, and Ramblin' Jack Elliott. Master of ceremonies Millard Lampell—Seeger's onetime musical colleague in the 1940s-era Almanac Singers—noted with evident nostalgia, "What's happening tonight is more like the old days when everybody sang together." In a poignant commentary on the commercial overkill that accompanied the boom's demise, he observed that only a benefit concert could bring all of these artists together, "because they're all worth thousands and thousands of dollars—everybody's got a piece of their asses."[21]

A second article offered a glowing look at the recently concluded ninth annual Philadelphia Folk Festival under the headline "Philly Folkies' Community Vibes." Using mimicry that managed to sound somewhat more loving than the dismissive caricatures that sometimes appeared in national media, the magazine exalted the festival's focus on the "straight natchal blues, straight natchal bluegrass, and straight natchal grass-roots music." Eschewing both rock and roll and the revival stars who honored Guthrie in Hollywood, Philadelphia's biggest attractions were bluesman Luther Allison and the contemporary British revivalists Fairport Convention, whose electrified versions of traditional tunes drove the crowd to furious jigs and morris dancing. Though both performed at high volume, neither was a huge star, and their sound was steeped in vernacular tradition. Doc Watson, bluegrasser Ralph Stanley, the political Utah Phillips, and the contemporary sounds of Happy Traum and his brother Artie helped fill out the schedule. The dominant Philadelphia "vibe," however, came from the audience. "Banjos, fiddles, jews harps, dulcimers, guitars and clanging beer cans provided 24–hour music for cooking, smoking, balling and sleeping. Community and relaxation were the prevailing moods of the festival."[22]

All of this suggests a residue of commercial promise in folk music revivalism, at least for a select few performers. Much of Rounder's growth would stem from this still romantic yearning for the return of folk's commercial glory and for the bygone days it idealized. Yet a significant part of the label's appeal, particularly over time, grew from the more tangible desire of vernacular musicians for an increased commercial presence. In the month of Rounder's birth, while *Rolling Stone* lovingly examined vestiges of the great boom, *Billboard*, the industry's unabashed commercial chronicler, discussed the sorry state of the country music industry, foreshadowing one alternative source of Rounder's eventual strength. In a special section titled the "World of Country Music," Paul W. Soelberg, a principal in a country artist management firm, examined the problems posed by country's commercial growing pains.

Soelberg targeted country music radio, an industry unto itself that had exploded in size in the midsixties. As he saw it, this burgeoning format encompassed an excessive number of disc jockeys, program directors, and station owners who were not only wholly ignorant of country music's storied past but also possessed of an outright antagonism toward the form. Intent on "modernizing" the music in search of that always elusive mass market, these programmers fled the hillbilly image as they experimented with an ongoing series of marketing terms such as *metropolitan country* or *countrypolitan*, designed to demonstrate that country music had arrived uptown. In practice, their bias led them to ignore older artists and styles and the fans who still loved them. Disclaiming any responsibility to appeal to specialty audiences or to educate listeners about country music's wide range, they focused on a narrow band of soundalike music that they believed would sell to the largest number of consumers. As a result, Soelberg concluded, "entire county music sub-categories such as country gospel, western swing, or bluegrass, were . . . summarily eliminated from programming." Artists and labels that desired radio play learned to avoid the disfavored forms, thus contributing to the music's demise.[23]

Though initially disclaiming any particular interest in commerce, Rounder sought to fill this void. In October 1971, one year after its debut, the label released three additional records that, in their fidelity to commercially outmoded musical forms, seemed directly responsive to Soelberg's concerns. The banjo and fiddle duo of Snuffy Jenkins and Pappy Sherrill recorded *33 Years of Pickin' and Pluckin'*, which demonstrated that a well-made album could still provide a measure of professional opportunity for country artists performing older styles. DeWitt "Snuffy" Jenkins and Homer "Pappy" Sherrill, born in 1908 and 1915, respectively, were old-time players from the Carolinas who began their careers in the midthirties, working the medicine-show circuit on behalf of the manufacturers of nonprescription home remedies. By the end of the fifties they were veterans who, separately and together, had placed dozens of tunes on commercial recordings. The country music industry had passed them by, however, and they never developed a folk-fan following during the boom. By 1971 they performed only occasionally, while earning their livings as South Carolina automobile salesmen.[24]

Pat Ahrens, a friend and banjo enthusiast, introduced them to the Rounders, who journeyed south and rented a professional studio to record the duo. Jenkins and Sherrill were very excited about the project, and the relaxed sessions displayed their virtuosity in a variety of early styles, from prebluegrass banjo strumming to swing-tinged fiddling. In Ahrens' view, the two were very proud of the resulting record, which she believes helped revive their dormant careers. Though Rounder lacked meaningful commercial distribution, Ahrens helped the newly energized performers use the album and its 1976 Rounder follow-up as calling cards, alerting specialized promoters to their continued viability. This provided entrée to southern bluegrass festivals as well as to ongoing revival venues, such as the Philadelphia and University of Chicago folk festivals. The two appeared with the Joffrey Ballet in *Country Dance*, choreographed by Twyla Tharp, and they took the stage of Carnegie Hall as part of a 1985 retrospective titled *Southern Mountain Music*. Once seemingly forgotten, Jenkins and Sherrill thrived artistically in the ongoing revival of the seventies and beyond, a scene that Rounder helped nurture through an increasingly steady stream of releases.[25]

Also in 1971, Rounder took its first steps into bluegrass. This revival staple would eventually form a major part of the label's catalog, as Rounder embraced, and encouraged, a "full spectrum" approach to the genre, ranging from the most traditional to the most progressive. Old-time music stems from the folk ballads and dance tunes with which people entertained themselves in the days before records and radio. Though the fledgling recording industry embraced it enthusiastically, its boom-era cachet arose from its identity as a survival of preindustrial social music. Bluegrass, by contrast, was born as a commercial form through the innovations of Bill Monroe and his Blue Grass Boys. Monroe, known today as the father of bluegrass, began performing on the commercial country music circuit in the 1920s. By the late 1940s he had honed the relatively casual old-time style into a then revolutionary ensemble sound. Mayne Smith, in what is probably the earliest scholarly article on bluegrass, described it as "more formalized and jazz-like than that encountered in earlier string band styles." The old-time instruments of banjo, fiddle, and mandolin play within "well defined roles" that shift pursuant to "predictable patterns." Band member Earl Scruggs' rapid-fire three-finger banjo picking helped define and popularize the sound, as did a tense, high-pitched, nasal vocal delivery. Revivalists began performing bluegrass in the mid-1950s, drawn by its old-time roots and—from the perspective of urban elites—its archaic southern sound.[26] In an irony typical of the revival, purists who exalt so-called traditional bluegrass generally mean the music played as Monroe performed it in the forties, arguably misunderstanding the bandleader's role as a consummate professional and a conscious artistic innovator.

Rounder's bluegrass journey began with *One Morning in May* by Joe Val and the New England Bluegrass Boys. Val (né Joe Valiante) was a Massachusetts native born in 1926 who worked as a typewriter repairman when not playing music. A mandolinist and high-tenor singer, he stood apart from a strict dichotomy between boom-influenced revivalists and so-called southern authentics. A generation older than the young music lovers who fueled the boom, Val's path to bluegrass came not through the revival but through his ardent love of early country music. He was in his twenties when he first heard Bill Monroe, and by the early 1950s he was performing with the Radio Rangers on the *Hayloft Jamboree*, a Boston country radio show that died before the revival peaked. Other influences included the Lilly Brothers, whom he met shortly after they moved to Boston and with whom he sometimes performed at the Hillbilly Ranch. During the boom Val moved freely across boundaries, playing comfortably with younger folk-influenced musicians and performing frequently at Club 47. In the midsixties he joined the Charles River Valley Boys, mainstays of the Cambridge scene who are perhaps most widely known among folk aficionados for *Beatle Country*, a collection of bluegrass renditions of Beatle tunes that Elektra released in 1966.[27]

For his Rounder debut Val and guitarist Herb Applin focused on the close harmony vocal duets that marked the genre's formative days. In an early example of Rounder's often detailed, historically oriented liner notes, the label offered a musical context for the collection. "The music of the New England Bluegrass Boys," the notes explain, "is early bluegrass. What we now know as bluegrass music is a specified style of country music which developed under the influence of Bill Monroe." Decades later these notes seem almost painfully simplistic, but they reflect the still ongoing education of Rounder's owners, who were grappling earnestly with their desire to spread the good word about the music they loved.[28]

Bluegrass Unlimited called the album "a delightful set" and "a cardinal illustration of the direction bluegrass can take, far removed of the demands of Nashville and it's [*sic*] blind commercialism." Ignoring distinctions posed by geographic region or labels such as "city singer," "revivalist," or "traditionalist," Rounder scored an artistic triumph. The label issued four more albums by Joe Val and the New England Bluegrass Boys—Val's only albums as a bandleader—before the musician's death from cancer in 1985. Demonstrating how even a small label could help create a personal and regional legacy, these albums helped Val solidify his reputation as a New England bluegrass pioneer. Today, in part because of Rounder, he is known widely among serious bluegrass fans and memorialized annually at the Joe Val Bluegrass Festival, presented since 1986 by the Boston Bluegrass Union.[29]

From the beginning, though music served as Irwin's prime motivation, Nowlin and Leighton linked their efforts to those of earlier leftists who promoted the artistry of an idealized "people," as part of a political agenda in opposition to capitalism, racism, and sexism. In Nowlin's mind, work at Rounder became "a surrogate [political] activity, working with people's music and having a part of it be explicitly political in terms of content but knowing that the other stuff was also political in the sense—as it still is—of working with minority cultures and music that's outside the mainstream." In a mission statement that appeared in album liner notes irregularly in the early and midseventies, Rounder declared itself "an anti-profit collective" and a "service group" that desired only to ensure the availability of "important traditions of American culture that are largely non-commercial." The label was "worker-controlled, with no bosses, and with all finances in common," and it aspired to stand as "an alternative to commercial record companies . . . to continue serving people's culture ethically and in an anti-profit mode in the new world we all are working toward."[30]

This was a heady, ambitious agenda that attracted others caught up in the ferment of the times. Pete Wernick, a young banjoist who met Irwin and Leighton in Ithaca in 1971, was drawn to them as much by their politics as by their musical tastes. "Those were highly politicized days," Wernick says, and he applauded the Rounders' desire "to help 'the people' have some ascendancy." "Cultural ascendancy," he recalls, "was something everybody believed in very easily." Wernick, born in 1946, was a New York

City native and an ardent revivalist. He considers Pete Seeger's Weavers a "major influence," and he was a regular presence at the Sunday-afternoon jams in Washington Square. While attending Columbia University in the 1960s he hosted the only New York–area radio show devoted exclusively to bluegrass.[31] In 1971 Wernick, then a doctoral candidate in sociology at Columbia, worked at the Cornell International Population Program in Ithaca. He met fellow banjoist Tony Trischka along the upstate New York musicians' circuit. Trischka was born in 1949 and grew up in Syracuse, New York. After taking flute, piano, and guitar lessons as a young child, his life, and his primary instrument, changed at age fourteen when he heard Dave Guard play the banjo on a Kingston Trio recording. He later embraced the music of Earl Scruggs, the Beatles, Jimi Hendrix, Cream, and the jazz fusion of Weather Report and John McLaughlin's Mahavishnu Orchestra.[32]

The two banjo players began performing together in the Contraband Countryband, which featured Wernick's future wife, Joan "Nondi" Leonard, on vocals. After crossing paths with Irwin and Leighton, the band performed at the first concert staged by the Ithaca Friends of Bluegrass. The Contraband, which later changed its name to Country Cooking, played what Wernick terms "good-time bluegrass" that was more "collegiate entertainment" than art. Envisioning something of greater musical depth, Wernick suggested that he and Trischka record their explorations in complementary twin banjos, something that no one was doing on record at the time and that few had ever done. They conceived an all-instrumental record using the best musicians available, resulting in a recording lineup that differed somewhat from the performing band. The Rounders were delighted to put out such an innovative record. The album, *14 Bluegrass Instrumentals* by Country Cooking, became the label's third release of 1971. "It was really just hippies," says Wernick, who saw the album initially as something they would offer their friends and sell at local gigs. Real records came from established companies like RCA or, at the least, Folkways; they were not recorded at the Cornell Student Union by a group of students and their friends. Despite a recording session so informal that it bordered on the amateurish, his attitude began to change fairly quickly. As the group members passed around headphones to listen to the tape playback they became giddy with delight, realizing that this indeed sounded like a record.[33]

Though noting the album's myriad engineering deficiencies, *Bluegrass Unlimited* praised its musical qualities, calling it "as good an instrumental bluegrass recording as one is apt to find anywhere." Wernick, who previously assumed he would pursue an academic career as a sociologist, now glimpsed the possibility of life as a professional musician. Country Cooking began touring more aggressively, and the band members eventually funded a second album themselves, this time using a sixteen-track professional studio. Fueled by its presence in the popular film *Deliverance*, the song "Dueling Banjos" had seemingly made the banjo a hot commercial commodity, at least for the moment. Assuming that he could capitalize on this phenomenon, Wernick shopped the sophomore album to major labels, hoping for money and promotional support that Rounder was unable to offer. He found initial interest, but ultimately no one was buying. Label executives considered "Dueling Banjos" a fluke that attracted attention because of the "dueling" and the movie tie-in, not because of the banjo. At that point Wernick reverted to the obvious alternative, Rounder, which offered an otherwise unavailable commercial niche. The founders were happy to release the album, though Wernick perceived some tension stemming from his aspirations.[34]

Barrel of Fun, Country Cooking's second Rounder release, came out in January 1974. Though bluegrass basics held it together, the album was broadly experimental. It offered more of the stylistic variety characteristic of the band's live act, including two cuts featuring Leonard's vocals, which deviated from the traditional bluegrass sound. The otherwise all-instrumental record featured, in small doses, steel guitar, piano, saxophone, and even a synthesizer. Wernick jokes that after the relative—in bluegrass terms—success of the first record, it was as if the band told the bluegrass world, "Now that we've got your attention, we're going to abuse it." In a largely positive review, *Bluegrass Unlimited* called the record a successful example of "abstract bluegrass." These young, urban northerners, the reviewer concluded, had distilled what they could from the style's traditional elements and used it to "create something different and unique."[35]

Wernick is proud of the second album's experimental genre bending, which he attributes to the band's immersion in the counterculture. Some band members had "seriously long hair and the looser attitudes that went with that." On the record jacket, in lieu of the formal, often dour poses struck by many bluegrassers, Country Cooking posed in a chorus line with their legs kicked high in the air. The band understood that older southern bluegrass fans, looking at that cover, might think, "Oh, no, an invasion of the freaks," but they enjoyed flaunting established rules of decorum. From the first album onward, Country Cooking took that image to the stages of southern festivals with largely positive results. Wernick recalls many southern hippies plus quite a few seemingly conservative older musicians who, ignoring cultural or political differences, just wanted to jam. The band's single greatest validation came unexpectedly from Bill Monroe, the taciturn, often stern, and sometimes scary bluegrass patriarch. At the first annual Delaware Bluegrass Festival in September 1972 a promoter warned the band members that headliner Monroe would not even look at them. After the band left the stage, however, Monroe approached. Directing himself to guitarist Russ Barenberg and bassist John Miller, he urged simply, "Boys, always keep looking for them new notes."[36]

With Country Cooking, the fledgling Rounder helped expand the artistic parameters of bluegrass while simultaneously building bridges between conservative traditionalists and experimental innovators. It also helped launch long-running and influential professional careers. Most members of the band have acquired lengthy artistic résumés. Wernick spent twelve years with Hot Rize, one of the most popular bluegrass bands of the 1980s. Still interested in innovation, he also leads a band that blends bluegrass and early jazz. He served fifteen years as president of the International Bluegrass Music Association, and he runs music instruction camps throughout the United States. *Bluegrass Banjo*, the instruction manual Wernick published in 1974, has sold more than two hundred thousand copies and was the first of his several books and instructional DVDs. Though he worked only briefly as a professional sociologist, his Ph.D. from Columbia has made him known to bluegrassers worldwide as "Dr. Banjo."

Musicians recognize Trischka as a major influence on progressive banjo players. A respected teacher, he has also recorded a string of albums for Rounder and other labels that apply the banjo to music that ranges from hard bluegrass to free-form jazz. He became a pioneer in the field of "new acoustic music," a term that fiddler Darol Anger coined to describe eclectic acoustic albums that fell outside conventional genres. Anger applied this admittedly flexible phrase to "original and folk and jazz-derived music on acoustic stringed instruments," performed largely by musicians "who have been playing bluegrass, or started out playing traditional oriented music, who have been interested in trying to take the boundaries of that music a little farther." Elaborating, mandolinist Andy Statman explains that though bluegrass itself began as a synthesis, it ultimately became "very stylized and more solidified and maybe a little bit rigid." New acoustic music, he adds, is another synthesis—one built on the bluegrass foundation "but taking different elements because it's people from a different time and place."[37]

Through its extended exploration of new acoustic music, Rounder demonstrated that it was willing to move far beyond the well-known repertoire and relatively casual picking that fueled the jam sessions so beloved by folkies and amateur bluegrassers. New acoustic tends to be virtuosic art music that demands an extraordinary level of musical sophistication. Rounder not only recorded and released it but, within the limitations of the label's marginal industry status in the 1970s and 1980s, also made a genuine effort to drive it into the marketplace. Anger acknowledges that he hoped his inventive nomenclature would help sell records. "Basically," he says, the phrase "was just a ploy to try and get these people's records that didn't fit into any other category into a spot in the record stores . . . because we know the larger music corporations aren't really interested."[38] Though the catchphrase failed to survive, many of the musicians whom Rounder helped nurture are still performing professionally. In addition to Trischka and the others mentioned above, onetime Rounder artists who pioneered the loosely defined new acoustic "style" include such well-known performers as banjoist Bela Fleck, mandolinist David Grisman, guitarist Tony Rice, and fiddler Mark O'Connor. Practitioners went on to explore not only jazz but also calypso, Jewish klezmer music, and classical forms, among other things.

Befitting the founders' political interests, they branched fairly quickly into topical songs. As champions of "the people," they loved finding obscure political material performed by the people's idealized representatives. "If some of these bluegrass or old-time musicians had a song that had a title that sounded like it could be political, we got excited about things like that," says Nowlin.[39] In 1972 they issued *How Can a Poor Man Stand Such Times and Live?* a collection of topical material recorded in the late 1920s by West Virginia fiddler Blind Alfred Reed. The title song, recorded just one month after Black Tuesday ushered in the Great Depression, reflects the political tilt of the album as a whole, as it rails against monied interests, high prices, religious leaders "who preach for dough and not the soul," and police officers who "kill without a cause." That same year Rounder issued an anthology of obscure political recordings that Aunt Molly Jackson had made for the Library of Congress. Jackson, a Kentucky labor agitator and coal miner's wife, had come to prominence within the short-lived, highly politicized folk music movement of the 1930s.

Not content to confine themselves to historical political commentary, the founders also began to issue music that addressed contemporary social issues. The first such album, released in January 1973, was *Mountain Moving Day*, an explicitly feminist rock record that was also the label's earliest departure from the acoustic sounds that had dominated the boom. "These were not 'the people,'" Nowlin says of the musicians. "These were kids like us." The project featured the New Haven and Chicago Women's Liberation Rock Bands, two groups that recorded separately and shared space on the album. The band members knew virtually nothing about the Rounders. According to Chicago band keyboardist Naomi Weisstein, "We knew they were sort of the successor to Alan Lomax but, mainly, we didn't care."[40]

In making this comparison, Weisstein suggests implicitly that the Women's Liberation Rock Bands were themselves successors to Molly Jackson and Woody Guthrie, political troubadours whom Lomax had recorded decades earlier. If so, they were successors who were emblematic of their own time. Those earlier performers had supported class-based calls for justice manifested, in large part, by the demands of organized labor. In a later era, when Mick Jagger sang of women "under his thumb" and Jim Morrison deified his penis symbolically onstage, Weisstein and her colleagues represented a newer brand of identity politics, espousing a broad message of female empowerment that energized a personal-liberation movement with which the musicians made common cause. Moreover, like the Rounder founders themselves, the musicians were steeped in the free-form artistic ethos of the counterculture, and they did not want to emulate the often didactic style of earlier topical performers. "One of the things that I had found so exciting about what we were doing," Weisstein says of the Chicago band, "was to try to have consciousness without going back into the old agit-prop, socialist realism kind of thing. . . . I think one of the things that stopped it from being socialist realism in our case is that we were very funny, we were really very funny, and even did [comic] monologues in our singing."[41]

By rock-and-roll standards, neither band was particularly aggressive musically. This was not the assaultive protopunk of Detroit's politicized MC-5. However, before the musicians struck a note, the band names telegraphed their explicit political agenda, confirmed by their lyrical themes. The album's poetic title track casts emergent second-wave feminism as an unstoppable force of nature, as the Chicago band sings, "All sleeping women now awake and move." "Papa Don't Lay That Shit on Me" is a funky vaudeville number that attacks a patriarchal social and economic structure, represented in part by the rock music industry itself: "Papa don't lay those sounds on me, don't you know they make me sick / Rolling Stones, Blood, Sweat and Tears, I've taken that shit for too many years." In the original spirit of folk music as an informal participatory exercise, the bands sought, through their interaction with the audience, to establish an identity as movement colleagues, not as leaders. At live performances, the crowd sang along and danced among the band members, who took requests and honored audience demands to "play it again." Concerts often helped support a multiplicity of causes. The message was that any woman could control her own destiny, if not in the musical arena than elsewhere.[42]

Not only was topical music consistent with the Rounders' personal sympathies, but it was also something that Folkways embraced. Ultimately, however, the founders moved beyond the already broad boundaries of that admired forerunner. Happy Traum and his younger brother Artie helped trigger this evolution with the 1972 release of *Mud Acres*, an album named after the condition of Artie's front yard in Woodstock, New York. At the time, with many young people contemplating the value of life in the country, the surrounding Catskill Mountains were home to a number of musicians linked to the boom, now seeking respite from urban life. Dylan lived there, as did the members of the Band, who composed their first album in "Big Pink," their famed house in the town of West Saugerties. Happy Traum, who was himself part of this artistic community, describes the collective vision that led to the album: "We had long wanted to put down . . . the kind of songs and instrumentals we play when we get together at parties and just pick and sing for fun. We wanted to record for a small record company with whom we could work informally, free from commercial restraint."[43] Artie had heard some Rounder releases. Impressed with their look and sound, he contacted the company, which agreed to release the record.

In January 1972 several musicians recorded the album in one weekend at a small studio in upstate New York. Participants included the Traum brothers; Jim Rooney, onetime stalwart of the Cambridge revival scene; Bill Keith, Rooney's sometime performing partner and the first native northerner to join Bill Monroe's Blue Grass Boys; former Greenbriar Boy John Herald; and Maria Muldaur, once a member of the Jim Kweskin Jug Band and still a few years away from her solo success. "I believe," Happy wrote, "we got what we went for—an album of songs that convey the sense of closeness, personally and musically, that we feel, as well as the fun of doing something for its own sake, as opposed to doing it for financial or other ends."[44] The album's subtitle, *Music among Friends*, is appropriate to the collegial feelings that inspired it, and to the record's warm, inviting sound.

The material recorded was fairly typical revival fare. There are songs associated with Guthrie and Lead Belly, early commercial country tunes, an acoustic blues number, and an original banjo duet by Keith and Artie Traum. The record was, however, somehow different from other Rounder offerings. Although Spark Gap, Joe Val, and Country Cooking all performed music that originated within cultures other than their own, they worked within the recognizable parameters of specific vernacular styles. On *Mud Acres*, however, the repertoire consists of a miscellany of cultural borrowings, akin to that which so troubled performer Sheldon Posen as he agonized over his personal authenticity. Rather than being an old-time, bluegrass, or blues album, it is defined best as an "urban revival album"—consisting of that grab bag of sources and styles that revivalists tend to meld into a singular performance aesthetic, one owing more to Greenwich Village or Harvard Square than to even an imagined American South. It was not particularly clear that this was the music of the downtrodden "people," nor was it the present-day topical music of the founders' leftist contemporaries. Acknowledging the distinction between this album and those of other northern urbanites then on their roster, the Rounders created a special series for styles that fell within the revival's wide orbit but that were, in Nowlin's words, "more contemporary, not so traditional."[45]

The creation of this series proved to be an initial step in Rounder's eventual embrace of that sometimes controversial folk world staple, the singer-songwriter. In 1977 the Traum brothers spearheaded the first of three *Mud Acres'* reunions. Of the fifteen tracks on that initial follow-up, *Woodstock Mountains: More Music from Mud Acres*, six were original compositions by participating musicians. Though the Traums and their friends were singer-songwriters in a literal sense, they were different from the acoustic pop star hopefuls who caused such angst in some folk music circles. They were "rooted," meaning that they incorporated recognizably traditional styles and motifs into their songwriting and performing. This made them more acceptable to the young Rounders who, in their earliest days, avoided the "smooth, pretty style" of the confessional singer-songwriters influenced predominantly by folk/pop artists such as Joni Mitchell.[46] Many of the latter made overtures to the label, but the founders generally referred them to Chicago's Flying Fish Records or to Philo Records, a Vermont company founded in 1972 that was more welcoming to the genre.

One of Philo's biggest "stars" was Mary McCaslin, a young Californian who was a major draw on the coffeehouse circuit of the seventies. McCaslin wrote evocative lyrics describing life in a mythic American West—songs that many committed revivalists could embrace for their regional or historical focus. Vocally, however, she bore similarities to Mitchell, and she also recorded tunes by the Beatles and songwriter Randy Newman. The Rounders had nothing against either the Beatles or Newman, but McCaslin's overall image seemed contrary to their more rooted aesthetic. Still, the two labels began to work together. As Rounder branched into record distribution, Philo became a client. When Philo filed for bankruptcy in the early 1980s, Rounder took over its administration in cooperation with a court-appointed trustee and eventually purchased the Vermont company.

The Philo name continued as a Rounder imprint and is now home to most of Rounder's contemporary acoustic singer-songwriters, including those with the "sweet, pretty voices" that the company once avoided. The first signing by the Rounder-controlled Philo was Nanci Griffith, who has had much success as a pop-oriented folk star. The second was Christine Lavin, a strong writer and all-around comic entertainer who had worked with New York's Fast Folk musical cooperative. Aware of distinctions that once seemed so important, Irwin observes that the slow "organic" development of the founders' relationship with Philo allowed them to ease into the singer-songwriter field. "It wasn't like, 'Poof, you're a singer-songwriter label.' We never," he jokes, "had the tarnish."[47]

With *Mud Acres* opening the door, Rounder's "more contemporary" series eventually became home to a miscellany of noncommercial music, ranging from the surrealistic tunes of those early idols the Holy Modal Rounders to the rockabilly stylings of Sleepy LaBeef and the avant-garde jazz of Sun Ra. In 1977 the series hosted the recording debut of George Thorogood and the Destroyers, a band that had an enormous impact on Rounder, both artistically and commercially. Thorogood was a young, white electric slide guitarist who played bluesy rock and roll expressed through a repertoire drawn from the likes of John Lee Hooker, Elmore James, Chuck Berry, and Bo Diddley, all post–World War II African American pioneers of electric blues and rock. He was hardly the first to tread this ground. In the 1960s the Rolling Stones and Johnny Winter, to name just two, attained fame with the identical approach. Thorogood was merely one more in a long line of white performers who mined a black-originated repertoire, even as many of the artists who created that repertoire were still working, generally with less success. Viewed cynically, his growling approach to Hooker's paean to "one bourbon, one Scotch, and one beee-ah" barely rose above the level of caricature. The Rounders initially paid him no mind, immersed in exploring vernacular sounds that were both more obscure and more conventionally "traditional."[48]

Cambridge school bus driver John Forward introduced artist and label. Forward visited Rounder's warehouse regularly, where he bought albums for personal enjoyment, and Rounder's small staff came to know him as the label's single best customer. As Thorogood's self-proclaimed number-one fan, Forward tried for a long time to interest the label in recording him. The founders enjoyed an amateur tape of the band that Forward provided, but they saw nothing distinctive enough to warrant a shift in their focus. Forward kept pushing, however, urging the Rounders to attend one of Thorogood's live shows where, he insisted, the musician truly blossomed. Finally, Nowlin relented and attended a performance that Forward had helped to organize. It took only two songs before he concluded that the bus driver had indeed found something extraordinary. Overwhelmed by Thorogood's energy, stage presence, and obvious love for performing, he called Irwin and told him to come to the club.

Eventually, each of the founders saw Thorogood in performance many times before they committed to making a record. They came to like him personally and to respect his passion. Still, notwithstanding the blues-based repertoire, they fretted over Thorogood's obvious identity as a rocker. They enjoyed the Stones and did not agonize over the "white boy playing the blues" clichés that had once dominated folk revival debates. Intellectually, Thorogood's work was not far removed from what Country Cooking had done with bluegrass. Indeed, the Ithaca bluegrassers had arguably taken more liberties with their sources than Thorogood did with his. The question remained whether, on a gut level, this was right for Rounder. This was not bluegrass, that folk world constant. It was rock, it was electric, and, assuredly, it was not something that Folkways would release.[49]

Given that a new generation of pop music fans is born roughly every four years, many young record buyers in the midseventies were unfamiliar with the African American artists who had inspired the Stones and other British Invasion bands just a decade earlier. Weary of a music scene that had grown increasingly pretentious, rock adventurers were moving toward early punk and new wave, as Led Zeppelin and other arena bands buried their blues "sources" in layers of psychedelia and heavy metal. On another part of the spectrum disco was ascending, becoming a phenomenon that captured the attention of the Stones themselves. In this climate Thorogood did manage to look a bit "traditional," at least in the expansive terms of the rock music industry. He honored his sources and played his rocking blues straight, never relegating it to raw material for strained experimentation. Lacking other commercial recording prospects, the guitarist pressed his case, pointing out that he represented the rhythm-and-blues "tradition" or the "roots" of rock. For their part, the Rounders had already demonstrated their allegiance to true vernacular originators, black and white, and they had nothing to prove on that score. They would have loved to record John Lee Hooker himself, but he was unavailable to the small Cambridge folk label. Thorogood was, and they were tempted.

For months, the Rounders debated. They feared going the route of Elektra, which they believed had veered off course after signing the Doors. They worried that friends and fans would become confused about their commitment to their mission or, worse, view them as sellouts. Eventually, they relented. They enjoyed the music, liked the band members, and wanted to do it. Their first attempt at recording showed their inexperience with rock. Adopting a configuration the band often used onstage, they recorded with just two guitars and a drummer. The playback revealed the need for a fuller sound, and Rounder returned to the studio to overdub a bass. From a commercial standpoint, nothing in either the industry landscape or Rounder's history suggested that the record would become anything other than a résumé builder for Thorogood—one that might help him get steady club work. Nobody dreamed seriously that it would be a hit.[50]

In numerical terms Thorogood's debut—released in July 1977—was not an immediate smash. *Rolling Stone* reported that it sold approximately forty thousand copies in the four months following its release. For Rounder, this might as well have been a million. The label had never before sold in such numbers. More important, the record was added to the playlists of hip FM stations, and, fueled by word of Thorogood's sensational live performances, it began to develop a cachet. Press was widespread and favorable. Calling the record a "notable debut," *Down Beat* declared Thorogood "an impressive and hugely entertaining performer, a strong persuasive vocalist in a straightforward ungimmicked style . . . and a gripping guitarist." Using a characterization that might have pleased the tradition-minded Rounders, New York's *Village Voice* said that he captured the precise point at which blues, country, and rock met, before they were diluted by ineffective imitators. Given the appropriately limited expectations, the record was an overwhelming success in terms of sales, praise, and impact, both artistic and commercial.[51]

Rounder released *Move It on Over*, Thorogood's second album, in October 1978. Its musical approach was virtually identical to that of its predecessor. In a back-cover essay signed by "The Rounder Folks" the founders sought to assure fans—and perhaps themselves—that nothing important had changed, despite the unexpected burst of success. In an effort to suggest that Thorogood was perhaps a bit of a folk artist himself, the Rounders took pains to present him as a "reluctant star," a genuine everyman uninterested in the "adulation" and "artificial pleasures" that accompany rock-and-roll success. The essay describes both the artist and the label owners as devoted to "the many local institutions that contribute to a community or neighborhood consciousness," a milieu that had historically produced "many excellent folk musicians, who usually went unrecognized among mass audiences and the mass media." The founders assured readers that they "still like 'old' music best" and prefer obscure "quality labels like Arhoolie or [Nashville's] Excello more than the bustling, blustering conglomerates." Stressing that they remained "fiercely independent," they expressed hope that the network of small record distributors of which they were then a part could be "strengthened financially and more sought after by stores that care about music."[52]

Read against the backdrop of the founders' initial concerns about Thorogood, the essay's many truths seem joined by equal parts hope, rationalization, and self-defense. Beyond any doubt, the Rounders loved old music and small labels. They valued community participation, artistic and otherwise. They saw Thorogood's music as an art form shamefully ignored by much of the music industry. In releasing it they performed a service that no major label was then willing to undertake, at least until Thorogood demonstrated his commercial potential. The wholly unexpected success, however, heightened their initial fears that onetime admirers would see them as sellouts, as it enmeshed them in the commercial music business to a previously unimaginable degree. In 1979 Thorogood's sophomore album passed five hundred thousand units sold, earning Rounder its first gold record. Artistically, its impact was twofold. Determined to demonstrate their commitment to their original mission, the founders continued to release a steady stream of traditionally based vernacular music from a wide array of international cultures. They also concluded that more contemporary—and perhaps more commercial—sounds could coexist with those displaying a fidelity to older traditional styles. Although they undoubtedly enjoyed the additional income, they also understood that such commercial material could help finance more esoteric albums and, if chosen carefully, could itself constitute a meaningful cultural contribution.[53]

Producer Scott Billington credits the Thorogood albums with bringing Rounder a level of professional credibility that allowed it to record "roots artists with the potential of commercial success." Billington's initial production credits had consisted of two stripped-down acoustic albums. One features Joseph Spence, a Bahamian guitarist that he and Nowlin had recorded in a Nassau hotel room. The other stars bluesman Johnny Shines in a live solo performance taken from a Boston Blues Society tape. Characterizing these as "documentary-style" recordings, Billington says, "I wanted [to make] something that spoke to someone in a more contemporary way."[54] Walking through the door opened by Thorogood, he traveled to Bogalusa, Louisiana, in 1981 to produce Gatemouth Brown's Grammy-winning big-band record. This, in turn, led to a "spiraling number of musical contacts" that helped Rounder attain a preeminent position in the Louisiana music scene of the 1980s and 1990s.[55]

Billington is particularly proud of his work with zydeco, the African American dance music indigenous to southwestern Louisiana. The genre took shape in the 1950s, when the famed Clifton Chenier began blending traditional Louisiana French accordion tunes with the jazz and rhythm-and-blues sounds popularized by the likes of Duke Ellington and Ray Charles. Until around 1980 Billington was only vaguely aware of zydeco, which he considered "an odd type of French blues." He embraced it after witnessing a dynamic performance by Buckwheat Zydeco and the Ils Sont Partis Band at the New Orleans Jazz and Heritage Festival and thinking, "Yeah, this is something that the world should hear." He subsequently produced two Rounder albums by Buckwheat, who worked within the broad framework established by Chenier. It is through his work with several other artists, however, that Billington helped to promote a new and distinctive zydeco sound.[56]

One of the most satisfying of these partnerships was with accordionist Andrus Espree who, billing himself as Beau Jocque, recorded five albums for Rounder before a heart attack felled him in 1999 at the age of forty-six. Espree gained fame in Louisiana dance halls with a high-energy stage show built around nonstop, pounding rhythms in which the bass drum was as prominent as the accordion. With his deep, booming voice, he barked out minimalist lyrics that were often little more than shouted refrains, developing neither melody nor story line but serving merely as one more percussive device. Many of his tunes, such as "Git It, Beau Jocque," "Beau Jocque Boogie," and "Beau Jocque Run," consisted of brief lyrical phrases that did little more than exalt the presence of the charismatic front man. This approach, which owes far more to funk and hip-hop than it does to blues or jazz, let alone Louisiana French folk tunes, brought young black Louisianans streaming into clubs in the 1990s, condemning all previous stylistic variants to at least momentary oblivion.

Some sticklers for purity dismissed Beau Jocque's music as "zyderap" or, perhaps more charitably, as "noveau zydeco," a term designed to distinguish it from supposedly more authentic earlier forms. To Billington, however, Espree merely embodied one legitimate approach to the future of southwestern Louisiana vernacular expression. Though he considers himself a fan of traditional music, the producer is no fan of rigid, frozen-in-place purity. What he loves more than anything is "somebody coming out of [a] tradition and just lighting a fire under the whole thing." "There will always be a great artist coming along working within one of those [traditional] fields," he says, "with something very exciting to say to people. But I feel that the genres themselves in terms of being able to grab attention in the media are kind of tired." With a practicality borne of more than three decades in the record business, he adds, "We can't make the same record now that we would have made twenty years ago. I mean, maybe some music is timeless, but people just don't want to hear the same thing forever. I feel that today more than ever the success of an artist is as much personality based as musically based."[57]

Critics might see in Billington the triumph of commerce over heritage, ignoring the reality that commerce and heritage have commingled for centuries. Indeed, zydeco, like bluegrass before it, stemmed from the artistic and commercial innovations of ambitious professional entertainers, working within a framework provided only in part by their personal cultural heritage. To Sean Ardoin, an inventive African American zydeco bandleader, and a member of a famed Louisiana musical family, the advances Billington captured on record are an accurate reflection of the region's artistic progression. "We're 'noveau' as opposed to what?" he asks with disdain. "We are the indigenous people who support and create and refine the music. . . . We are what the people in southwestern Louisiana call zydeco, yet some writer not from here wants to put us in a box and label us noveau?"[58]

Despite early concern on Billington's part, Rounder supported his yearning for experimentation, largely because the founders never confined themselves to purism either. Indeed, Billington came to consider Irwin "a musical soul mate." "Ken," he says, "may go for a more unvarnished sound," whereas Billington often prefers "a more musically polished sound." In the end, the producer adds, they both want "something soulful, that says something to people, that communicates something to people, and that makes them feel something. There's different ways of getting that."[59]

Eventually, Rounder abandoned the "antiprofit" posture of its early years. The founders learned about distribution, marketing, and promotion as they sought to survive and prosper. But they have remained true to the traditional/contemporary/experimental artistic mixture that became Rounder's hallmark as it distinguished itself from those labels that influenced it—the predominantly traditional Folkways, on the one hand, and the far more mainstream Elektra, on the other. By repeatedly welcoming under its umbrella artists as diverse as George Pegram, the Women's Liberation Rock Bands, the Traum brothers, Gatemouth Brown, Mary McCaslin, and Beau Jocque, Rounder simultaneously marketed heritage and challenged old ideas about tradition. Pulling together vernacularity, topical songs, community music making, acoustic pop, and avant-garde experimentation, Rounder, perhaps more than any other commercial entity, has helped not only to reflect but also to shape the expanding definition of folk music in the decades following the great boom.

FOUR

Toward an Authenticity of Self:
Old-Time Music in the Modern World

Notwithstanding the increasing elasticity of the term *folk*, old constructs die hard, and the concept, along with its companions "tradition" and "authenticity," has continued to bedevil scholars, musicians, and entrepreneurs. In this chapter I examine how postboom revivalists have negotiated these concepts in the context of the ongoing old-time country music revival. Within this arena, activists pursue all of revivalism's historical endeavors—they document and preserve repertoire and musical style, they strive to understand other cultures, and they attempt to satisfy personal yearnings for community, artistic experimentation, and professional success.[1]

Ever diverse, Rounder has encouraged all of these efforts through a steady stream of old-time releases. Early in their musical exploration Irwin, Nowlin, and Leighton fell in love with both the so-called authentic singing of Clarence Ashley and the more "surrealistic" old-time vision offered by the Holy Modal Rounders. Over time they came to understand the culturally freighted distinction between urbanites who never penetrated the revival's romantic shroud and the idealized rural musicians themselves, who invariably proved to be multidimensional human beings. Though George Pegram, Snuffy Jenkins, and Pappy Sherrill embodied the idea of the authentic, they actually occupied the vast middle ground between Cambridge revivalists and stereotypically traditional community entertainers. Jenkins and Sherrill had spent years as consummate music industry professionals. Pegram had sought commercial opportunity, though with less success, and was well acquainted with folk song collectors and folk festival promoters. Each man had recorded previously, and each was a self-conscious showman, knowledgeable about the use of the stage, aware of his impact on an audience, and happy to earn money from performing.

The Rounders prized their opportunity to record such musicians, but they also hoped to record skilled nonprofessionals who were presumably less "contaminated" by the music industry's lures and demands. Fairly early in its history Rounder began issuing albums by unknown old-time musicians who had largely confined themselves to informal performances within their own communities. Mark Wilson, a university philosophy professor, became a longtime collaborator in this endeavor. Raised in Oregon, the son of an avocational jazz pianist, Wilson developed an interest in folk song while still a child. During the boom he listened initially to the Kingston Trio, but after discovering Lead Belly he gravitated quickly to more authentic performers. While a graduate student at Harvard, Wilson met Nowlin at Boston-area bluegrass shows, as Nowlin sold Rounder's first releases from a tabletop.

Although Wilson enjoyed bluegrass and old-time music, he had no interest in the boom's more commercial aspects. "I never liked the urban folk scene," he says. "I've never had much to do with it." He heard groups in the "spirit" of the Holy Modal Rounders, but he hated their irreverence, which he considered a "wise guy" attitude that was "denigrating to the music."[2] Time has not tempered this disdain. Decades after the boom, Wilson continues to characterize the music of revivalists as "ingrown," criticizing their marked tendency to learn mainly from one another. Dismissing revivalist fiddling as either "bland" or "pointlessly frenetic," he charges that it "frequently lacks the virtues that supply genuine traditional music with its special élan" and "fails to appreciate the intrinsic subtleties of the American dance tradition."[3] He decries the revivalist tendency to sentimentalize traditional performers, a practice that he believes detracts from their genuinely interesting lives. He also dislikes the rural caricatures prevalent within some revival circles. Citing a discussion with Roscoe Holcomb, the Kentucky banjo player who enjoyed renown during the boom, he notes Holcomb's puzzlement over photographers who posed him routinely in front of his somewhat dilapidated old barn while ignoring the gorgeous Kentucky scenery all around.[4]

Despite Nowlin's connection to the revivalist Spark Gap Wonder Boys, he and Wilson developed a friendship built around a shared love of traditional music. Wilson began his formal involvement with Rounder by writing and editing liner notes. He attended some of the label's early recording sessions and, distressed by the absence of technical engineering expertise, developed his own skills in this area. In the early 1970s he began recording those musicians who met his rigid aesthetic. He concentrated on the "country people"—specifically those from "the last couple of generations that grew up before rural electrification, for true tradition." In this respect, he says, "I'm what they used to call a purist, I guess. I've always felt that we had an obligation to help get traditional artists on records, so that they could experience a direct benefit from sharing their heritage with others." Wilson has since supervised many of Rounder's recordings—both collections of ballad singing and the instrumental fiddle and banjo music that accompanied dances and parties in an earlier era. Particularly as recorded by the local musicians whom Wilson favors, it is presently about as noncommercial a sound as one can find. Some of Wilson's productions have sold in the hundreds of copies, and sales of more than two thousand constitute a best-seller. He credits Rounder with being one of the few companies willing to release such truly traditional music on a consistent basis.[5]

By playing close attention to tune, technique, and the stories musicians tell, Wilson hopes to discern the nature of early styles and determine how later ones developed. He acknowledges the influence of professional musicians and the mass media, but after several decades of avocational field research he has concluded that scholars overemphasize such influences due to excessive reliance on the most readily available historical sources. With respect to the informal community music making that Wilson reveres, there are no newspaper accounts, concert programs, or recordings, leaving a gap in our understanding of musical practice, which Wilson strives to fill. "In my opinion," he writes, "some modern writers on the banjo's history overemphasize the importance to folk tradition of the music that can be found in the nineteenth century tutors [published banjo manuals]. In fact," he adds, there exists a great disparity "between what can be found in [older] instruction manuals and how the instrument in question was actually played contemporaneously." The vast majority of banjo tunes that Wilson has heard during his field research "seem to have reached their performers completely beneath the radar of the [published] tutors and the [professional] songsters."[6]

Reflecting Wilson's conviction that an understanding of musicians' lives is essential to a complete understanding of their music, the liner notes to his recordings generally include detailed biographical or, where possible, autobiographical essays. He favors notes that rely on the artist's own words to describe both the music and the context of its creation. Typical are those by Buddy Thomas, an impoverished fiddler who died of heart failure in 1974 at the age of thirty-nine. In explaining how he learned the old-time tunes of his region, Thomas illustrates the importance of face-to-face transmission. "A lot of my fiddle tunes," he recalls, "I learned from Morris Allen up there in Portsmouth [Ohio]. He's getting near eighty but he's still a pretty good old fiddler. Back in the thirties, he was a bachelor and had a good job in a steel mill and he used to like to get all the fiddlers together. . . . And I then got to hearing him and different good fiddlers around Portsmouth and the fiddle sounded so pretty that I just had to get into it and learn those tunes."[7]

Beyond his desire to provide a more accurate picture of cultural transmission, Wilson hopes to promote "simple cultural justice." Illustrating the class consciousness that surfaces so often in connection with the promotion of the folk arts, it troubles Wilson that revival professionals tend to reap the lion's share of public acclaim, as well as the bulk of the meager financial rewards available through playing old-time music. Those musicians who seek employment as entertainers, who are so often outsiders to the cultures they emulate, face the perpetual need to draw an audience. They accomplish this, Wilson believes, by distorting the art, hoping to maximize its admittedly narrow commercial appeal. The "folk," Wilson says, "deserve to have their music heard in its proper contours, not filtered through several layers of interpretive remove."[8]

Of necessity, professional emulators are generally skilled at self-promotion. Wilson, by contrast, strives to record the best traditional musicians he can find—a group that does not necessarily overlap with those interested in pursuing professional performing careers. The musicians that he favors often dislike the personal grandstanding necessary to hold the attention of a club or festival crowd. He describes the experience of Joe Cormier, a Boston-based fiddler who performs from within the traditions of his native Cape Breton Island. At a relatively rare commercial performance outside his own community, a promoter asked Cormier to do more than sit stock-still and fiddle. He wanted some kind of "show" or, at least, a smile. As Wilson recalls, Cormier replied that he "came to play the fiddle, not act a clown." As a consequence of this professional/amateur divide, Wilson often encounters situations in Appalachia "where 'folk festivals' are largely dominated by [revivalists], even if excellent traditional musicians may live nearby," a commercial disparity that strikes him as deeply unjust.[9]

Despite the sincerity of Wilson's concerns, it is difficult to characterize all revivalists as either callow "wise guy" replicators or striving professionals. In the late sixties and early seventies a small and thoroughly local old-time music revival scene developed among graduate students attending the University of North Carolina at Chapel Hill and nearby Duke University. Like Wilson, these musical activists sought to explore admired—and perhaps idealized—musical communities. They also hoped to draw on the artistic resources of these communities in an effort to heighten their own collective bonds. Among these was Florida native and future folklorist Alan Jabbour, raised by a father who had emigrated from Syria and a mother who had grown up in the Deep South. As a youth Jabbour studied classical violin but, prompted by the civil rights movement and his mother's heritage, shifted to old-time fiddling as part of a quest to understand his native region. While pursuing scholarship and musical adventure Jabbour met Henry Reed, an octogenarian Virginia fiddler with an extensive repertoire of otherwise unknown tunes that he had learned traditionally. The young student befriended Reed, played music with him, and spent time with his family. He also recorded Reed in informal performance and then taught the elderly fiddler's tunes to the circle of North Carolina friends with whom he played music.[10]

Several bands formed within this circle, the most well known being the Hollow Rock String Band featuring Jabbour on fiddle, and the Fuzzy Mountain String Band, affectionately dubbed the Fuzzies. Relying on a network of personal musical connections, members, inspired by Jabbour's experience with Reed, often made weekend visits to local musicians residing throughout North Carolina, Virginia, and West Virginia. Band members immersed themselves in the lives of these revered sources. They got to know their families, ate with them, and played music with them. Then, as Fuzzy Mountain fiddler Bill Hicks recalls, they would "come home on Sunday, review the field tape for the newest gem, and, by Wednesday, present a new tune for the group to start working on." Preservation minded and deeply respectful of their sources, the bands valued fidelity to the "original" sound and style, and they expended considerable effort making certain they played the tunes "right," which meant exactly "as the source played them." Aware of the treasure trove of tunes that Jabbour had discovered, everyone was, to paraphrase Fuzzies banjoist Tom Carter, looking for their own Henry Reed.[11]

In 1968 Ken Davidson's Kanawha Records issued *Traditional Dance Tunes*, an album by Hollow Rock that introduced Reed's repertoire to the world. Shortly thereafter, the group disbanded, as members left North Carolina to pursue varied professional opportunities, with Jabbour going on to an illustrious career as a government folklorist. The Fuzzies remained intact to carry the revivalists' old-time torch in North Carolina. After Rounder's inaugural releases, the band met the label founders at a West Virginia music festival, and all agreed that the Fuzzies would release a Rounder album. They recorded this eponymous debut in a band member's living room, and Rounder issued the predominantly instrumental collection in May 1972, with notes that carefully identified each Appalachian traditionalist who served as the source of a tune. In 1973 the label released a Fuzzy Mountain follow-up titled *Summer Oak and Porch*. One year later it issued an album by a new version of the Hollow Rock String Band, with Jabbour again playing fiddle on a collection of tunes drawn predominantly from Henry Reed's repertoire.

Depending on one's point of view, these recordings either honored or exploited the bands' sources. Observers sympathetic to Mark Wilson might insist that such interpreters soften the distinctive edges of the music, stripping it of depth while making it more salable. Others disagree. Richard Spottswood, a discerning listener whose earlier critique of Spark Gap expressed his own qualms about revivalists, believed that Fuzzy Mountain managed to transcend any limitations of origin. Reviewing the band's first album, he concluded not only that their playing was "impeccable" but also that they approached the music with "genuine taste and feeling."[12] Inevitably, there are those who find it disturbing that any listener would choose to enjoy old-time music through performers new to the genre, notwithstanding the availability of recordings by the old-time masters themselves. However, one constant of commercial folk music revivalism—and of the commercial music industry generally—is that consumers enjoy listening to musicians with whom they can identify. At least for the more casual listener, the music may appear worthy of attention precisely because people like themselves are performing it. Many will dig no deeper; others will, and in the process may gain a greater appreciation of the older players and the worlds they inhabit. Beyond any doubt, Jabbour and his friends helped turn Henry Reed's tunes into old-time standards, and Reed himself is now a traditionalist icon, despite never having recorded a commercial album.[13]

Though both Hollow Rock and Fuzzy Mountain performed for audiences on occasion, concert performance was not their reason for being, and neither band was a professional touring ensemble in the conventional sense. Their primary purpose was to explore the music they loved and, according to banjoist Carter, foster "a sense of community." As described by Fuzzy Mountain fiddler Hicks, "The band was the twice weekly [jam] session, and big parties on holidays, with children, relatives, family, smoked oysters, turkey, and country ham. The band, in a way, was a controlled jam session." Both Hollow Rock and the Fuzzies concentrated on instrumentals and the development of a "unison ensemble sound" in which banjo, fiddle, and mandolin played a generally unvarying lead melody, while the guitar kept the beat. This approach, perfect for informal group playing, fuels old-time music jams to this day. Without vocals, instrumental soloing, or harmonic arrangements, any player capable of executing the melody can join in, mid-song. The addition of a second or even a third fiddle or banjo, for example, might make the tune louder but would not change its structure.[14]

Notwithstanding vastly different musical interests, the North Carolina old-time revival scene is akin to the cooperative Songwriter's Exchange that developed a few years later in New York City, though the latter was somewhat more focused on commercial promotion. In each case, the use of music as a mechanism for advancing the musicians' personal search for community exemplifies the small-group artistic expression that Dan Ben-Amos defined as the essence of folklore. The various "North Carolina albums" are thus field recordings of a sort. They document folk revival practice in action by preserving the informal playing of a distinctive "folk group"—the young, educated traditional music emulator. Over the course of the next generation those albums became legendary sources for nonprofessional, jam-loving old-time music fans. In the words of John Bealle, who was active in the Indiana old-time music scene in the 1970s, "The impact of these unassuming Rounder recordings was astounding, with sales reaching old-time music enclaves worldwide." Perhaps to the chagrin of avowed purists like Mark Wilson, people who never enjoyed direct access to southern traditionalists could learn their tunes—ostensibly "played right"—through the LPs of these devoted acolytes.[15]

A different branch of old-time revivalism places a premium on conscious professionalism, public performance, adaptation, and innovation. In the 1970s the Highwoods String Band best illustrated this approach, and attained widespread revival popularity playing colleges and festivals. In the early 1990s, more than a decade after the group broke up, it became the subject of a hotly contested debate over the meaning of tradition and authenticity. To best understand this particular cultural skirmish, one needs to recall the New Lost City Ramblers, undoubtedly the preeminent revival string band of the great boom. Unlike Hollow Rock and Fuzzy Mountain, the Ramblers were a diversified stage band, and, as "first generation" revivalists, its members took seriously the need to educate their audiences about the range of traditional southern music. Generally performing in dress vests, starched white shirts, and creased slacks, the Ramblers, in the words of historian Philip F. Gura, presented "full string-band sounds, banjo solos, banjo-fiddle duets, unaccompanied ballads, early commercial country music," Cajun tunes, and bluegrass. "The way the NLCR executed their program," Gura writes, "was a curious mixture of stage show, illustrated lecture, academic and creative folklore, corny country jokes and complicated patter improvised on the spot. . . . It was an odd combination of seriousness, antiquity, intensity, and hilarity."[16]

Though intensely active during the boom, the Ramblers performed infrequently in the seventies. In that decade it was Highwoods that carried the old-time flame to stages around the world. The band's genesis lay in Berkeley, California, during the late 1960s, where a thriving counterculture drew Walt Koken, Mac Benford, and Bob Potts from disparate parts of the country. Koken and Benford, who had met previously during sojourns to Union Grove, drew their initial inspiration from the Kingston Trio. Despite arrangements that "missed a lot of the real power and beauty that old-time music really had," the trio, in Benford's words, "were the first clue that there was something different" from the even blander pop music of the fifties. Adds Koken, "I played Kingston Trio music because that's what I heard, but when I heard something better—more soulful, much more beautiful, I wanted to play that." Joined at times by a shifting aggregation of accompanists, Benford, Koken, and Potts—playing banjo and twin fiddles, respectively—began busking on the streets of Berkeley, eventually dubbing themselves the Fat City String Band. Though Fat City played coffeehouses and festivals along the West Coast, most of their performances occurred on the streets, where spare change constituted a considerable portion of their limited income.[17]

At the time, the boom's often rigid rules had broken down. Emerging free-form radio blended genres to an extraordinary degree, and rock groups borrowed openly from America's traditional repertoire. It was an era, Benford recalls, when "it was just kind of 'Open your ears, boys and girls—there's a big world out there.' It was a real interesting time for music, because everybody was looking for something 'far out' that would take them to a new place, a whole new set of experiences." It was also a time when youthful California audiences wanted to lose themselves in dance, in the carnivalesque style of the day. Playing on the streets forced the members of Fat City to learn how to hold a crowd that had not come specifically to hear them, had not paid admission, and was free to wander away without offering a single dime. To capture this audience the band played old-time music with driving rock-and-roll energy. One early fan was Mike Seeger of the New Lost City Ramblers. "The first time I heard that trio," he recalls, "I thought it was the most amazing thing I'd heard, rhythmically." Unlike the Ramblers, Fat City eschewed the more didactic trappings of the boom. It did not conduct minieducational seminars on solo fiddle styles or unaccompanied singing. Band members did not offer history lessons recounting musical transitions. They did not wear costumes—neither the hillbilly wear that would have transformed them into cartoons nor the reverential business wear of the Ramblers. They dressed, instead, like themselves and their audience, in the jeans and flannel shirts favored by most other Berkeley hippies. If this was a "costume," at least it was that of their own extended cultural clan.[18]

In the fall of 1971 Fat City split up, worn out from close quarters, frequent travel, and poverty. Koken went to Ithaca, New York, where he renewed a friendship with Cornell student Doug Dorschug and met Dorschug's friend Jenny Cleland. Dorschug, a Connecticut native who played guitar and banjo, had discovered old-time music through a fairly typical path for a young northerner, one that wound from Burl Ives, Pete Seeger, and the Kingston Trio to the southern radio stations that reached northward at night. Cleland, a newcomer to old-time music, was a multi-instrumentalist who had enjoyed the revival through square-dancing and high school hootenannies. In short order, the three formed a band, and Koken then coaxed Potts and Benford—now living in San Francisco and Maryland, respectively—back into the fold. Cleland's acoustic bass and Dorschug's guitar added a booming rhythm to the banjo and twin fiddles of the original trio. After a period of rehearsal, the newly formed quintet took to the road. Wanting to avoid confusion with an East Coast band also called Fat City, they rechristened themselves, drawing from a line in an old Charlie Poole song, "Gonna go to the high woods when I die." Mike Seeger saw the change as one tied closely to the times. "In those years," he said, "that presented a wonderful image. It was the drug years—'High.' And 'woods' made it feel like out in the country."[19]

Echoing Peter Stampfel's description of the Holy Modal Rounders, Koken explains that Highwoods wanted "to take the old-time tunes and songs which had prevailed in the Appalachian region for over 100 years before being swamped into oblivion by modern day media and pop music, and present them as a dynamic art form to the American public."[20] The band began touring with a commercial sophistication that had been foreign to Fat City. Old-time performer and music critic Kerry Blech, in a retrospective remembrance, writes that the musicians had "great individual talent and vitality that coalesced as a throbbing entity on stage. They were exciting, they were having fun, and they showed it." Irwin and Leighton met Koken in Ithaca, and Rounder ultimately released three Highwoods albums between 1973 and 1976, which helped the band spread its music and secure gigs. *Bluegrass Unlimited* reviewed all three records favorably, noting that the band had the "uncommon ability to maintain on an album the same electricity that can charge up their live performance."[21]

By being their hippie selves, the band members forged a special connection with their audience, reaching listeners who would not have readily embraced either costumed "professionals," academic tutors, or genuine southern traditionalists. "By gum, they were us up there on that stage," writes Blech. "It was as if they had stepped right out of the audience." The musicians fostered this connection after their shows ended, developing a reputation as hard partiers who were always willing to keep the festivities going until sleep overcame them. Their energetic performances, quality records, and easy accessibility led to an enduring influence within the relatively small world of committed old-time revivalists. Seeger considers Highwoods "the most important" old-time band of their day. "They encouraged and inspired their generation and younger to take up old-time music," he says. Musician Brad Leftwich praises the "documentary efforts of scholars" but argues that Highwoods was more helpful in demonstrating that old-time music was a "living tradition." "Not only did Highwoods inspire legions of old-time musicians to form flannel-shirted, twin fiddle bands, their success gave dozens of those bands the itch to perform. Whether or not they scratched that itch," he adds, "many Highwoods fans have continued to play old-time music for fun."[22]

Recognition brought Highwoods high-profile appearances at the Smithsonian Festival of American Folklife and the long-running National Folk Festival, along with participation in a State Department–sponsored goodwill tour of Central and South Americas. Such bookings suggest a fair measure of acceptance by those charged, officially, with promoting traditional artistry. However, in the mid-1970s a change in the government's arts policy altered the band's fortunes. In 1974 Alan Jabbour became director of the new Folk Arts Program within the National Endowment for the Arts, responsible for funding traditional artistic expression. He confronted a world in which much of the public associated the word *folk* with revival pop groups such as Peter, Paul and Mary, whereas others considered "folk art" the province of the untrained, sometimes associating it with subpar technical standards. Neither understanding encompassed an appreciation of artistry that was culturally specific, maintained traditionally and without thought of monetary reward, and often of high quality.[23]

Given extremely limited funds, Jabbour and his government colleagues concluded that they met their responsibilities best by funding those artists who learned more or less traditionally within their own communities. Using the organic and pastoral metaphors still common when discussing folklife, Jabbour says that this decision sprang from a desire to fund the "roots," in the hope that the "branches" would thus thrive as well. Mindful of government funding trends, the private, nonprofit National Council for the Traditional Arts followed suit. In 1976 Joe Wilson—no relation to Rounder's Mark Wilson—became director of that organization, and he and his board, which organized the National Folk Festival, revamped its booking policy. There was, he says, "a major policy change, and it amounts to more than withdrawing the annual invitation to Highwoods. Basically, it was a decision to put more emphasis upon the traditional, to get as close to the original as possible, to present the rare rather than the commonplace."[24]

Highwoods banjoist Benford bristled at the change. Though proud of his influence among his peers, he insisted that older southerners who grew up with early country music also embraced the band. "Our music . . . took them back to times and places in their own pasts," he said, "and they were good about expressing their gratitude. It was their conviction that we were keeping something they valued alive that convinced us we were an authentic part of the tradition." Friends such as North Carolina fiddler Tommy Jarrell and Kentucky banjoist Roscoe Holcomb, elders whom staunch traditionalists revered, had gone "out of their way to let [Highwoods] know we had been accepted into the 'family.'" In Benford's view, folklorists failed to understand the significance of this acceptance, adhering instead to outmoded beliefs that placed the band "outside the tradition, because we weren't born into it." Speaking in 1979, Benford argued, "Well, I've been playing old-time music for almost 20 years now, and I think that's enough time to develop a feel for it. It has to do with an attitude, not where you were brought up. History," he added, "will show that we were an important link in that tradition." Contending that young southerners had largely ignored old-time music for a generation, he maintained, "this music is finally being revived by younger people in the South. And they didn't learn it from their parents—they learned it from the records of the Highwoods String Band. The tradition needed a spur from outside the culture in order to keep that culture alive. But the folklorists haven't figured that out yet."[25]

In 1989, more than ten years after Highwoods disbanded, Benford revisited this controversy in the pages of the *Old-Time Herald*. There, he castigated those cultural gatekeepers—Joe Wilson among them—who "describe a world that simply does not exist in real life anymore. People can no longer be born into culturally distinct, isolated geographic areas. [Such areas] just don't exist. We are now all part of the homogenized blend, like it or not."[26] Wilson penned a blistering response. Not an academic folklorist, he took pains to dissociate himself from any theoretical school, grounding his argument in his personal bias for the roots. "You can see everything else labeled folk," he writes, "but it is hard to see the originals." Who, he asks, would prefer to see a copy of the Parthenon as opposed to the splendor of the Athenian original?[27] In response to those who note that few, if any, remaining "originals" are free of popular influences, Wilson disclaims any interest in an idealized authenticity of style and repertoire. "Purity I'm not seeking," he says. "But nevertheless there are things that come from a little closer to the bone." He sees little that is truly traditional among the many who market themselves at the annual Folk Alliance conferences. "It's mainly people who have learned styles and are reproducing those kinds of things, and I think that's OK. If you're raised out in the mainstream, and it's a little bit polluted, and you hear something from a crystal spring somewhere, and you want to get closer to that, it's OK to wiggle in that direction. But it's not the same as the deeper thing," he adds, "the thing that comes from the working folks with the sweat on them and all of it—it's not exactly the same."[28]

For Wilson, Benford's blithe acceptance of cultural homogenization sums up all that is wrong with revivalists. Most self-identified "folk" performances, he maintains, "make everything look and sound like everything else. . . . Then the event looks like all the rest and is boring and dies without anyone noticing."[29] At the root of Wilson's preference lies a highly personal, class-based belief in equity, which he shares with Rounder's Mark Wilson. Born during the Great Depression in eastern Tennessee and raised in lower-class circumstances, Joe Wilson strives to promote those relative unknowns who labor for a living while making music avocationally because they find meaning in its connection to community. "The people who are skilled at marketing are the people you hear of," he says. "They're the people who make the money because that's their purpose. And God bless them, fine for them. They can go into business and do whatever they want to do, but they don't necessarily need my hillbilly ass to help them. There're some other folks that I'm interested in. I've had to sort out my work."[30]

Like that of Mark Wilson, Joe's passion sometimes infers that all revival-ists are guilty of egregious cultural plunder, and suggests a divide reminis-cent of the heated Dorson-Botkin debates of the 1950s. In the spirit of that earlier controversy, the Benford-Wilson dispute prompted an outpouring of anguished commentary in the pages of the *Old-Time Herald*. Most remarks came from revivalists, presumably because they felt under siege and perhaps because they are the ones who read the magazine. *Herald* associate editor and one-time Fuzzy Mountain fiddler Bill Hicks noted that Wilson sought to "crush and pulverize" not only Benford but also "probably 90 percent of this magazine's readership." At least one magazine correspondent, however, was sympathetic to Wilson. "I feel it is unwise," he wrote, "for us to confuse coat-tail riding with real tradition." Folklorists, he added, "study forms of music that have existed for centuries without commercial exploitation and one doubts that Wilson is the only one who refuses to buy the idea that it is their job to help revivalists be successful." Although this description of the folklorist's mission is somewhat inconsistent with modern theory, the writer's—and Wilson's—commitment to those standing apart from entre-preneurial activity is rooted in the discipline's earliest focus.[31]

Notwithstanding such support, the majority of commentators disagreed with Wilson. Some found him guilty of the same excessive romanticism and cultural colonialism that he criticized in others. In response to Wilson's contention that Benford could have integrated himself into rural culture more fully had he chosen to spend twenty-five years residing on Pipers Gap Road near Galax, Virginia, one Pipers Gap resident hinted that perhaps Wilson had lost touch with those whom he revered. "If you drive down [that roadway] today," he wrote, "you will see a stretch of suburbia/exurbia pretty typical of anywhere in the country. There are only two log houses between here and the Blue Ridge Parkway, both recently built and out of my price range. Not a tarpaper shack in the whole ten-mile stretch." By far, the most common critique held that Wilson saw division where most musicians, whether revivalists or authentic traditionalists, saw none. New Lost City Rambler Tracy Schwarz expressed the prevailing sentiment, noting that the "old masters" whom he had encountered over roughly thirty years of performing always gave freely to both folklorists and revival musicians, perhaps, he speculated, because they recognized "the importance of the moment," when the interest of revivalist devotees rendered obvious the value of the traditionalist's art.[32]

Some commentators noted that revered traditionalists could also be savvy self-promoters, fully capable of protecting their own interests. *Herald* editor Hicks argued that many of the southern traditionalists embraced the professional opportunities that revivalists offered. He pointed specifically to Tommy Jarrell, the elderly North Carolina fiddler, banjoist, and singer whom Wilson cited as one of the "originals" entitled to respect. At the start of his public career Jarrell had recently retired after spending forty years engaged in highway construction for the state of North Carolina. Widowed, with grown children, and in possession of a pension and secure health insurance, Jarrell relished his musical career. In addition to his work with Alan Jabbour, he toured with Blanton Owen of Fuzzy Mountain and with Mike Seeger, jammed with Mac Benford, and performed under the sponsorship of Joe Wilson. He was, Hicks wrote, a "spell-binding entertainer" who "damn well knew it," and he used his revival connections to build the second career that brought him immortality within the old-time music universe. In an irony that Hicks found particularly meaningful, Wilson himself had heard Jarrell praise the advocates who, in Wilson's words, "recorded his music and put it in the hands of players everywhere, those who took him west and north to concerts and festivals, those who made his movie, all who gave something back to this most generous man." As he spoke of these predominantly revivalist benefactors, Jarrell reportedly told Wilson, "Not a goddamn thing would have happened without them."[33]

As a young government official in the 1970s, compelled to safeguard the meager funds at his disposal, Alan Jabbour was among those who drew hard lines between "authentic" and "imitative" musicians. He later rejected that approach, and lamented that bureaucrats tended to reduce the categories invented by earlier scholarship into rigid and insensitive formulas. Jabbour does not reject scholarship, but he urges lovers of vernacular culture to keep it in perspective. The word *folk*, he believes, has been of tremendous importance in spotlighting hidden corners of our cultural arena. It remains a helpful term when used carefully by those who understand its nuances, but Jabbour cautions against investing any word, whether it be *folk, tradition,* or *revivalist,* with inordinate power, lest it be used inappropriately to exclude. He saw this tendency toward exclusion wielded against young musicians who fell in love with the fiddling of Henry Reed and Tommy Jarrell, only to find their enthusiasm ghettoized by those who told them, "Well, you're not really folk—you're a revivalist." Those condemned, he observes, "react with wounded anger, and you're then into a world of antagonism and bad blood. Well, that's not doing anybody any good, culturally."[34]

To those who might dismiss Jabbour's argument as the special pleading of one who is himself a revivalist, he offers the case of Frank George. A native West Virginian born in 1928, George grew up performing older southern tunes. He was, however, at most only one generation older than the young revivalists who began heading south in the 1960s. Meeting these visitors at fiddling contests, George delighted in sharing his knowledge with and learning from those whom he saw simply as fellow musicians. Developing an interest in Scottish music, he studied the bagpipes, the pennywhistle, and the fife, marking himself as a traditionalist with respect to his "own" music but a revivalist with respect to the music of others. On a personal level people responded well to George, who was not only passionate about music but also fun to be around. Still, demonstrating that cultural prejudice can run in every direction, some revivalists considered this particular West Virginia fiddler to be less authentic than his elders. Authentic traditionalists, to borrow Bill Nowlin's self-aware characterization of George Pegram, "fit all the stereotypes." They were old, eccentric, and noticeably different from their urban admirers. Frank George was none of these things. He was too young, and he looked too much like his visitors. His wide-ranging curiosity and unwillingness to pigeonhole musical styles made him, in the eyes of some, too cosmopolitan to serve as an exemplar of regional traditionalism. George was thus caught betwixt and between those who sought idealized authenticity and those willing to accept the mantle of the idealized authentic.[35]

Inevitably, such distinctions allow for the unfortunate dismissal of both a Frank George and a Mac Benford. Rejecting such division, Jabbour urges us to recognize and respect the reality of omnipresent cultural interchange. People, he says, "have always been multicultural, subject to multiple cultural influences from all directions." Within this framework, those unfamiliar with a tradition learn from those who are more familiar, thus helping to move the tradition forward even as it crosses boundaries. For those in the act of discovery, the journey is one form of "creative rebellion" against mainstream culture. For the teachers, it is a way to "hoist the flag until someone comes along to pick it up."[36]

Jabbour's approach seeks factional reconciliation. It does not compel criticism of Joe Wilson's and Mark Wilson's commendable desire to spotlight those who are otherwise unlikely to gain deserved attention. Nor does it dismiss well-meaning people whose only crime is to so admire a form of artistry that they seek to emulate it. Instead, it urges the acknowledgment of mutual benefits. Speaking of his own experience as a student in North Carolina, Jabbour recalls older local musicians who were troubled because their grandchildren had little interest in their region's vernacular tunes. They thus accepted the attention of young revivalists with pride and pleasure. Remembering his roughly contemporaneous experience, Fuzzy Mountain banjoist Tom Carter says, "We gave the [local] musicians a great deal. We gave them something by constantly showing up, in a sense, renewing their lives and giving them a certain recognition in their own community." However, he concedes, "we took a lot too. . . . There were some revivalists who fully adopted the rural lifestyle, but most of us took only what we needed and that was the music. We took the tunes and turned them into power. In this way, the music helped us acquire prestige in our own circles."[37]

Perhaps, accommodation between innovators and preservationists, between revivalists and staunch champions of original sources, may lie in Carter's honest self-awareness. In expressing his irritation with the Highwoods String Band, Joe Wilson recounts a conversation he had with Benford, in which the banjoist purportedly said that he just wanted to earn a living from performance, like the members of the Skillet Lickers did in the 1920s. Dismayed by the statement, Wilson notes that the musicians Benford cited also worked as farmers and mechanics and one—the blind Riley Puckett—sometimes performed alone on the street, seeking alms in a tin cup. To cure revival musicians of their "romantic vision," Wilson, somewhat tongue in cheek, advocates that they adopt the day jobs, as well as the tunes, of the musicians they emulate. Whether or not his reaction truly reflects the context of Benford's remark, Wilson seems most offended by those revivalists who, in his view, equate themselves with their sources. "What's the purpose," he asks, "of trying to become what you are not?" By contrast, he speaks well of Bruce Molsky, a New York City–bred performer with whom Wilson has worked. Playing fiddle, banjo, and guitar, with which

he accompanies his occasional singing, Molsky is among the most industrious professionals on the old-time revival scene and one who, Wilson says
with approval, "knows exactly who he is."[38]

Molsky, born in 1955, is a Cornell-educated civil engineer raised in New
York City. At one time, resistant to the idea of categorization, he hated being
called a revivalist. He accepts it now as the inevitable offshoot of leading a
public life in association with a particular interest group. He concedes that
the great boom not only exposed him to old-time music but also influenced
the shape of his career. Though he has met and played with several older
southern musicians whom revivalists consider authentic "source" performers,
his earliest old-time influences consist of recordings and his Cornell-based
friendship with the members of Highwoods. A Rounder album titled *Parkersburg Landing* is a significant influence, one that he shares with many other
old-time fiddlers. This 1975 release contains then thirty-year-old home
recordings by the late Ed Haley, a previously unknown Kentuckian whom
many musicians praise as one of the greatest traditional southern fiddlers.
Speaking of Haley's impact, Molsky says, "[We revivalists] have our top ten.
. . . There's a finite set of old source material that's out there so everybody's
always got their nose in the air, and when somebody like Ed Haley comes
along, you know, it's natural we all jump on that stuff."[39]

Molsky grounds his work in a personal desire to celebrate the cultural
heritage of the powerless, a concern that stems in part from the pluralist and
humanitarian ethos of the great boom. Though he shares this motivation
with Wilson and Wilson, he manifests it through his own cultural borrowing.
"Poor Man's Troubles" is the name of a fiddle tune, but Molsky, a man with
considerable economic options, made it the title of his 2000 Rounder album
as a tribute to the relatively poor, rural people who gave birth to the music
he loves. One of Molsky's early musical groups was called Big Hoedown,
after the old term for a rural dance. Mulling over the word *hoedown*, he
says it's "a good word. At the end of a hard workweek, people put their hoe
down. It's a very stark kind of reality, or my romantic notion of it is a very
stark reality; you work hard and you play hard." Attuned to the possibility
of excessive romance, and appearing to understand that people might find
his claimed affinity to be an exploitive absurdity, he carries on, attesting to
Joe Wilson's observation that he knows who he is.[40]

In performance Molsky bears Wilson out still further. He dresses in
conventional street clothes. Give him a stereotypical pocket protector, and he
could be an engineer once again, hard at work on a "casual Friday." There's

no cowboy hat, no string tie, no vest or overalls. "I'm not a costume kind of guy," he says. Rooting among his musical paraphernalia while onstage in Austin, Texas, he makes a joking reference to the cell phone and Palm Pilot lying in an instrument case. Asked about that later, he shrugs. These are part of his life—tools that help him stay organized while on the road. "Part of my desire to put this old music on the map," he says, "is giving it some meaning in the present, and I want people to see the fact that I use a cell phone and a Palm Pilot, because they do too." He sees no incongruity between the normal appreciation of modern amenities and the desire to enjoy "scratchy old recordings. You know, one thing does not preclude the other. It makes sense to me. It's how I lead my life."[41]

Molsky does not condemn those who seek strict stylistic preservation, but he realizes that at some point their efforts can clash with the drive for innovation and the desire for one's own voice that are common to all great musicians. He knows that attempts to preserve tend to focus on one moment frozen in time and often on one musician, standing in isolation. It is an approach, he fears, that when taken to extremes can make traditional music sound like something that is near death. He prefers that people look at traditional styles as points along a continuum that is marked by steady change. Many of our most revered traditionalists, he points out, were themselves great innovators and cultural borrowers. The idolized Ed Haley, for example, possessed a vast repertoire of traditional tunes but delighted in surprising his audience. "I like to flavor up a tune," he reportedly said, "so that nobody in the world could tell what I'm playing." "Listen to [Haley's] playing sometime," says Molsky, "and listen to all those damn triplets in there. And then you do a little research, and you find out that he was a real fan of ragtime, so that music made its way into his playing. That was pop music of his day." Any musician, he adds, "lets what's interesting creep into their music, whether they want it to or not."[42] That willingness to innovate is what separates strict preservationists—whether they are traditional performers or revivalists—from true musicians, who always perform in the present, within the context of their own lives.

At the center of *Poor Man's Troubles*, an album dominated by tunes from an older rural South, lies Molsky's own composition "Brothers and Sisters." He derived this polyrhythmic guitar solo from the choral singing of the Zimbabwe National Choir, on a 1967 album titled *Africa in Revolutionary Music*. Mark Wilson, for one, dismisses the resulting blend as a blatant effort to appeal to a contemporary audience of self-identified cultural connoisseurs.

There is, he says, "so much more genuine intellect and musicality" in the playing of the unknown traditionalists whom he records who draw solely from the wellspring of their own heritage.[43]

Molsky, for his part, is merely trying to be himself. He recognizes that whatever appeal he possesses does not come from strict fidelity to a particular style or from any pretense that he exemplifies a culture or class to which he does not belong. Instead, it comes from an authenticity of self. It comes from his willingness to present himself as what he is: a native northerner, an urbanite, an educated man, a skilled musician, a concerned citizen—who finds in old-time music a source of beauty, an artistic challenge, and the opportunity for an implicit sociopolitical expression that he considers personally meaningful. "I have to just trust my gut," he says, "that what ties together a lot of the music in my show is me, [my particular] musical approach and personality. There's a lot of polyrhythm in my fiddling, so playing a polyrhythmic African guitar piece is not that far afield, if you look at it that way." He understands that some people might ask why this American fiddler is playing African music. "But I don't care about that. Nobody's complained, and I'm always interested in hearing what people have to say about it. What I'm trying to do is develop a show that includes traditional music without compromising it but also couching it in some things that might be a little bit more accessible or interesting or unexpected. Unexpected is good."[44]

In concluding a detailed examination of "cultural borrowing" in various contexts, anthropologist Michael F. Brown cautions against the tendency to take "too rigid a view of cultural ownership, especially when technological and social changes are making cultural boundaries ever harder to identify." Sounding much like Alan Jabbour, Brown argues that in pluralist societies, such rigidity both constrains creativity and creates antagonists. None of us, he suggests, would want to live in "a world ruled solely by proprietary passions."[45] In epitomizing an authenticity of self, Molsky appears to constitute one solution to Brown's concern. By looking backward, moving forward, and shaping his own artistic and sociocultural vision, he bridges the divide between Joe Wilson and Mac Benford. He helps shorten the years and span the geographic distance between the experiences of the long-gone Ed Haley and those of all the old-time musicians who have followed him, whether they are rich or poor, northerners or southerners. He offers an approach with the potential to knit diverse factions together in a world ruled not by proprietary passion but by shared joy.

FIVE

Like Politics in Chicago:
The Folk Alliance Strives for Unity

Throughout the 1970s and 1980s committed vernacular music proponents searched for ways to ensure both the economic survival and the artistic vitality of their musical passions. Entrepreneurs built their small record labels and specialty publications. Nonprofit organizations offered classes or staged concerts. Hobbyists tended to their song circles and jam sessions, occasionally bringing in a guest artist to perform for a small fee. Collectively, these activists made up the loose-knit folk music "industry," which tried to maximize professional opportunities for performing musicians. Although they did not necessarily yearn for the return of the national spotlight, many of them did want the intangible comfort of knowing that they were part of a unified movement, larger than their own small revival circles. From a pragmatic standpoint, they wanted to enhance communication among themselves, believing that they could do a better job if they had ready access to practical information regarding performers, programming, and promotion. To fulfill any of these goals, some degree of communication across local lines was essential. Unfortunately, given that so many activities were ill-funded and dependent on volunteers, communication was difficult.

In an effort to foster needed connections, Californians Elaine and Clark Weissman spearheaded the 1989 creation of the Folk Alliance. A self-styled trade organization for the vernacular music industry, the Alliance serves as a forum in which a diverse and often fractious community struggles to contain its divisions and work for common goals. The organization's survival is remarkable given the many similar efforts that failed in the years following the great boom. In 1977, for example, one folk song–society activist wrote to dozens of organizations suggesting the exchange of newsletters and the sharing of ideas with the goal of "mutual growth." Foreshadowing the Alliance, he envisioned a "state-wide or regional league of societies, pooling resources" and, possibly, "a low-profile convention once a year with songfests, workshops on organization, incorporation, etc." Regrettably, nothing came of this overture. The Philadelphia Folksong Society was the only organization that replied.[1] A few years later, performer Michael Cooney used his *Sing Out!* column to solicit names for a proposed "database of performers and clubs, coffeehouses, etc." Recognizing the difficulty facing anyone who tried to keep track of the many local scenes, he sought help from readers. "Is there anything happening in Tucson?" he asked. "Portland? Houston? Kansas City? I'd really like to hear." Cooney subsequently reported a handful of responses, but no publicly available database ever appeared.[2]

In 1980 New Lost City Rambler Tracy Schwarz urged fellow performers to boycott those venues that failed to pay a fair wage.[3] Though Schwarz identified a genuine problem, it was not one necessarily rooted in promoter avarice and thus not something that even a fair promoter, acting alone, could solve. In the absence of media attention and adequate promotion, tiny folk audiences were usually unable to generate sufficient revenue to allow large fees. Suitable venues were often widely dispersed, resulting in high travel and lodging costs that prevented performers from profiting at those venues that did exist. It did not make economic sense, for example, to journey from the East Coast to the Southwest to perform a single concert, given that even a "fair" fee would be relatively small.[4] Any solution demanded a multifaceted approach—more venues, more high-caliber booking agents, better promotional skills, and enhanced communication within the industry so small-scale performers and presenters could find one another and reach an audience.

In September 1980 Minneapolis folk activists sparked a concerted effort to address the overall economic plight of the working folk performer. Expressing a variety of concerns, including low fees, the cost of travel and lodging, music industry chicanery, and the need for health insurance, thirty-one performers held a "rendezvous" at which they formed the nucleus of

Hey Rube! an artists' guild "devoted to the advancement of traditional performing arts as a trade." The playful name came from the historic cry for assistance used by carnival performers. The organization hoped "to perpetuate through the artist the public's participation in the folk traditions, and to create and maintain a good working environment through the exchange of information and mutual support." Working with an initial mailing list of two hundred interested people, a twelve-member steering committee began developing a permanent structure. Activists assembled a nationwide list of folk music venues, helped establish a group health plan for touring musicians, put out an intermittent newsletter, and organized several musician get-togethers. It was an industrious and worthy effort but one that proved to be short-lived. Traveling folk musicians could afford neither the time nor the money needed to write and distribute the newsletter or to attend regular meetings. The venue list, which proved useless without constant updating, prompted promoter complaints about unceasing calls from musicians who were completely unknown to them, and who thus could not be booked. By the fall of 1984, Hey Rube! was dying.[5]

Stephen Baird, a Boston musician, coffeehouse manager, street performer, and all-around industry enthusiast, found Hey Rube!'s grand aspirations intriguing but flawed. A major problem, as he saw it, was that the organization's "national Gig List" served merely to encourage the more efficient division of existing work, as opposed to the more fruitful approach of "working together to create new work." More significantly, Baird saw Hey Rube! as an undemocratic "artists-against-the-world routine." It granted voting rights to full-time professional performers but relegated "facilitators"—club owners, record companies, agents, managers, disc jockeys—to nonvoting "associate" status. To Baird, these businesspeople were "pillars" of the folk world. He viewed their marginal status within Hey Rube! as a suicidal failure of community, separating performers from the technical and financial resources they needed to survive. Nonetheless, Baird saw promise in Hey Rube!'s goal of industry organization and he set out to improve the model on a manageable, local scale. Distributing flyers around Boston in the spring of 1982, he convened a meeting of performers, coffeehouse proprietors, and anyone else interested in discussing "common concerns and issues within the acoustic, traditional and folk music community." The meeting led to the birth in April 1983 of the Folk Arts Network (FAN), which took root and grew into an ambitious local service organization.

With Baird as its director, FAN conducted seminars on business practices, introduced artists to the media and financial communities, and compiled a comprehensive directory of local folk musicians and organizations.[6]

Encouraged by FAN's success, Baird reached out to other activists. One was Margo Blevin, director of the Augusta Heritage Center, a program dedicated to preserving the culture and heritage of West Virginia. Augusta offers year-round instruction in traditional music, dance, crafts, and folklore. It also funds apprenticeships between students and masters in diverse traditional arts, records traditional musicians, and presents them in public performance.[7] In the late 1980s, the precise year lost to her memory, Blevin attended a Boston meeting organized by FAN for the purpose of discussing immigration rules that made it prohibitively expensive to bring traditional musicians into the United States from abroad. She returned to West Virginia tremendously excited by this "wonderful meeting" and the prospect of "what people could do when they get together and talk about these things." Around the same time, Blevin wrote to musicians John McCutcheon and David Holt, along with others interested in traditional music, suggesting that they organize so they could better share information and ideas. People were interested, but the usual problems prevailed—their schedules were too tight, their funds too limited, and their organizations too understaffed. Once again, an effort at industry organization never grew beyond the talking stage.[8]

Sonny Thomas, a professional social worker and the director of North Carolina's Fiddle and Bow Folk Music Society, also believed that folk music could benefit from better coordination. Thomas helped found Fiddle and Bow in 1981, believing that an ongoing association of fans would draw professional musicians to the area for performances. Organized as a coffeehouse with a membership base, Fiddle and Bow provided touring musicians with one more place to play while traveling to or from larger markets in Atlanta or Washington, D.C. However, the club faced that age-old problem—with relatively few professional folk venues in the region, many musicians could not afford to tour in the area. Like others, Thomas understood that he could draw more talent if he could assure performers of several paydays at multiple venues within an easy day's drive from one another. Toward that end Fiddle and Bow hosted a weekend get-together for folk promoters, drawing people from West Virginia, Virginia, Georgia, and South Carolina. They found that they all did things differently. Some staged weekly shows on a shoestring; others presented one well-funded concert each month. Realizing their differences, no one saw any potential in networking, and no one had the wherewithal to keep trying. They parted having had a good time but with no plans to continue and with no one responsible for keeping the effort alive.[9]

Given the pressures on a largely volunteer population chronically short of money and time, any successful effort to organize folk revivalists on a large scale required a tenacious and visionary personality. In the mid-1980s that visionary surfaced in the person of Elaine Weissman. In the summer of 1988 readers of *Sing Out!* encountered a one-column notice that Weissman placed in the magazine's back pages headed "Important Announcement!!! Formative Meeting of a North American Folk Music Association." It called on "interested leaders" of folk music organizations to attend a "signal event in the history of folk music"—a meeting in Malibu, California, designed to "open lines of communication . . . and create a strong voice for the folk music community." Referring to unspecified "national and international issues threatening folk music," the notice called for "integrated action" embracing "all segments of the industry," including "artists, agents, media, recording, government, festivals, societies, arts councils, and individual supporters."[10]

This tiny notice was only one small component of Elaine and Clark Weissman's effort to create a continent-wide folk music organization. Recalling the frequent sojourns that he and Elaine made to festivals as an adjunct to his business travel, Clark explains, "We got behind the scenes and talked to the organizers. And we found out that they had problems with volunteers, they had problems with the arts organizations, they had problems with musicians, the musicians had problems with the organizers." Moving on to another festival, the couple realized "they would have the same problems—different color, different city, different finances but the same problems." In addition to festival personnel, they talked to "endless numbers of folk societies. We at one time were members of about seven hundred of them, just swapping newsletters and talking to them. And they had the same problems." Ultimately, the Weissmans asked themselves, "Why are we divided? We all have the same problems. We're people trying to enjoy this kind of music, which is unaccepted somehow in the community. There's a lack of a food chain—of financial sustenance—to this business, and it has to be restructured, and we need the massive strength that we have to make it happen."[11]

Clark credits Elaine, who died in 2005, with the birth of the Alliance. Long before the Malibu meeting, she took to the phone in what turned into a years-long campaign to enlist support. Margo Blevin was tremendously impressed by the passion with which Weissman approached her task. The two did not know each other, but Weissman called anyway, delighted when she found a sympathetic believer in the need for communication and unity. Blevin recalls her saying, "All the people involved with traditional music and dance should get together and talk, all in one place. We never see each other, we never meet each other—you do your festival, I do my festival." Blevin was willing, but her schedule always seemed to preclude immediate commitment. Weissman kept calling. She called several times a year for roughly three years, and at the end of each conversation she would ask, "'Where and when?' She is a very practical person," Blevin explains. "Where, when?" Finally, Weissman issued a challenge, paraphrased by Blevin: "I'm ready to move. Are you with me or aren't you? It's going to be in Malibu . . . and it's going to be on such-and-such a date. Will you do it with me? Will you help?" The two made up a list of the "must call" people, and Weissman then made another round of calls, claiming commitments from anyone who had even hinted they might attend. Ultimately, Blevin believes, people came because they feared being left out.[12]

Weissman's effort culminated in a meeting of approximately 130 folk music activists at Camp Hess Kramer, a 120–acre retreat in Malibu, held from January 19 through January 22, 1989. Sandy and Caroline Paton spent some time with the Weissmans shortly before the conference began and attained some insight into their goals. The Patons had been active professionally in folk music circles since the 1950s as song collectors, performers, and founding owners of Folk-Legacy Records. In Sandy's mind, the purpose of the proposed organization was "to make more professional the promotion of traditional music—of folk music—in the various organizations around the country that pay tribute to it," whether they be festivals, coffeehouses, or local folk societies. "Many of the people that were doing folk music programs," he adds, "were not really terribly sophisticated in promotion, and [the Weissmans believed] that exchanging ideas with others who were doing it—maybe more successfully—could help increase their market share." The underlying goal was to reach the general public, thus increasing "the interest in folk music, the awareness of it . . . as an alternative to more commercial forms of music."[13]

The Weissmans organized the conference around a series of themed discussions. There were separate sessions on both small and large folk societies, festivals and schools, camps and art centers. There was a session directed to the work of agents, one focused on media, and another that discussed government grants.[14] Participants were all true believers, eager to talk. "It was a block from the ocean," Blevin recalls, "and we never went to the ocean until the last day. We were in this room, in this pressure cooker of a space, talking nonstop with people who cared passionately about the same things that we did. So it was tremendously exciting," she says, "and if we had done nothing else but just sit and talk to each other for a weekend, that would have been really valuable."[15]

Whereas the formal sessions provided an ice-breaking framework and a hint of what could be, the overriding necessity was to do that which had not yet been done: create an ongoing structure. After a couple of days spent in workshops, it appeared that the Weissmans' careful organization might defeat this goal. "The nearly fatal flaw of the weekend," Blevin says, "is that it was overorganized." There were so many formal sessions that there was "literally no time in the schedule left to discuss, absorb, evaluate, and vote on whatever we were there to produce." Eventually, a small group rebelled. Following a private discussion, they recommended abandonment of the schedule in favor of a plenary session focused on ultimate goals. Seeing overwhelming support for this proposal, the Weissmans "graciously scrapped their meticulously crafted schedule. A flip chart and easel were dragged out, and the work of forming, defining, and naming the new organization began at once. This is the precise moment," Blevin explains, "that the gathering became an organization."[16]

There was not, however, any immediate agreement regarding the nature of the incipient association. Blevin was one of several traditionalists who hoped it would resemble the fiddling contests or music camps held at Augusta and elsewhere. George Balderose, a booking agent who represents performers of traditional music, envisioned a regularly scheduled folk music festival with time set aside for meeting and sharing information. Thinking in business terms from the start, he thought that his agency could be an early beneficiary of the emergent Alliance because it would allow him to meet promoters he did not know, as well as those he knew only through phone conversations. As far as Balderose could determine, the Weissmans had no particular model in mind beyond something that was "big."[17] Just how big the Alliance would become, and what it meant to be "big," became a source of conflict throughout the weekend and in the years ahead. It was one of several issues concerning the fledgling association's identity that was wound up with deeper questions regarding the nature of folk music, the meaning of a folk community, and how the "idea of the folk" meshed with the reality of American life at the dawn of the twenty-first century.

Despite the open invitation placed in *Sing Out!* Weissman had not left Malibu attendance to chance, as demonstrated by her long telephone campaign and the final "must call" list crafted with Blevin. As a result, most attendees favored folk music with a traditional flavor, as opposed to the more contemporary sounds of the singer-songwriters. They tended to play influential roles in established folk arts organizations, both commercial (such as Balderose's booking agency) and nonprofit (such as Augusta Heritage). They also tended to be over thirty-five, white, and influenced to a considerable degree by the great boom. But there were differences among them, the starkest being that between those who saw themselves as proponents of the so-called backyard or back-porch players and those with a more overtly commercial orientation. As Anne Blaine of the Vancouver Folk Music Festival put it, there was a fear of "the *p* word—*professional.*" In the more expansive words of Sonny Thomas, "There was some hesitancy [in adopting a business model] on the part of people who see folk music as kind of a participatory, back-porch kind of thing . . . and some reluctance to make it [businesslike] for fear of what would happen to it. There have been some negative things along those lines."[18]

In short, the backyard players were afraid of creating an organization that would bring back the worst commercial excesses of the sixties. In general, the larger an organization, the more the backyard partisans considered it suspect. To have a large budget, the theory went, an organization needed to draw a large audience, which meant that it needed to cater to broad tastes, which meant that it needed to enter the realm of show business, not folk music. As summarized by Juel Ulven, founder of the all-volunteer Fox Valley Folklore Society of Illinois, the Malibu gathering was marked by a struggle for supremacy between big and small organizations, and the competing sides tended to view one another with considerable suspicion.[19]

This divide was not always black and white. Instead, it reflected relative points along a continuum, with many facing the eternal paradox of desiring promotion while fearing its impact. Some who emphasized professionalism accused backyard proponents of possessing a naïveté so extreme that it could keep the organization from accomplishing anything.[20] Others saw hypocrisy in the laments of relatively privileged, well-educated urbanites who seemed intent on preserving not just musical styles but their idealized image of an older, decidedly harsher rural lifestyle. Jim Hirsch, then the executive director of Chicago's Old Town School of Folk Music, an aggressively self-promoting nonprofit with a multimillion-dollar budget, maintains that some backyard proponents were interested largely in their own standing as defenders of tradition, adding derisively that none of these people had emerged personally from the American backwoods.[21]

Hirsch's position alludes to another reality that disturbed some conference participants—the fact that certain attendees appeared to have agendas that went beyond the simple love of music. Ulven was astonished by some of the struggles he witnessed in Malibu, which looked to him like stereotypical Chicago power politics. Sonny Thomas was surprised to find that "there were some people that wanted to feel like they were . . . power brokers in the folk scene—which back then was a pretty strange notion and maybe still is, considering the nature of the genre." There was, he recalls, "a lot of argument and debate about how things would be worded and the political correctness of everything, which certainly has to be a concern, but it's not something that I would have thought people could be screaming at each other over, which actually happened. There were some very tense moments in those meetings."[22]

At times, these divisions indicated little more than differences in personal style. Those successful in business, or in meeting the fund-raising and promotional demands of larger nonprofit organizations, could display an aggressiveness foreign to those who came to Malibu because of their involvement in a local folk music society or coffeehouse. But stylistic differences resisted any neat dichotomy. Blaine, from the relatively large and long-running Vancouver Folk Music Festival, saw an East versus West divide. In her view, some of the easterners brought an aggressive intensity to the discussion that she had never before witnessed. Despite her proposed geographic divide, Blaine found similar intensity in California's Weissmans, as well as in Chicago's Hirsch, whom she later came to consider an admired friend. Dianne Tankle of the Philadelphia Folksong Society noted that during an initial group phone-number exchange, one participant provided only his office number, not his home number. Perhaps, she surmised with concern, folk music was nothing more than a business to him. Whatever its source, tension and discord created particular distress among those who valued folk music as a source of community.[23]

The distinction between big or commercial or slick, on the one hand, and small or community oriented or, perhaps, "folksy," on the other, manifested itself in the group's first concrete action, the election of a steering committee to draft the articles and bylaws that would govern the organization. The Weissmans arrived in Malibu with a set of proposed bylaws in hand. Some believed that their proposal favored larger organizations, and this aroused tremendous concern among those most fearful of commercialism's excess. On the first night, the Weissmans asked a hand-chosen few to meet privately. The tenor of the resulting gathering suggested that this group would form the steering committee, recalls Hirsch, who was himself one of the invitees. Thereafter, the Weissmans invited certain individuals to address the larger group, investing those chosen with a potentially influential cachet.[24] The perception of favoritism heightened existing fears that the largest participants would dominate any national organization. By the third day these concerns led to an express revolt, which saw small-group representatives openly condemn both backroom politicking and the seemingly biased bylaws.[25]

Democracy carried the day, and the group decided to hold an open election. They discussed whether they should allocate steering committee seats based on "interest" or geographic region, but in the end a consensus emerged to seat a twelve-member committee by allowing each registrant to vote for any twelve from among the twenty-five who chose to run. Additionally, the group allowed couples to run jointly for a single seat, possessing a single vote. The result was a fifteen-member elected committee—including three couples—that was reasonably diverse within the context of the older, white, middle-class revivalists in attendance.[26] Elaine and Clark Weissman won a joint seat. Other committee members included Augusta's Blevin; the Vancouver Folk Music Festival's Blaine; Dianne Tankle and her husband, Robert Cohen, from the Philadelphia Folksong Society; and Balderose, whose small booking agency had a roster weighted toward traditional artists and who was himself a performing bagpiper.

Sonny Thomas, Juel Ulven, and Shelly Romalis, an anthropologist from the University of Toronto, each won seats, and each was as close to a representative of the backyard singer as could be found among the myriad organizational affiliations present. Each had a day job unrelated to music, and each represented an organization composed solely of volunteers. "The Woods," Romalis's folk music and dance camp, came together for only four consecutive days each year, when it offered lessons in traditional musical genres, along with opportunities for group singing and playing. Thomas's Fiddle and Bow was tiny in scale and catered to a purely local audience. Given his druthers, Thomas would have preferred to present music from the

Celtic and eastern European traditions that he enjoyed, but he recognized that neither that music nor the Appalachian string band sounds that once flourished on the club's North Carolina doorstep drew a consistent audience. He staged as much vernacular music as was feasible, but economic necessity compelled him to focus on a steady stream of guitar-playing singer-songwriters. Although that group had its own commercial difficulties, its members were most likely to be aggressive professionals armed with recordings and press kits.[27]

Due to a fairly broad audience base in its suburban Chicago home, plus the fact that it favored participatory events such as group sings and dances, Ulven's Fox Valley was able to hew closer to relatively noncommercial traditional sounds. Ulven founded the organization in 1975 and enmeshed it in multiple aspects of folklife, including storytelling as well as music and dance. Fox Valley, sometimes in conjunction with other groups, hosts roughly one hundred events a year, including weekly participatory "sings," regular contra dances, storytelling sessions, and an annual festival. A strong traditionalist, Ulven sees folk music not as a particular performance style but as a functional device that accompanies other aspects of life, such as work or worship. He knows that much of this music can sound foreign to contemporary ears, accustomed as they are to the more passive reception of hook-laden pop songs. That's why Fox Valley's dances and group sings place such emphasis on participation. True folk music, Ulven believes, seldom works well as entertainment before passive audiences. If that's what you want, he maintains, you're better off hiring the Rolling Stones.[28]

Although Sandy and Caroline Paton did earn their living from folk music, they sought and won election as professed advocates of the backyard and were as suited for the role as any longtime folk music professionals could be. Born in 1929, the intellectually curious Sandy began a career as an itinerant singer of folk songs in the 1940s. "I was becoming aware, politically, of the importance of paying attention to the working class and the underprivileged. I thought [folk] music spoke to that; these were songs of working people, not art songs, not songs removed from life. It was music that spoke to the needs and concerns of people who were very real to me." In 1957, at a concert in Berkeley, California, he met graduate student Caroline Swenson. He was performing. She was an audience member who asked him the source of a tune. They were married within a few months and soon embarked on a tour of the British Isles that cemented Caroline's role as Sandy's singing partner. Hearing the "big powerful voices" of British ballad singers moved Caroline to try her own hand at harmony. "I was always afraid to sing in public until I met those singers. Their power really was a revelation to me. And what they cared about was the song."[29]

Caring about the song became the Patons' lifework. With their friend Lee Haggerty, they founded Folk-Legacy Records in 1961. Modest in scope, Folk-Legacy has released fewer than two hundred recordings, all of which contain songs found in oral tradition or new songs that sound like they could be hundreds of years old. Many of the performers are nonprofessionals, singing songs learned through family or community tradition. In the words of *Sing Out!* the label's distinctive sound presents "a soft acoustic sweetness, a melodiousness, and arrangements that put the song out front." Whether it's an unaccompanied ballad or an intricate vocal harmony fronting an instrumental arrangement, the song itself is always the star. The Patons decry performers who seem to say, "Look at me—I'm singing the hell out of this song," preferring those whose style quietly asks their audience to "listen to this wonderful song." Their approach represents the antithesis of the pop music star system that the two disdain. Folk-Legacy has, predictably, never been a high-dollar operation. It has done just fine, however, for two people in whom life, song, and the business of folk music are fused.[30]

Robert Cohen and Dianne Tankle, husband and wife activists from the all-volunteer Philadelphia Folksong Society, also won a joint seat. Eclectic in their tastes, Cohen and Tankle perceive folk music in terms far broader than either Ulven or the Patons, a position influenced heavily by the multifaceted nature of the great boom. Once involved extensively in eastern European folk dancing, Tankle, like her husband, became a huge Kingston Trio fan. They welcome a wide variety of sounds and styles under the folk umbrella. Eschewing a relatively precise, functional definition, Cohen cites the much maligned dictum that all songs must be folk songs because horses never sing them. Pressed further, he acknowledges that some songs and styles fall outside any reasonable definition of folk music, while adopting an "I know it when I hear it" approach that focuses on whether a song has a "folkie sound." Pushed still harder for specifics, he can only allow that this sound derives from "the whole gestalt." However imprecise this may seem, many folk fans share Cohen's approach, and its adherents often manage to display a surprising level of agreement about what is and is not folk music in contemporary terms.[31]

Jim Hirsch—wiry, fast-talking, and possessed of an aggressive, salesmanlike persona—was initially the most distrusted member of the steering committee, due to a staunchly market-driven philosophy that drove some of the backyard advocates to distraction. In 1989 Hirsch was the director of Chicago's Old Town School of Folk Music, a venerable revival institution. Founded in 1957, the school began by teaching a variety of "folk instruments"—predominantly guitar, banjo, and fiddle. Students learned in groups, and everyone joined in a collective "songfest" when an afternoon or evening class schedule concluded, a tradition soon dubbed "the second half." Regular teacher-student coffee breaks became another early tradition, as did occasional all-night parties, all of which contributed to a deliberately cultivated atmosphere of community. As much a social club as a school, Old Town, in the words of cofounder Frank Hamilton, served as a "giant meetinghouse for musicians, storytellers, folk dancers, folklorists and professional folk entertainers who would gather to share their knowledge with the public." As the boom gathered steam, virtually every movement figure of note performed on the school's stage, including stylists as diverse as Pete Seeger, Bill Monroe, and Mahalia Jackson. One-time students who found fame include Byrds founder Roger McGuinn, singer-songwriter John Prine, and veteran recording artist Steve Goodman, who wrote the legendary "City of New Orleans," a tune that Arlo Guthrie made famous.[32]

Until the mid-1970s the school seemed charmed. A growing demand for music lessons encouraged expansion beyond its original urban base. Branches opened in the Chicago suburbs, and optimistic administrators acquired real property, with its accompanying debt and maintenance expenses. By the late seventies, however, increasing oil costs and the rise of disco and new wave brought this success to an abrupt halt. Declining enrollment resulted in a huge drop in the tuition payments that constituted the bulk of the school's income. Forced to take stock with a degree of professionalism previously unknown, the school found itself with tax troubles, decaying buildings, and a huge operating deficit. Its board responded in a typically idiosyncratic manner. It hired Hirsch as the new director—a man who, by his own admission, was seemingly unqualified for the job. Hirsch's career at Old Town began in 1972 as a guitar teacher at the school's suburban Evanston branch. He became branch director in 1978, despite the absence of either appropriate experience or a college diploma, having dropped out of Southern Illinois University before completing its degree program in "acoustic music." However, in four years he had made Evanston financially self-sufficient, and in 1982 the board hoped he could do the same for the school as a whole.[33]

Possessed of a demonic work ethic and an almost bionic aura of self-confidence, Hirsch set about his task in a manner never before seen at the Old Town School. In his first month as director he took no salary and began reducing staff and slashing operating expenses. His hunt for new revenue streams mitigated the resulting tension. Thinking counterintuitively, he responded to dwindling enrollment by expanding the nature of classes offered, adding children's programs and songwriting workshops in a successful gamble that new types of classes would draw new students. He rented space in the school to outsiders and turned a previously casual system of musician referrals into a business, taking a percentage of the musician's fee for performing jobs obtained. The largest single tangible change Hirsch engineered had to do with the school's approach to donations. The casual system he inherited had resulted in contribution totals of $5,000 per year at best. With the help of a fund-raising professional, Hirsch organized a program targeting corporate, foundation, and individual donors. Within a couple of years he was raising more than $100,000 annually and had set even higher goals. Spurred by the complete deterioration of the school's downtown home, Hirsch initiated a capital fund drive, raised $650,000 between 1985 and 1987, and paid for the building's total renovation.[34]

He arrived in Malibu in 1989 as the antithesis of the backyard player—an aggressive financial wunderkind whose innate business acumen had transformed a somewhat funky folk music parlor into an entertainment and educational goliath. With a large measure of respect, Ulven argues that Hirsch is more fund-raiser than folkie—someone possessed of an instinctive and uncanny ability to raise money. Hirsch's success is accompanied by what some consider a distressing tendency to see his path as the only path. He combines a penchant for sales jargon with a propensity to lecture others on the need to be professional. Some who were content with their small, volunteer-driven song circles were appalled, but the strength of Hirsch's vision helped propel the Alliance toward an ethos of professionalism and an acceptance of marketplace realities.[35]

The balance of the committee consisted of two strong individuals whose attitudes greatly influenced the Alliance's initial direction. A onetime union electrician, Mark Moss was president of the Penn State Folklore Society during the midseventies. He was also a founding member of the Lehigh Valley (Pennsylvania) Folksong Society and spent more than ten years as a *Sing Out!* volunteer. By the summer of 1980, just past its thirtieth anniversary, *Sing Out!* was on the brink of extinction. Circulation had declined sharply. Subscription revenue failed to cover monthly operating expenses, and advertising revenue had also fallen. The magazine owed roughly $20,000. Creditors who had allowed debt to accumulate for years now sensed imminent bankruptcy and were demanding immediate payment. The situation was so dire that the magazine made a dramatic and desperate appeal to its readers for contributions.[36]

In the fall of 1980 Moss became coordinator of the Friends of *Sing Out!* a position focused on helping readers promote the magazine, whether by drumming up donations, encouraging sales by their local retailer, or other means. A contemporaneous editorial praised Moss, thanking him for "his enthusiastic efforts organizing festival booths, transcribing interviews, tracking down songs, helping with benefits, and getting us through rough times." He and others threw themselves into the fund-raising effort. For approximately two years the "magazine" consisted of nothing more than an occasional newsletter, before emerging debt free in the spring of 1983 with a new design and with Moss as editor.[37] *Sing Out!* has always been a staunchly collaborative effort, but Moss earned the lion's share of the credit for the periodical's rejuvenation. He is a knowledgeable and articulate observer of the folk music scene, thoroughly familiar with both traditional American music and the more contemporary sounds of the singer-songwriters. His editorial position gives him a high-profile platform from which he strives to reconcile the goals of community-based music and business professionalism. At the time of the Malibu conference he had served six years as editor. He has gone on to hold that position longer than anyone in the magazine's history.

The remaining committee member was a man with a unique ability to straddle the revival's disparate worlds. Born in 1955 in Raleigh, North Carolina, Art Menius developed such a strong early fascination with country music that he makes the unusual claim, "I cannot remember not knowing [Bill] Monroe's versions of 'Uncle Pen' and 'Muleskinner Blues.'"[38] After earning a master's in history from the University of North Carolina at Chapel Hill, Menius became a researcher for that state's Department of Cultural Resources, writing social histories linked to North Carolina historic sites. From there, he joined Linear Productions, where he helped develop *Fire on the Mountain,* a television series focusing on early country music, produced for the Nashville Network in the early 1980s. To prepare, Menius steeped himself in country music history, working his way through a self-designed program of study that he claims consumed up to fourteen hours per day through much of 1983. In 1984 Linear Productions undertook a consulting assignment designed to help the then fairly disorganized bluegrass "industry" better understand its market. Menius studied bluegrass festivals throughout the nation, delineating their geographic and artistic differences. He then prepared a survey applicable to each festival type and in the summer of 1984 set out to interview festivalgoers around the nation. The resulting 2,106 completed questionnaires constituted the largest comprehensive survey of bluegrass fans then undertaken.[39]

Next, he became publicity director for *Liberty Flyer*, a syndicated radio show featuring live acoustic music, roughly two-thirds of which was bluegrass. The show eventually ran on 113 stations, and, Menius says, "That's where I developed my bluegrass association and radio contacts." In June 1985 talent agent Lance LeRoy invited him to a Nashville meeting called to discuss the formation of a bluegrass trade association. By that fall, the International Bluegrass Music Association (IBMA) was up and running, and Executive Director Art Menius was its first hire. It was his job to weld a loose network of relatively small independent record companies, talent agencies, promoters, and specialty publications into a genuine industry that could enhance public appreciation of bluegrass and thus provide musicians—and their support structure—with a greater opportunity to earn a living.[40]

With its pronounced roots in traditional southern folk tunes, bluegrass's commercial development sets it apart from present-day mainstream country music. As Mark Fenster notes in his analysis of the IBMA, many bluegrassers are "concerned with the music as a cultural entity rather than as a mere commodity," and they desire "a nonintrusive commercial structure by which bluegrass can be successfully produced and distributed without despoiling the music of its integrity and traditions."[41] In other words, to be successful Menius needed to straddle the worlds of mass marketing and community tradition, of backyard picking and professionalism, the very skills that would well serve the fledgling Folk Alliance. As it happens, Menius is an ardent, unabashed advocate of commercial promotion who does not believe that this necessitates the compromise of musical or cultural values. What intrigued him about the Alliance was the possibility of moving beyond bluegrass, with the hope that all niche or independent musics could band together "to create a big market of the little markets." "My intent," he says, "was and always has been to advance the business aspects and improve the bottom line. . . . My position is that a market exists for this music, and that market can be increased. . . . I remain steadfast that the route of selling records and tickets is the only true route to preservation of roots."[42] In this he aligns himself strongly with Hirsch, of whom he says, "Jim has stood for more than a decade on the front line of developing folk music institutions that business people can respect and, thus, donate funds to."[43]

The significance of Art Menius stems from the fact that, despite his staunch commercial outlook, he did not threaten the backyard singers and small-group volunteers. Although Hirsch's city-slicker, salesman style sometimes made him an object of suspicion, folk revival romanticism rendered Menius untouchable. His North Carolina upbringing, his accompanying southern drawl and easygoing manner, and his close affiliation with a regionally based "traditional" genre made him seem like the personification of the folk. If Hirsch, in caricature, was a fast-talking outsider whose blasphemy might sell out the music, Menius was roots incarnate who could never desire anything but preservation of the traditional sounds that were his birthright. As Balderose sums it up, "Art embodied a love of traditional music, and that kind of really came through. It's like he was born in the holler, and he's never left, but he's intelligent and he can bring that kind of cultural background to intelligent discussions, very intelligent discussions about organization, and that impressed a lot of people, because he had his foot in both camps. He was," Balderose continues, "a good organizer, but he was apparently a traditionalist as well, and he could recite chapter and verse of every bluegrass performer that ever lived."[44]

Throughout 1989 the steering committee, with Moss as chair, met via telephone and at two weekend gatherings held at Tankle and Cohen's Pennsylvania home. Utilizing a subcommittee structure, the group addressed membership categories, voting rights, and programs. Moss suggested the word *Alliance*, and he and Cohen hammered out a set of proposed bylaws. These contained an ambitious, sometimes muddled mission statement that mixed long-standing scholarly constructs with modern theoretical refinements and pragmatic commercial considerations. They began by declaring that the Alliance existed "to foster and promote traditional, contemporary and multicultural folk music, dance and related performing arts in the U.S. and Canada." By positing "traditional" and "contemporary" as distinct categories, the bylaws appeared to confine tradition to the past, divorced from all present-day artistic expression.[45]

The second sentence, however, acknowledged that "living cultural expressions and traditions are shared through folk music and dance." Read in conjunction, these sentences honored tradition's ongoing role while accepting the existence of a folk music apart from the purely traditional. The reference to multiculturalism was, arguably, a redundancy, since the culturally neutral terms *traditional* and *contemporary* could encompass a wide range of vernacular music. Still, given the revival's historical emphasis on Anglo-American forms and the blues, it was a political necessity, particularly for an organization that—notwithstanding the conspicuous absence of Mexican and Central American involvement—aspired to a continental reach. Overall, it was a statement suited to the revival, blending old and new academic constructs with the commercial realities inherent in marketing "folk" as a music industry genre.[46]

Three early decisions had an enormous impact on the organization's eventual structure. The first was the decision to leave the word *folk* undefined. The Weissmans advocated this, and the organizers agreed fairly quickly. Menius believed strongly that any attempt at definition would cripple the fledgling group. "Understand," he maintains, "that we're dealing with a community so fractious that a split exists between folks who like archaic commercial music versus those who only like back porch archaic music versus those interested only in contemporary performers of the same styles. Any definition at all destroys any chance of success for the organization."[47] The second significant decision was that which structured the planned annual gathering as a commercial trade show. Menius advocated this as well, in accordance with his abiding faith in the value of commerce. From the start, he explains, he saw the promise of the Alliance "in marketing terms." In considering the organization's subject matter and constituency, he thought not about musical genres as such but of "music released on certain labels, handled by particular distributors and agents, presented in certain venues, covered by particular media."[48]

The third noteworthy decision was that which allowed individuals to become voting members. Some founders envisioned the Alliance as an "organization of organizations." Most committee members, however, feared that such an approach would promote an exclusivity that contradicted the revival's egalitarian ethos. In the end, the committee extended voting rights not only to organizations but also to any individual "presently professionally active in the field of folk music, dance, and the related performing arts." Defined explicitly to include "performers," this opened membership to the countless ambitious singers and musicians who later flocked to the annual conference in the hope of personal career advancement. Collectively, these three decisions created an organization open both to committed cultural advocates and to anyone—performer, agent, or record mogul—who sensed commercial advantage in defining themselves or their art as folk, at least for the few days per year that the Alliance met in conference.

At the organization's second annual conference, held in Philadelphia in 1990, the approximately two hundred registrants approved the bylaws by a near unanimous vote. Menius became president of the newly constituted board of directors. He left the board in early 1991 and accepted a salaried position as Alliance "manager" that placed him in charge of day-to-day operations, which he ran from Chapel Hill, North Carolina. Fairly rapidly, a predictable divide opened between members. On one side stood self-described traditionalists who favor folk music that retains some identity as the unique cultural product of indigenous groups. On the other stood the singer-songwriters, whom many traditionalists disdained, and continue to disdain, as pop musicians using folk venues as way stations in their struggle for success. Despite the historical linkage between the great boom and the contemporary acoustic writer-performer, the number of singer-songwriters drawn immediately to the Alliance caught some organizers off guard. Notwithstanding the egalitarian decision to admit individuals, the largely tradition-minded, organizationally based activists present in Malibu assumed that the goal of the new association was to help members better achieve their organizational ends.

Shelly Romalis envisioned a forum in which revivalists and academic folklorists would work together to foster an appropriately sensitive nexus between commerce and the traditional arts. Serving on a subcommittee charged with selecting performers for the organization's annual conferences, she received a rude awakening when she saw how quickly applications began to come through conventional business channels. Hoping for an organization "that didn't constantly sell, sell, sell," she did not anticipate the "wonderful résumés or publicity packets" submitted by ambitious entertainment professionals who identified the Alliance as a suitable locale for self-promotion. "I know that all of this [promotional material] is terribly necessary if you want to sell yourself, but it just seemed like a pop orientation." Romalis soon concluded that the organization was attracting people who saw it as a device through which they might—and she adopts a loud carnival barker's voice here—"bring back the folk boom." With different personal goals, she left the Alliance after a few years.[49]

Ulven also served on the showcase committee during the Folk Alliance's early years. He too was surprised at the speed with which professionally aggressive singer-songwriters embraced the organization as one more commercial opportunity. He recalls roughly sixty applications for eighteen performing slots at the second conference, with the majority coming from singer-songwriters. He reviewed close to three hundred submissions for the fourth conference, and the percentage of contemporary songwriters among them had increased. The sheer quantity of material made the need to wade through bad writing inevitable. Ulven found many of the lyrics so personal, so inner-directed, that he could not imagine them interesting anyone but the writer. He tired quickly of songwriters bemoaning their own broken hearts and, with a traditionalist's interest in material that endures, he asked himself if anyone would be singing these songs a few generations hence.[50]

Ulven voices a common concern. Writing in the Alliance newsletter in 1993, performer Mike Agranoff bemoaned the prevalence of "me" songs within the folk scene, to the exclusion of more inclusive "us" songs. Randy Pitts, who booked a multitude of guitar-strumming troubadours as creative director of Berkeley's Freight and Salvage in the 1990s, jokes that the writers of the sixties who focused on "songs of political action" have been replaced by a later generation who favor "songs of personal indulgence." Anguish over "me" songs has grown so prevalent that it has provoked satirical comment in the form of "Those Festivals," a song written by the politically conscious Peter Siegel, which laments the fact that "in modern folk the singer is the center of the song."[51]

Those interested in folk song as a window into vernacular communities, a means of fostering fellowship or a tool for social activism, tend to dismiss "me songs" as the products of "navel gazers singing their diaries," a phrase heard often in discussion among revivalists. The contempt directed toward such material is evident in a review of *Night in a Strange Town*, an album by Canadian songwriter Lynn Miles on Rounder's Philo imprint. Calling the work a "crushingly banal vanity production," the reviewer is content to explain his critique by referencing just a few lines from one fairly typical song:

> I drew a map of my heart
> I painted it melancholy blue
> and the biggest room is empty
> and it's waiting for you.

Satisfied that this brief fragment proves his point, the reviewer follows it with only one word: "Cut!" He makes no mention of Miles' gorgeous voice, her fine sense of melody, or the quality of the album's musicianship. These are apparently not even relevant to a critical aesthetic that elevates lyrical subject matter above all else. With her overriding focus on the personal torment of heartbreak, Miles apparently falls short of this reviewer's idea of an acceptable folk album, and her perceived thematic inadequacy allows him to dismiss her CD in its entirety.[52]

Jody Stecher, a New York–born, great boom–bred instrumentalist, singer, and writer who performs within a wide range of traditional and contemporary vernacular styles, has thought a great deal about the role of composition within the folk music world. Strongly supportive of new music, Stecher has no objection to singer-songwriters. Nonetheless, he sees a problem with many contemporary writers that extends beyond lyrical triteness. The "divide" between traditionalists and "your average troubadour," he says, stems from the fact that so many of the latter have "not heard the old music." Even those writers who have listened casually to older material often fail to examine the compositional features that produce art that is capable of withstanding the test of time. Consequently, they lack an essential stylistic vocabulary that, if employed, could link their work to a vast artistic mosaic that reflects our collective humanity. Though many present-day writers are "clever and intellectual," says Stecher, their work "doesn't stir anything in me that's primal, that's deep, that has to do with my general humanity as opposed to this person's specifics." Those who do make the effort to absorb older material have, in Stecher's opinion, simply undertaken the fundamental homework essential to the songwriter's craft, which often results in art that is "stronger and more powerful than something that comes out of individual imagination."[53]

Sandy and Caroline Paton admire new songs that reflect the "values" of traditional song. Wading into ambiguity's murky waters, Sandy explains that one finds such values in songs that reflect the "attitudes and concerns of community, rather than individuals." It's the "sort of thing you find in labor songs," he adds, or even in songs of "courting and complaint," provided that they address broadly universal themes. Drawn to songs that serve as vehicles of communal expression and fellowship, Sandy and Caroline each favor songs suitable for group singing. Sandy refers to this quality as "the accessibility of a song," which he finds in "choruses that people can join in on and share the song that way." Caroline, who acknowledges that all of this is hugely subjective, adds that one often hears these varied qualities in lullabies, which she considers almost perfect examples of folk or folklike songs. In addition to being straightforward in message, easy to sing, and usually noncommercial in sound, they serve a universal function that is useful to every human who has ever cradled a small child.[54]

Art Menius anticipated singer-songwriter involvement in the Alliance but "honestly expected only more rooted singer-songwriters" to participate. Here he touches on terrain as ambiguous as the concept of "the folk" itself. Revivalists, as I noted previously, tend to call a song "rooted" if it appears tied in some fashion to the historical construct of folk song as understood by either academic folklorists or an earlier generation of folk music activists. In practice, this means tunes that use stylistic elements derived from discernible vernacular traditions, lyrics that describe the lives or histories of a people, or songs that serve political ends. Like the related construct of authenticity, rootedness lies along a continuum, allowing singer-songwriters of varying circumstances to earn the coveted status even if they lack the more obvious markers of vernacularity derived from race, ethnicity, or regionalism.

The ideal of rootedness is embodied in the work of Gordon Bok, a songwriter well-versed in the "old songs" who listens widely and performs a great many songs written by others in addition to his own tunes. Bok chased stardom fleetingly in the sixties, when Noel "Paul" Stookey of Peter, Paul and Mary produced his first album for Verve Records, an MGM subsidiary. Later, he settled into a quieter recording and performing career. Alone or in collaboration he has recorded roughly twenty albums for the Patons' Folk-Legacy Records. Like Lynn Miles, Bok has written songs that address the purely personal. As a lifelong sailor and sometime commercial captain, he has also recorded many self-composed songs about the sea and the seafaring people he has worked with on the waters off his native Maine. Disdainful of stereotypically boisterous sea chanteys, which he calls "yo-ho-ho songs," Bok has crafted finely detailed lyrical portraits of a distinctive world filled with flesh-and-blood men and women with joys and concerns that are a mixture of the universal and the unique, the concrete and the mythical.

In "The Ways of Man" he sings of the hardship and perils of a fisherman's life and of regional cycles that repeat, year after year.

> But the days grow short and the year gets old
> And the fish won't stay where the water's cold
> And if they're going to fill the hold
> They've got to go offshore to find them.

In "Hills of Isle Au Haut" he tells of one place, "away and to the westward," which offers respite from those same hardships—a place "where the fishing's always easy / they've got no ice or snow." Bok's quiet, richly descriptive songs, steeped in traditional elements, will never top a contemporary hit parade, but, like the cowboy songs sought by John Lomax at the dawn of the twentieth century, they constitute a regional literature illuminating a relatively hidden corner of American life. Unlike Lomax, who compiled his collection from others, Bok draws his details from his own world, making him a virtually perfect exemplar of a living folk artist, albeit one who is comfortable in the recording studio and on a concert stage.[55]

Offering his own example of a rooted singer-songwriter, Menius mentions Tish Hinojosa, a Texas-born Mexican American raised by Spanish-speaking immigrants as the youngest of thirteen children.[56] Unlike Bok, Hinojosa is an ambitious commercial artist whose up-and-down career includes albums on major labels A&M Records and Warner Communications, as well as several releases on Rounder. She, too, has written her share of songs focused on love and loss, but those interested in roots music tend to exalt that part of her work that draws explicitly from her ethnic heritage. Her 1992 Rounder release, *Culture Swing*, positions her deliberately as a representative of two overlapping cultures. Embellished with Aztec imagery, the liner notes begin with a quote from Americo Paredes, a scholar of indigenous Texas-Mexican border ballads, who writes that Hinojosa's "art is deeply rooted in the traditions of our ancestors. In her songs," he continues, "the spirit of our people is given voice." With her strummed guitar and wide-open, bell-like voice, Hinojosa seems an inheritor of the Baez-Collins-Mitchell folk revival aesthetic. Yet her production is flavored by elements of conjunto, country music, and Texas swing. Her lyrics, sung in a mixture of English and Spanish, are miniaturist evocations of immigrant life along the border. The album opener, "By the Rio Grande," talks of the river's symbolic hold on the lives of those whose cultural influences stem from each of its banks. "Something in the Rain" tells the story of migrant farmworkers, felled by backbreaking work and the pesticides they breathe in the course of their struggle to earn a living. "In the Real West" is a southwestern-flavored dance tune celebrating the simplicity of "a clean white shirt on a Saturday night / and a long cold beer that's pure delight."[57]

Hinojosa's various records shift between those that emphasize her cultural roots and those that adopt a more universal pop song aesthetic. Notwithstanding these shifts, she appears able to maintain a core audience that appreciates her more indigenous-sounding work. In keeping with the flexible nature of rootedness, many fervent admirers of musical traditions are forgiving of purely pop aspirations, provided that a performer returns to the roots with reasonable regularity. White revivalists tend to be conscious of the politics of culture, making them hesitant to ghettoize an indigenous performer by insisting on absolute purity at the expense of the opportunity to reap the commercial world's financial rewards. As a born-and-bred exemplar of the cultural hybridity reflected in her diverse musical streams, Hinojosa possesses a personal authenticity that affords her considerable leeway. In that context, an overt pop composition, or an entire pop album, is only one small aspect of a broader persona that, in her case, encompasses demonstrable respect for both her lived heritage and the concept of community. This allows roots-oriented revivalists to embrace Hinojosa as a fully realized individual, anchored in her own heritage yet part of the larger world. It allows such fans to accept the reality of the commercial culture within which admired artists work while continuing to revere the idealized folk cultures that shape their own passion.

One clear beneficiary of the broad flexibility accorded the concept of "rooted" is Nanci Griffith, a child of the white middle class, raised by politically liberal parents who loved the Weavers and other sounds of the great boom. After two self-released albums, Griffith signed with Rounder's Philo imprint and has also recorded for several major labels in a commercial career that has waxed and waned. She opened her first Rounder release with "Ghost in the Music," a haunting lament celebrating the unfairly forgotten Native Americans and immigrants who helped build the United States. "Year Down in New Orleans" is a remembrance of lost love, but it carries its story through a finely detailed sense of place. With references to "clover in the fields south of New Orleans" and "fields of summer cane," Griffith reminds listeners of a regional distinctiveness too often forgotten along forgettable highways.[58]

Her 1993 release, *Other Voices, Other Rooms*, is an unabashed celebration of her personal roots within the folk revival itself, covering songs made famous by icons such as Guthrie and Dylan and those influenced directly by the boom, such as John Prine and Janis Ian. To some critics, Griffith is simply one more pop-oriented, commercially ambitious singer-songwriter who has helped bastardize the idea of the folk. She lacks Bok's real-life immersion in a distinctive regional and occupational culture and Hinojosa's ability to draw upon a lived ethnic heritage. However, she reveres the revival openly, understands its values, and acknowledges her musical influences proudly. Over the course of approximately fifteen albums that have encompassed blatant pop sentimentality and even light rock, she has hit the revival touchstones of old-time instrumentation, finely detailed storytelling, and political awareness often enough to retain an enormous measure of folk world credibility.

Notwithstanding the ever increasing number of contemporary song-writers seeking to showcase, the Folk Alliance has sought to ensure that traditional or at least vernacular music is well represented. As the number of showcase applications from singer-songwriters has continued to grow, selection committees have awarded a disproportionate number of official performance slots to those on the more traditional side of the spectrum.[59] Nonetheless, the rise of the unofficial—or guerrilla—showcase has altered the balance. Beginning with the inaugural Alliance meeting in Malibu, attendees have performed informally and spontaneously throughout the conference grounds. In Calgary in 1992, *Dirty Linen* magazine hosted a hospitality suite with featured performers, an early instance of organized entertainment outside the formal program. At Tucson in 1993 the Scottish band Wolfstone advertised a specific unofficial performance on the conference premises. This unabashed attempt to attain commercial attention distressed conference organizers.

Other artists, however, were eager to follow Wolfstone's lead. Wedded to an ideal of egalitarianism, the Alliance board succumbed. As the 1994 Boston conference approached, many performers not only planned unofficial showcases well in advance but also promoted them with paid advertising in the conference program. Others simply relied on handbills posted or distributed at the conference itself. With the Alliance reputation growing and a conference located in the populous and accessible urban Northeast, attendance doubled that of Tucson, and there seemed to be unofficial show-cases throughout the hotel, day and night. Singer-songwriters crooning their "me songs" of love and loss were seemingly everywhere.

Boston is the source of a now legendary, as yet unduplicated, singer-songwriter success story, which fueled hope that a few days at the conference might jump-start a successful career. In February 1994 Dar Williams was a twenty-six-year-old Wesleyan graduate living in Northampton, Massachu-setts. A clever, literate, though still developing songwriter with a gorgeous soprano, Williams had spent years playing at unknown coffeehouses and informal "open mic" nights, where she sold her self-financed, self-released debut album, a collection of songs that seemingly chronicled every aspect of her personal development. That album garnered favorable attention on the coffeehouse circuit, prompting a small but tangible "buzz" that suggested—to those who pay attention to such things—the presence of a talent worth examining. At the Boston conference, Williams gave three unofficial showcase performances that transformed her life in a manner that seems miraculous. "I remember going to the Folk Alliance in '94 and coming home a completely different person. Everything was different. I was offered management, record label, and booking in one sitting, basically."[60] That summer she performed at the Newport Folk Festival, now reborn as a relatively star-studded affair with corporate sponsorship. In 1995 she toured as the opening act for Joan Baez and was profiled in *Billboard*. By the end of the decade Williams employed a backing band and had earned a spot on the much publicized Lilith Fair, and her three solo albums had collectively sold more than three hundred thousand copies, a stratospheric total for even the most established folk artists.[61]

Boston cast differing visions of the Alliance into sharp relief. Menius recalls it as the place where the "singer-songwriter hell issue" became apparent. Blevin saw an "air of hostility and competitiveness" that marred the gathering, with people "aggressively looking for gigs, aggressively looking for agents, not attending workshops at all and being there only to showcase, and that was something that just kind of snowballed." Boston, she concluded, "was hard."[62] *Sing Out!* columnist Ian Robb wondered if the Alliance was forgetting the many nonprofit folk clubs whose aims were "cultural and social, not financial."[63] Moss expressed dismay over "self-promotion run amok." Though acknowledging that business development had a legitimate place within the folk world, he urged all concerned to "find a way to prevent the music from being swallowed whole by a lack of focus, clarity, and real understanding about the genre. I believe," he said in Boston's wake, "that the Alliance needs to redouble its efforts to truly represent the full spectrum of its purported constituency, giving equal weight to the traditional music, academia, and participative folk music programs, along with a measured level of service for the myriad of contemporary singer songwriters who singularly want to sell their services."[64]

Alliance board president Phyllis Barney sought to calm the rising negative tide, insisting that the organization was committed to "nothing less than a cultural revolution to convince people that folk music and dance is a valuable cultural resource to be respected and celebrated." Rejecting any suggestion that folk music had to become "monochromatic pabulum in order to succeed," she affirmed the Alliance's dedication to a "broad community" as opposed to a "limited few." She noted the diverse array of vernacular music available in Boston, the many workshops offering varied types of technical assistance, and the opportunities to network with those advancing widely disparate cultural, social, or business agendas. Calling the conference a "kaleidoscopic view of the community," Barney reminded critics that it was never intended as the sole event that any folk activist attended in a given year. Instead, it was the one place where diverse agendas came together. She challenged all who loved folk music to involve themselves in "shaping the initiatives of the organization for the coming years."[65]

In 1995 the Alliance made an ambitious move from North Carolina to Washington, D.C., prompted by the allure of an international city that offered enhanced visibility and greater networking opportunities. After an extensive search, the board hired Barney, its own president, as the organization's first executive director, with duties that exceeded Menius's narrowly defined role as conference manager. Menius stayed on to produce the 1996 gathering. He then negotiated a buyout of his contract and resigned, while remaining an Alliance member and regular conference attendee. Barney had most recently spent seventeen years with the U.S. Fish and Wildlife Service, where she served as an expert in fishery management. She had attended the formative Malibu gathering as a folk fan, avocational house-concert presenter and festival volunteer, and the creator of an early electronic bulletin board that linked fellow fans. Her personal warmth, forthrightness, and attention to detail made her a beloved figure to many, and throughout her tenure Alliance members often referred to her affectionately as "Goddess" or "Queen."

Barney needed all of her considerable interpersonal skills as she attempted to balance often conflicting visions in which culture, community, and commerce struggled for position. What began as an effort to draw together traditional music lovers dedicated to finding better ways to promote vernacular culture has become, in the minds of many attendees, a mass audition for contemporary performers seeking commercial opportunity. Singer-songwriters—many with no discernible vernacular roots—vastly outnumber tradition bearers, and the troubadours fill hotel rooms with song into the early-morning hours. It is common to see a solitary performer, guitar case in hand, hustling down a corridor, off to his or her next showcase. Late at night, these corridors take on a surreal tone. Showcase organizers stand in doorways like carny barkers on a midway, urging those within the crowded hallways to step into their rooms. Listeners sometimes linger for mere seconds before moving on. Some rooms fill to overflowing. In others, artists perform uncomfortably in front of two or three people. Amid much good music, there is a great deal of terrible music. Confronted all at once by large numbers of acoustic guitar–playing singers, it is easy to understand the oft-heard complaint that so many of them sound alike and offer poetry of no particular distinction.

Menius, who is no fan of stereotypical navel-gazing songwriters, nonetheless blames traditionalists for much of the divisiveness, noting that they have always been too ready to "take their balls and bats (or banjos and mandolins) home."[66] In addition to Shelly Romalis, Juel Ulven ended his active participation, unable to see how the cost of attendance benefited his Fox Valley Folklore Society. After the 1996 Washington, D.C., conference, the Patons stopped attending as well. At the 1999 conference in Albuquerque, this separatist tendency sparked a discussion that might have altered the nature of the Alliance permanently. Roughly two dozen people out of sixteen hundred registrants attended a meeting of the Traditional Music Peer Group, a gathering open to any attendee who wanted to discuss traditional artistry. Moderator Jeff Davis noted that those interested in tradition had grown increasingly frustrated with their place in the organization, a remark that sparked an outpouring of grievances. At Phyllis Barney's request, onetime board member Charlie Pilzer raised the possibility of a separately scheduled "miniconference," dedicated to the preservation of tradition. After an exploration of this idea, with frustrations vented and alternatives explored, sentiment within this small group turned away from separatism. There were already too many demands on the time and money of devotees, and no one needed another event to attend. Mark Moss took a typically forceful stand that seemed to move the group decisively away from the idea. Rather than leave, he argued, traditionalists should hold their heads up, raise their own profile, and pursue their goals within the existing framework.[67]

The prospect of separation seems to have awakened traditionalists to certain realities. Whereas raw numbers suggest that singer-songwriters dominate the conference, the Alliance has always offered traditionalists many opportunities. The 1999 Albuquerque attendees who debated the possibility of an alternative conference could also have attended workshops on Nordic, Hispanic, or Native American music, to cite just a few examples of the vernacular forms presented. They could have partaken of sessions that discussed techniques useful in recording nonprofessional traditional musicians or offered advice on how to best present traditional music at large festivals. They could have discussed problems inherent in doing fieldwork among the traditional musicians of Mexico in a session focusing on interaction with Mexican cultural institutions. They could have learned something about the history of the banjo, enjoyed an oral history session with New Mexican accordionist Antonia Apodoca, seen a performance by traditional Zuni dancers, or listened to Acadian music as performed on Prince Edward Island, Canada. Still other activities were of interest to a broad range of attendees, whether traditionalists or not. Organizational representatives could attend sessions on board development or fund-raising, promoters of all stripes could gather to discuss concert production, and performers—whether contemporary songwriters or banjo-picking preservationists—could obtain tips on stagecraft or staying healthy while on the road.[68]

Philosophical tensions ebb and flow, but many Alliance members appear to have settled into a mood of acceptance, accommodation, and collaboration with respect to disparate musical and cultural interests. Traditionalists now seem quick to spurn anything that suggests the creation of a "trad ghetto," such as the proposal—floated briefly—for special conference badges identifying self-described traditionalists. Now when trad fans gather, their discussions tend to focus on programming strategies appropriate to a commercial world in which traditional music often struggles to find an audience. One hears much excited talk, for example, about the promise of mixed performances, in which traditional and vernacular musicians share stages with more accessible singer-songwriters, country performers, and even rock bands—an approach that was popular at the height of the great boom.

Performer and Alliance stalwart John McCutcheon credits the conference with reconciling fault lines within the revival, providing a setting where people can "enter into important discussions about the direction of the community and grapple with the issues." McCutcheon serves as president of Local 1000, a division of the American Federation of Musicians established specifically to address the needs of touring musicians in the acoustic music world. As a union officer he concedes that it would be impolitic of him to pick sides in folk's sectarian wars, but he is convincing in his call for mutual respect among all struggling artists. "I don't think there has to be sides," he argues. "There will always be people . . . who don't like your voice or your instrumental skills or whatever. There will be people who'll say, 'Oh, why don't you go back to playing traditional songs.' . . . I hope they'll all succeed," he adds "and I hope that somebody who's writing their diary can pay their bills, have kids, pay their rent, eat well, and take a vacation. And I hope, at the same time, there are twenty new bluegrass bands that can make a living next year. There's a lot of room." Although McCutcheon's own compositions center frequently on the value of community, he offers an impassioned defense of the much maligned navel-gazing singer-songwriter. "There's a tremendous need for poets in these nonpoetic times," he says, "and if you can open somebody up to what music has always done, by touching them in a place that only a twenty-two-year-old—'I just broke up with my boyfriend, and I don't know what to do'—writer can do, God bless 'em."[69]

Margo Blevin, who found the Boston meeting so disheartening, took stock of what the Alliance has to offer and remains a believer. Of the regular opportunity to meet with colleagues, she says, "How much more effective could you be than that? That is a primary thing—to take people out of their little isolated location and their single-minded activity and show them what other people are doing and open up a window on new possibilities." Always able to find a meaningful workshop or performance, Blevin adds, "I never come away from there without a notebook full of contacts, ideas, grant ideas, [and] breakthroughs." If there were no Folk Alliance, she says, "You'd have to spend your whole year going around visiting organizations and going to festivals and getting nothing else done. And here you can get so much of that done in one weekend. It's enormously valuable for me."[70]

Still, vocal critics remain. There is a rising belief that the Alliance needs some significant success apart from the conference itself—one that provides tangible and enduring benefits to its industry constituency. Unknown performers are realizing that a costly trip to the conference's madhouse setting can hardly spark the careers of a few hundred musicians, all desperate for small café or house-concert gigs. Benefits from attendance, where they exist at all, are likely to arise slowly, as a musician's reputation spreads within the community over a period of years. Better-known performers and established agents bemoan the fact that many large-concert presenters do not attend, since they usually have more efficient means to learn about an act and assess its suitability for their venue. Notwithstanding Blevin's positive perception, many attendees criticize the workshops, noting that moderators are often unprepared and that some sessions recur year after year, offering new insights only sporadically.

Perpetually short of funds, the Alliance has struggled with limited success to offer services beyond the annual gathering. It has established a program that simplifies members' efforts to obtain nonprofit status. In conjunction with other cultural organizations it has participated in intermittent negotiations with the U.S. Departments of State and Homeland Security regarding the visa problems of foreign artists who wish to perform in the United States. An annual booking-agent training course seeks to add to the ranks of qualified agents, and thus satisfy the demands of emerging artists who cannot find competent representation despite, in some cases, genuine talent. This is a long-range effort, and its ultimate success remains uncertain, but it is a well-meaning attempt by the Alliance to satisfy a structural need within its industry.[71]

As the Alliance matures, it remains to be seen whether ongoing debate about its purpose and efficacy will prompt its demise or spur it to greater achievement. In 2005, the organization made significant changes that may influence its future direction. After shifting the conference locale every year, the board decided that, beginning in 2007, it would hold the event in Memphis, Tennessee, for at least four consecutive years. To facilitate this, the organization moved its offices to Memphis so staff can develop ongoing relationships with that city's artistic, business, media, and tourist interests. By leaving the costly Washington, D.C., area, and entering into a multiyear contract with Memphis conference and hotel facilities, the Alliance hopes to free a considerable amount of money for new endeavors. The move may also serve the needs of those members who have complained of the necessity to "reinvent the wheel" every year in a perpetually unfamiliar conference location. Artists and entrepreneurs can now learn what to expect from the exhibit hall, showcase venues, and local services and can plan accordingly.

Perhaps the most dramatic change was that Phyllis Barney resigned to enter law school, after ten years at the organization's helm. Her replacement, Louis Jay Meyers, has more industry experience than Barney had at the start of her tenure, which is appropriate given the Alliance's steady growth. Most notably, Meyers was a longtime codirector of South by Southwest, the large music industry conference held each year in Austin, Texas, which is one of the industry's premier opportunities for networking and artist showcasing. Designed initially to spotlight independent rock artists, it has increasingly welcomed the participation of major record labels. Meyers is open about his desire to transform the Alliance into a younger and more aggressive organization, one that is ready to seize professional opportunity. He speaks with apparent confidence of his intention to provide year-round services that give people a reason to retain their membership in the years they do not attend the conference. He hopes to make better use of the organization's Web site to spotlight members. He urges better partnerships with media and is particularly insistent that the Alliance focus its publicity efforts on business publications, as well as those devoted to music and culture. He is excited about the untapped potential of European markets. There is much in Meyers' approach that alarms the "back porch" players who have always played a role in Alliance affairs, but he claims sensitivity to the aspirations of tradition lovers and professes to value the smaller, less commercial components of the folk world.[72]

The departure of any longtime executive affords an opportunity for organizational reinvention. It can also, however, prompt a period of disruption, and, for the Alliance, the Meyers hiring proved tumultuous in the short term. Barney projects openness and tends to surround people with warmth. Meyers, by contrast, can appear distant and defensive, prompting some people to distrust him. More tangibly, an independent audit in 2006 raised questions about his skill as a fiscal manager. Roughly simultaneously, some board members developed concerns about the quality of his personnel management. These issues came to a head in November 2006 when, after heated discussion, the board reorganized the Alliance's management structure. It created a new position of chief operating officer, with responsibility for "administrative, management, staff and fiscal functions." It invited Meyers to continue as executive director with his responsibilities limited to conference management, member programs, marketing, and public relations.[73] In essence, the board compelled Meyers to surrender overall control of fiscal and personnel management. He accepted, and the board ultimately filled the new position with two individuals who have worked as contracting consultants, not employees.

Mindful of its responsibility not to air personnel difficulties in public, the board made no announcement of its concerns or of its discussions with Meyers. The membership learned of the transition after the fact, prompting an uproar on the Alliance Listserv. Fervent Meyers supporters initiated and drove that discussion, and some of them alleged that the board's actions were unethical or even illegal. Other members praised the directors. Noting the confidential nature of personnel matters, they pointed out that the directors were dedicated volunteers charged with difficult oversight responsibilities. Overall, the restructuring and its aftermath led to considerable tension and acrimony. Between December 2006 and May 2007, seven of the sixteen elected board members resigned before the end of their terms. *Sing Out!*

editor Mark Moss was among them. Moss's departure was especially poignant given his past service as chair of the Alliance's founding steering committee and his central role in drafting the organization's mission statement. Following his resignation, a weary and disillusioned Moss allowed *Sing Out!*'s Alliance membership to lapse, ending all formal ties to the organization he helped found. Unhappy with existing management, he concluded that the Alliance had become a dysfunctional organization, plagued by petty, self-interested politics and incapable of accomplishing its mission.

As one founding member departed, another returned to active service. The remaining directors selected seven individuals to fill the board vacancies. Among them was Art Menius, who had served alongside Moss on the steering committee and had been the Alliance's first manager. Menius believes that the "root cause" of the turmoil surrounding Meyers lies in the long-standing tension over whether the Alliance exists to foster cultural equity or professional advancement. Though this position tends to minimize legitimate concerns about leadership temperament and management skill, it does contain a measure of truth. In Menius's view, commerce serves culture, and he maintains that the Alliance has shifted too far from the "conventional trade association model" that he has always championed. The Alliance, Menius says, overreacted to the incursion of singer-songwriters by striving too hard to appear "seamlessly multi-cultural, multi-ethnic, multi-national with deep regard for scholarly study of music and dance and an openly leftist political agenda." Though he sees nothing wrong with such aspirations per se, he believes they have diverted the organization from "core music and business focused activities." Focusing on one of Meyers' acknowledged strengths, Menius calls him a "brilliant conference manager," and he hopes that the new director can succeed in turning the Alliance into the "folk music industry's chamber of commerce."[74]

In 2007, the reconstituted board offered Meyers a two-year contract renewal, affording his once-precarious tenure a fresh start. Barney appears resigned to the fact that her stewardship is now fodder for perpetual second-guessing. She takes Menius's remarks in stride, seeing them as an expression of the "essential tension" that has always existed within the organization. They remind her, she says, "of the day that I got two post-conference letters. One from a singer-songwriter complaining that we did too much for traditional musicians, the other from a trad musician saying they'd never come back because all Folk Alliance cared about were singer-songwriters. Rather than choosing one point of view at the expense of the other," she explains,

"I sought to balance them." Mindful of the Alliance's diverse constituencies, she stresses the continued need for balance. "It will be interesting to see where the organization goes now," she muses. "I am hoping it continues to balance the many and varied interests of its members and supporters. The passion that people have for the organization is a great asset, and will help it reach its next evolution."[75]

SIX

Consolidation Blues:
Folk Music in Contemporary Markets

From the vantage point of more than three decades as a performer, rock musician Don Henley has declared that the contemporary music business is in a state of crisis. Looking back toward his professional start in the late 1960s, Henley remembers when his industry treated music as "vital to our culture." Radio stations were "local and diverse." Record companies developed "cutting-edge artists." Music stores were "magical places offering wide variety." Today, Henley complains, all is different. The labels, radio stations, and record retailers of yore have fallen before the juggernaut of commercial consolidation—growing and merging for the sole purpose of maximizing profit, while treating music not as art but as nothing more than their commodity of choice. Local radio is a thing of the past, as absentee corporate owners substitute centralized programming for community voices. Where there once existed a plethora of big and small record labels, a handful of multinational corporations now dominate. Mass merchandisers have replaced the once "magical" record stores. Overall, Henley sketches a world of profit-driven cultural homogenization that devalues art, those who create it, and the very idea of uniqueness.[1]

Whether the music industry of Henley's youth was truly art loving and altruistic may be debatable, but many people share his despair at the industry's current obsession with quick profits. Whereas our earliest folklorists feared the literal disappearance of diverse groups and their unique expressive features, today's revivalists fear the disappearance of those media outlets that help give voice to diverse cultural expression. The consolidation of the media and that of the music industry as a whole provoke fear and disdain akin to that which folklorists once expressed about urbanization and industrialization. As demonstrated during the founding of the Folk Alliance, there exists concern that size compels the need for the acquisition of large sums of money, thus encouraging a singular interest in music that appeals to the greatest common denominator, as opposed to that which is idiosyncratic and community based. Despite such concerns, many revivalists desire strongly to participate in the marketplace, prompting a constant struggle to locate acceptable middle ground.

For anyone needing proof that commercial radio has no interest in traditional American music, verification arrived in the medium's response to *O Brother Where Art Thou?*—the movie soundtrack that has sold more than seven million copies, an extraordinary accomplishment in any genre. The disc, which blends old-time fiddling with blues and spirituals, features current and former Rounder acts Alison Krauss, the Cox Family, and Norman Blake. Folk/country favorites Emmy Lou Harris and Gillian Welch also appear, as do bluesman Chris Thomas King, gospel stalwarts the Fairfield Four, and bluegrass legend Ralph Stanley. The album's best-known track is "Man of Constant Sorrow," an ancient song that Stanley, with his brother Carter, first recorded in 1951, when it was already old. In the film Hollywood heartthrob George Clooney lip-synchs the song to the voice of Dan Tyminski, the guitarist in Krauss's band. After a year of rising sales and favorable press, the album dominated the 2002 Grammy telecast, receiving five awards, including a designation as Album of the Year.

At the time of the album's late-2000 release by Mercury Records, the Universal Music Group—Mercury's parent company—was a Rounder distributor. The label knew how to market mainstream country and pop records, but it had no expertise with an idiosyncratic roots-music grab bag. Recognizing its limitations, the company sought Rounder's assistance in reaching the folk and bluegrass communities. Rounder agreed to assume a major role in promoting the disc, understanding that a successful soundtrack might provide a boost for Krauss, its best-selling artist, as well as for its entire stable of old-time, bluegrass, and blues musicians. The label's promotional staff called their roots radio and press contacts, while Ken Irwin discussed the album regularly on BGRASS-L and other Listservs. He encouraged fellow list members to spread the word, directed them to relevant items in the press, tracked the record's weekly sales progress, and in general reinforced the impression that its commercial and cultural impact was a meaningful community event, offering recognition, validation, and the promise of further success.[2]

Album producer T-Bone Burnett anticipated that mainstream radio would have little interest in *O Brother*. In a preemptive challenge to the medium's conservative impulses, the soundtrack's liner notes accuse Nashville's corporate "infidels" of appropriating the phrase "country music" to describe "watered-down pop/rock with greeting-card lyrics." Not surprisingly, radio executives did not take the bait. Contemporary country music is indeed a form of pop/rock, and, at the time of the soundtrack's release, no major broadcast executive would have seriously expected mainstream listeners to embrace the album's eccentric sounds. However, as the disc gained press, accolades, sales, and multiple Grammy awards, perceptions changed. *O Brother* was no longer merely the archaic-sounding album that country radio refused to play. It became, instead, the award-winning hit—and then the pop-culture phenomenon—that radio refused to play. Country Music Television, VH1, and MTV all programmed a video of "Man of Constant Sorrow," featuring the lip-synching Clooney fronting the film's fictitious Soggy Bottom Boys. Radio kept its distance. Mercury twice released the song as a single—once before the Grammy telecast and once after. A few stations eventually added "Sorrow" to their playlists, but it generally received few spins per day, and programmers tended to drop it fairly quickly.[3]

Nashville DJ Eddie Stubbs termed radio's reaction a "disgrace," prompted by the obsessive commercial consciousness that revivalists malign. Country music radio's largest single market consists of young mothers who make family buying decisions—an audience that advertisers are unwilling to lose. Those mothers, research reveals, enjoy the pop-flavored tunes that country radio favors, not *O Brother*'s archaic twang and death-obsessed spirituals. One hit album, which many executives presumed was either an artsy fad or a response to George Clooney's good looks, was not going to alter standard commercial operating procedure. Moreover, so many radio programmers have grown up on a diet of "safe" radio that their own knowledge of country music's artistic roots is often severely limited. Since those roots sound foreign and unappealing to programmers, they are hardly prepared to risk their ratings—and their jobs—by gambling that audiences may eventually embrace such sounds. Ironically, Paul Soelberg cited this identical problem in his 1970 analysis of the then dismal state of country radio, published at the time of Rounder's debut. More than thirty years later, as the Rounders helped promote the best-selling roots music anthology in history, they confronted this identical prejudice.[4]

Although the multifaceted phenomena of media and music industry consolidation are deserving of full-length study, my more limited goal is to illustrate the manner in which they color revivalist discourse. In this regard, a primary concern is the dwindling number of eclectic local radio stations that offer diverse programming and feature announcers who are knowledgeable about community concerns. Folk music disc jockeys tend to see their own programs as islands of cultural idiosyncrasy and pluralism amid airwaves that are otherwise awash in homogeneity. The best program hosts do more than broadcast an eclectic array of hard-to-find music. They also serve as educators, capable of explaining the roots of the music they play and something of the cultures from which it derives. Even those broadcasters who concentrate on contemporary Anglo singer-songwriters assert proudly that their offerings stand apart from the mainstream of mass-mediated culture. Folk radio also serves the vital function of nurturing the revival community within a listening area, by interviewing community activists, spotlighting local musicians and venues, and providing notice of nearby performances, thus fostering the sense of group identity and purpose on which revivalism thrives.

Changes in both law and radio station economics since the mid-1990s have posed an unprecedented threat to the continued existence of such unconventional local programming. Most dedicated folk shows are broadcast only once a week, generally on the weekends when listenership is low. Of ninety local folk radio shows listed in the summer 2004 issue of *Sing Out!* sixty-five appeared on the weekend, and all but a handful received no more than two to four hours of airtime per week. The disc jockeys who program these shows, many of whom converse on the Internet and at the annual Folk Alliance conference, sometimes sound like the beleaguered inhabitants of a community under siege as they exchange survival strategies centering on station politics and the incessant need to raise funds. Many direct their frustration at the Telecommunications Act of 1996, which vastly increased the number of radio stations that a single entity could own. With unprecedented investments at stake, the owners of multiple stations sought to maximize revenue, minimize costs, and eliminate risk. Stations now broadcast more commercials than ever before and often eliminate live announcers, offering pretaped shows that periodically insert local weather and traffic reports in order to give the illusion of a local presence.[5]

If there is a popular villain in this media consolidation narrative, it is undoubtedly Clear Channel Communications, the Texas corporation that dominated commercial radio by 2003, owning more than twelve hundred stations—then roughly four times more than its nearest competitor.[6] Clear Channel focuses on nationally syndicated programs, many of which have all-talk formats. Historically, its music programming has concentrated on the hits, in a conscious effort to attract the largest audience possible. By avoiding tunes that listeners might find unusual or even unfamiliar, the company strives to ensure advertisers a broad and relatively constant audience.[7] Bennet Zier, manager of an eight-station Clear Channel group in the Washington, D.C., area, explains that the company adheres to the "old saying: You don't get hurt by what you don't play."[8] The result, says media critic Michael Bracey, is "the disappearance of entire segments of music. It's hard to find bluegrass, traditional country, opera and jazz on the radio. And those are huge segments of cultural heritage that are gone from the airwaves."[9] In addition to bemoaning the loss of heritage, members of the revival community feared dire political consequences when, in 2003, the Federal Communications Commission considered a further relaxation of media-ownership rules. In a comment typical of many on the FOLKDJ-L Listserv, Mark Moss condemned the "amazing arrogance on the part of those who believe they have the right to take a free and open media away from us." Noting that he had signed anticonsolidation petitions and written to his elected representatives, he concluded, "Maybe I'm tilting at windmills, but I refuse to passively live out George Orwell's vision."[10]

Folk music once found a fairly welcoming environment on nonprofit public radio, but it is now endangered there as well. Faced with declining government funding, station executives have sought to maximize reliable private revenue streams. Professional marketing consultants have delivered the same message they brought to commercial radio: idiosyncrasy threatens ratings. The typical public radio listener, consultants advise, wants "news and information." If that listener tunes in and hears folk music, he or she will turn the dial, perhaps never to return. Consultant David Giovanni, one of public radio's premier programming gurus, advises clients who wish to maximize their audience to "lose what's on the periphery. Focus on a single audience," he says, "and serve that audience extremely, insanely well, all the time." Asked if it would be a mistake for a station to court two different types of listeners, he responds, "That makes it harder. A radio station should be something for the same person all the time," he insists. "You become less and you become better."[11] To a folk music community that values vernacular pluralism and artistic diversity, the idea that less is better is both absurd and dangerous.

Whereas the narrow mind-set of radio executives prompts ongoing concern, the consolidation of record labels is another area in which revivalists tend to believe that less is definitely not better. In this regard the "big four" record companies, which collectively account for approximately 80 percent of the revenue earned through disc sales, are particular targets. In early 2006 the big four consisted of the Universal Music Group, Sony BMG Music Entertainment, the EMI Group, and the Warner Music Group—diversified, international entertainment conglomerates that now own many of the once-independent labels known to consumers. Universal, for example, owns the legendary Motown, while Warner owns onetime folk stalwart Elektra, as well as rhythm-and-blues pioneer Atlantic. Criticism of the big four follows a predictable pattern—their costs are so high and their interest in profit above all else is so great that they are congenitally risk averse. They avoid the daring and tend to follow any successful artist or style with a soundalike, wanting nothing more than to replicate prior success. Timid when it comes to investing in long-term career development, which may never pay off, the majors typically drop any artist who does not become profitable quickly. Bob Dylan, whose first album sold only about five thousand copies upon its initial release, would not have the opportunity to record a second major-label album today. Bruce Springsteen, who was largely unknown until his third release, would today remain a New Jersey bit player instead of attaining international stardom.[12]

While the major labels collectively dominate sales, the folk scene encompasses an ever changing cast of smaller labels numbering in the hundreds. Rounder is one of the most enduring of these, some of which are nothing more than single-artist "do-it-yourself" enterprises. An examination of FOLKDJ-L's annual airplay summaries provides one measure of the role such "indies" play in the folk world. In 2005, 272 self-defined folk disc jockeys reported a total of 146,403 individual airplays. Of the ten most heavily played labels, only one—Columbia in the fourth position—was affiliated with one of the big-four label groups.[13]

If he has his way, folk music disc jockey John McLaughlin would eliminate any major label presence on the folk airwaves. Except in rare instances, such as a tribute to an unusually worthy artist, McLaughlin refuses to play major label product on his weekly folk music show. With a four-hour show broadcast once a week, McLaughlin—like most of his peers—controls a very limited amount of airtime. Since he can fill that time easily with good music from independent labels, he prefers not to give the majors more commercial access than they already have. He concedes that this requires him to forego some desirable music, but that is a price he is willing to pay in order to promote struggling and truly independent artists. Behind McLaughlin's stance—which he refers to as "tiny blows against the empire"—lies an innate political perspective consistent with that which has historically made common cause with the folk. "I don't like multi-nationals, instinctively," he says. He adheres to the oft-heard belief that, notwithstanding an occasional artistic gem, the major labels have no genuine interest in art. It is all "product" to them, he observes—"cabbages or kings, ships and shoes and sealing wax, what do they care?" He is equally harsh toward artists who manage to gain entrée to the majors, dismissing them as something akin to enemy collaborators, blinded by the lure of personal profit.[14]

Judging from the commentary posted on FOLKDJ-L, McLaughlin's absolutist position has won sympathizers but no converts. Though many vocal folk DJs agree that major media organs and music industry financiers care little about culture, there is no widespread rebellion against large-scale capitalism. Folk music broadcasters appear content to work within the prevailing economic system while voicing opposition within the established political framework. Although some may consider that approach naive or self-defeating, it reflects the truism that revivalists as a group, like Americans generally, do not live lives on the barricades of open rebellion. Their more modest goal is to promote those aspects of culture that they admire, wherever they find them, and they tend to applaud folk musicians who manage to make a decent living through their art.[15]

My goal is to illustrate the nature of revivalist concerns, but I must acknowledge that change is brewing within the radio and record industries, though the extent and impact of that change remains unknown. *O Brother's* seven million in sales may be an unrepeatable anomaly, but the album was an enormous hit, and many roots music devotees are now convinced that there exists a hidden market for their passion that they might reach, at least occasionally. Musicians and fans see promise in satellite and Internet radio, which are entering the marketplace with genuinely diverse, commercial-free programming. Such stations offer entire channels devoted to early country music, singer-songwriters, bluegrass, and blues, among many other things, often spotlighting truly obscure musicians. Though revivalists appear to overwhelmingly applaud this variety, the absence of a local focus remains a concern. Thus far, such stations provide diverse music and knowledgeable disc jockeys, but they cannot tell you which unknown folkie is playing in your town next week, and they are unlikely to spotlight your local club.

Nonetheless, the rise of these alternatives, along with a growing backlash against narrow radio playlists, has caused the broadcast industry to blink. Beginning in 2004, many commercial stations began adopting the so-called Jack format, which boasts larger than normal playlists while expanding the scope of "oldies" radio and mixing pop music genres. The name identi- fies the computerized disc jockey, which sometimes goes by Bob or Dave or some other easily remembered moniker. "Jack" might play a rock hit from the 1970s that follows a hip-hop hit from the nineties and precedes a country hit from the eighties. Broadcasters like to claim that the format approximates an iPod on shuffle, but the emphasis remains on broadly fa- miliar and commercially successful tunes. Jack is simply one more version of nationally focused "hit radio," and this new marketing gimmick is not going to mollify those folkies who desire truly eclectic local broadcasts.[16] In early 2006 Clear Channel shocked the folk and bluegrass communities with the announcement that an AM affiliate heard in parts of Kentucky, Ohio, and West Virginia was adopting a format focused on "traditional country, western swing, rockabilly, Texas singer-songwriter and alternative country- rock." The ultimate success of this limited experiment remains uncertain, but it is a hopeful sign when broadcasting's "evil empire" is at least willing to explore the possibility of deriving profit from such hitherto "alternative" musical sources.[17]

Record label executives, alarmed by declining CD sales, are also increas- ingly aware of the need to broaden their focus, and are demonstrating a renewed interest in postcollegiate audiences that often display surprisingly broad musical tastes. This audience is at least partially responsible for the success of the old-school Cuban music collection *Buena Vista Social Club* and the later, larger, success of *O Brother*. Norah Jones is one beneficiary of this outreach strategy. With her softly sung blend of jazz, pop, and country, Jones sounds like nothing else on the current hit-music scene, yet EMI subsidiary Blue Note released her debut album in 2002. In an extraordinary market- ing success, Jones has sold millions of CDs and seems poised to become a lasting star. The same strategy helps explain the vitality of Warner-owned

Nonesuch Records, a small major-label subsidiary with an eclectic roster that ranges from the avant-garde classical ensemble Kronos Quartet to the long-popular Emmy Lou Harris, a veritable goddess among fans of rootsy country and folk. Although these projects are all admirable, the big four still require a steady stream of successes, forcing them to focus predominantly on sure things while relegating the unsigned majority of artists to obscurity. The well-established Harris, a critic's favorite, lends cachet to a company roster, but she is unlikely to sell the number of records needed to keep the larger corporate ship afloat. The marketing of Jones required a considerable investment, which her label would have lost had she not defied probabilities and succeeded. Financial considerations preclude too many such risks.[18]

While narrow radio playlists and limited major-label rosters combine to constrain commercial opportunity for musicians, there is no guarantee that even with a record contract an artist will find space on store shelves. Record stores have always sold the hits, but—with allowances for the usual nostalgic idealization—the overstuffed shop that also carried eccentric music and was always willing to hang a poster advertising a local performer did actually exist. It was in such shops that the Rounder founders received much of their musical education—reading liner notes and listening to Folkways LPs—and where they found initial outlets for their label's offerings. In the decades following the great boom, such local retailers were crucial partners in keeping the folk scene alive.

Tower Records, born as a single store in 1960, pioneered the concept of the "deep catalog" superstore, attracting staunch music partisans through its large and diverse inventory. As the nineties began, Tower found itself in tight competition with similar deep-catalog giants, such as Britain's Virgin and HMV chains, then expanding aggressively in the United States. At a company conference in 1991, Tower president Russell Solomon articulated his survival strategy. "Tower cannot have a competitor who has a better selection," he told his store managers. "Don't let your catalog down."[19] As the decade progressed, the music superstores faced competition from a new breed of nontraditional music retailers such as the Borders and Barnes and Noble bookstore chains, video purveyor Blockbuster Entertainment and the electronic and appliance giants Best Buy and Circuit City. To varying degrees, these new market entrants joined the almost fetishistic competition for musical inventory, insisting that they would help broaden the consumer market. Instead, they began to cannibalize one another.

Best Buy and Circuit City became enmeshed in a price war that roiled the industry, as they discounted discs so heavily that they sold some popular CDs below their own cost. They could afford this because they had little economic interest in music sales, as such. They viewed CDs as heavily advertised loss leaders, priced solely to draw potential customers in the hope that some might eventually purchase a new stereo system or washing machine.[20] Other nontraditional music retailers soon entered the price-slashing fray, and at the end of 1994 *Billboard* reported that CD price wars had "squeezed music retailers' profit margins as thin as discs."[21] The following year, in which nonmusic stores sold 28 percent of the CDs in the United States, the retail explosion of a few years earlier began to contract, and the weaker "all music" stores started to fail. By one account, roughly three hundred music stores in the United States closed their doors in 1995, marking the beginning of a still ongoing trend.[22] Approximately twelve hundred record stores shut down in 2003 and 2004. Although Internet music sales and illegal downloading may be factors, the trend dates back years, and its roots lie in retail consolidation on a massive scale. Eventually, even the once-dominant Tower Records succumbed. In 2006, following a bankruptcy filing, the chain closed its doors.[23]

Eclectic local stores remain, of course, but they are fast-vanishing anomalies. For the most part, particularly away from the diversity of larger cities and university towns, Americans buy their music from the chains, where selection has grown increasingly limited. Wal-Mart was the nation's largest brick-and-mortar music retailer in 2004, controlling 20 percent of major-label CD sales. Best Buy and Target round out the top three retailers. This trio collectively accounts for roughly 50 percent of such sales, almost doubling the market share that all nontraditional music retailers combined had enjoyed just ten years earlier. They thrive due to their ubiquitous presence, national advertising, bulk buying power, discount pricing, and the revenue from many other product lines. With continued retail contraction, the pressure to compete through diversity has disappeared. Whereas a typical Tower outlet might have stocked sixty thousand titles, a Wal-Mart stocks approximately five thousand, eschewing struggling artists, most independent labels, and even the back catalog of major stars. Wanting only to serve its goal of drawing people through the doors, it focuses primarily on those popular titles necessary to achieve that limited end. With the big three mass-merchandisers dominating sales of the hits, the purely local retailer finds it increasingly difficult to compete. Mike Dreese, owner of Massachusetts-based Newbury Comics, which despite its name is a well-established deep-catalog music retailer, is blunt. "The only question is whether our death is in seven years or eight," he said in 2004. "Everybody's lights are out in ten."[24]

From his unique vantage point Ken Irwin has witnessed the transition. What he calls the "corporatization" of music retail has led to "less knowledge and less passion" on the part of store staff. Wal-Mart and its ilk simply do not employ salespeople based on their ability to recommend quality bluegrass or zydeco to interested customers. His label's ability to promote music within the stores has also changed. In earlier times a Rounder staffer would mail a poster to a store clerk with whom he or she was often personally acquainted, at least through a telephone relationship. If the clerk liked it, he would tack it to the wall. Now that clerk has no such discretion. In-store promotions—posters, listening posts, end-cap displays—as well as shelf space itself, have become commodities, which stores sell to those record distributors with whom they enjoy ongoing and profitable relationships. Consequently, idiosyncratic small-selling artists, who are increasingly excluded from terrestrial radio and major-label rosters, are unlikely to find a place in stores either.[25]

As Rounder grew, it endeavored to remain true to its identity as a purveyor of noncommercial vernacular eclecticism, retain the support of its historical customer base, and survive amid increasing industry consolidation. This led to occasional brickbats from vocal commentators who believe that folk-oriented businesses have duties beyond those common to all honorable commercial interests. I know of no one in this context who condemns profit outright, but some commentators expect folk entrepreneurs to utilize business practices that exemplify overtly a deep respect for the past and a strict communitarianism.

In 1993, *Old-Time Herald* founder Alice Gerrard contemplated the economic difficulties inherent in bringing old-time music to the marketplace. A onetime Rounder artist, she recalled the label's early days as a time of "youthful vision, great ideas, unlimited energies, dedication and passion about the music, willingness to sleep on floors and in vans, to run around reissuing and recording huge amounts of material, to operate on a shoestring." Contemplating changing times, she acknowledged that the label was "now interested in operating with a profit margin." Sounding more wistful than critical, she conceded that "a part of us . . . feels they should continue to operate at some philanthropic level, that they owe it to the community and greater good to continue operating from dedication and passion only, and not from profit motives." Reflecting revivalism's egalitarian ideals, she added that "part of us feels that no one should make a commercial, profit-line venture out of this homemade people's music—music that is a part of all of us."[26]

Gerrard's tone was pragmatic and understanding. Other critics, however, harshly scrutinize any apparent "concession" to commercial needs for signs that Rounder is deviating from once-sacrosanct ideals. In 2004 a participant in an online blues discussion list posted a link to an article that discussed Rounder's expansion "into the lucrative pop-rock world." The article quoted Rounder general manager Paul Foley, who reported that though the company still released roots music, it was "not the small, bluegrass-folk label from Cambridge anymore." Though the Listserv correspondent wished Rounder well, he added that he was unable to feel much excitement about this change. Of the three posted responses, one was from a former Rounder artist who noted simply that the label had indeed changed, another said that the change prompted him to vomit, and a third accused the Rounders of consorting with the devil, which the writer was certain would cause the company's downfall. No one discussed the full range of Rounder's contemporary releases or whether, absent its current business practices, the label could afford to release any roots music whatsoever. To these commentators Rounder's embrace of more "lucrative" musical styles was simply a negative development and cause for alarm.[27]

In 1999 music journalist Dave Marsh excoriated Rounder for offering one of his friends an artist's contract that Marsh considered the equivalent of a standard major-label deal. He mocked the founders for failing to live up to their identity as "good collectivists," a characterization that the label owners had not used to describe themselves in more than two decades. Shortly thereafter, Marsh took Rounder to task for the termination of a longtime employee. Once again, he characterized the label as a "collective," arguing that it was "supposed to be the benchmark good-guy independent." He seemed particularly outraged by an e-mail in which Nowlin addressed Marsh's concerns by declaring, "I do, in fact, consider Rounder to be 'just another record company.'"[28]

In 1998, *Sing Out!* editor Mark Moss expressed concern about a contract between Rounder and Mercury Records, a division of the worldwide entertainment corporation Polygram, now part of Universal. That contract called for Mercury to distribute approximately one thousand records from Rounder's back catalog along with selected future releases. The deal provided some of Rounder's roots-oriented artists with the strength of Polygram's established nationwide distribution network, along with the marketing power of an international entertainment goliath. On its face, it seemed a clear victory for the small-scale tradition-based music at Rounder's heart. If Polygram could help sell such music, it might benefit not only the particular artists and genres involved but also, by adding to Rounder's bottom line, the label's entire array of vernacular and political song.[29]

Moss feared the contract could hurt, not help, some of Rounder's most unique artists. The one thousand back-catalog albums encompassed by the new agreement accounted for roughly 90 percent of Rounder's 1997 sales volume of twenty-four million dollars.[30] However, because certain albums sell far more than others, those same albums constituted less than half of the label's overall output. Seemingly, a minority of better sellers was getting enhanced attention from a label founded on the premise that the music, not its sales potential, was what mattered. Worried about that part of the Rounder catalog that fell outside the agreement, Moss wondered if Rounder could truly guarantee that music's continued availability, now that it stood apart from "the more successful material, which has provided the infrastructure necessary to promote and distribute the full line." More fundamentally, he worried about any deal that aligned "the Rounder collective"—like Marsh, he used a characterization the label had abandoned twenty years earlier—with the "megacorp" Polygram. Could Rounder's historical "focus on preserving and promoting quirky roots music be sustained," he wondered, if entrusted to those "enamored by the 'big fish eats the small fish' theory of good business?" Thinking beyond this one label, he urged folk music lovers to be especially vigilant, warning against the day when "we'll wake up to find all recorded music controlled by [international corporations] and our access to recordings by George Pegram, [union activist] Aunt Molly Jackson or [the old-time band] the Freight Hoppers has simply evaporated."[31]

Moss raised a legitimate concern, which I will discuss later in this chapter. I note preliminarily that to varying degrees all of the concerns described above rest on the fundamentally flawed premise that Rounder had undergone a relatively recent change for the worse. Though the pace of change at the label has arguably increased since the late 1990s, the company's history encompasses relatively constant change. This change has always been in the direction of increased involvement with established elements of the music business. Nowlin acknowledges that in Rounder's earliest days he found the idea of marketing distasteful because of its overt ties to the commercial world he hoped to avoid. However, the founders took to heart the advice of folklorist Archie Green, who told them early in their label's existence that if they wanted to introduce an alternative business model to the record industry, they needed to conduct business as well or better than their more established competitors.[32] Whether because of this advice, a desire to better serve the artists and cultures they sought to represent, burgeoning professional and financial ambition, an inherent desire to be good at what they do, or a combination of all of these, the Rounders began to professionalize almost immediately, a slow process that continues to produce change. As they attempted to master the existing commercial structure, they became the capitalists they once disdained. "One thing we definitely learned," Nowlin says, "is that working within the system, we ended up being shaped to the system in some ways."[33]

The founders succeeded to a degree they never imagined. In 2004 Rounder's gross revenue was approximately fifty million dollars, double the level attained just seven years earlier.[34] The label appears to have successfully negotiated the ongoing tension between romantic folk world idealism and commercial necessity, managing to increase revenue dramatically while continuing to market a fairly large amount of noncommercial vernacular music. In doing so, notwithstanding the comments of a few, it has retained a large measure of respect within the folk world. Most revivalists are pragmatists where present-day business realities are concerned. So long as Rounder continues to release a large amount of music that the folk world can embrace, most folkies will accept—or even admire—the label's success. If, however, the music tips too far from a revivalist ideal, the numbers of those complaining that the company has "gone corporate" will grow. In the balance of this chapter I dissect Rounder's success thus far in straddling the divide between romance and commerce.

After taking delivery in October 1970 of five hundred copies each of the Pegram and Spark Gap records, the Rounders set about the task of selling those LPs, despite having no idea what they were doing. They were thrilled when Discount Records in Harvard Square agreed to accept five copies of each album on consignment. They learned quickly, however, that there existed an institutional barrier that limited their ability to place the records in stores. The overwhelming majority of retailers had no interest in purchasing from individual labels. Instead, they obtained records through ongoing relationships with distributors—wholesalers who purchased from numerous labels, then resold the records to retail outlets within a regional or even local area of operation. Those distributors who represented major labels with better sellers enjoyed a market advantage, since retailers wanted their products. In some cases such distributors could use the leverage afforded by strong sellers to persuade retailers to stock a few lesser sellers. The stores enjoyed the opportunity that distributors provided for the consideration of a wide range of merchandise, which saved a tremendous amount of time. All parties enjoyed significant economies of scale.

Few established distributors would work with a "label" that consisted of three inexperienced young owners hawking two relatively homemade, noncommercial albums. The Rounders found initial support from people much like themselves. Jack's Record Cellar, an esoteric enterprise in San Francisco that sold jazz, blues, and country music, ran both a retail storefront and a small, regional distributorship. The Rounders considered it a coup when Jack's agreed to distribute twenty-five copies of each album. This arrangement, like the earlier consignment placement with Discount Records, did not bring the label any immediate revenue. Following standard industry practice, Jack's purchased the albums on credit, reserving the right to return them if they failed to sell. Still, this early distribution "success" is a remembered high point of Rounder's formative years. In practical terms, however, Jack's occupied a music industry niche only slightly larger than that of Rounder itself. From the standpoint of the overwhelming majority of retailers—and consumers—Rounder's debut albums may as well not have existed. The founders' attempts to remedy this situation moved along two tracks. On the one hand, they pursued a grassroots strategy that involved direct communication with individual consumers. On the other hand, they pursued an industry strategy, through which they attempted to enter the organized distribution stream.[35]

In pursuit of their grassroots strategy the Rounders took to the road in their van, making sales trips to folk and bluegrass festivals along a fairly wide swath of the eastern United States. Upon arrival, they would set up a table and display their wares. I cannot overstate the significance of these trips, which went on through much of the seventies. The Rounders, year after year, met and mingled with a highly targeted audience. Though they had records to sell, the Rounders also listened to music with the same sense of excitement as other festivalgoers. This had the dual benefit of helping them bond with their customers, who came to know them as music-loving peers, while allowing them to experience new music, much of which ended up on Rounder Records. The Rounders first saw the Fuzzy Mountain String Band and the now legendary Cajun band BeauSoleil on these trips, along with many other performers. When feasible, they visited the Archive of Folk Culture at the Library of Congress, where they educated themselves through field recordings, reading, and conversation. They met folklorists Alan Jabbour and Archie Green and government folk festival programmer Ralph Rinzler, each of whom offered encouragement and assistance. Rinzler, for example, eventually asked the Rounders to release the Cajun albums he was compiling from his Louisiana fieldwork, despite his long association with Moses Asch of Folkways Records. Irwin credits this invitation to the founders' incessant hard work at festivals, which helped shift their reputation from that of "hippie radicals" to "young hustlers," with the latter characterization offered in a positive light.[36]

Roundup Records, the company mail-order arm, grew from these trips. Seeing an opportunity, the Rounders collected names and addresses from those who visited their sales table. They then mailed mimeographed descriptions of their latest offerings, along with an address and phone number for the placement of orders. In the label's earliest days Mark Wilson received orders in Massachusetts, while the founders traveled. Wilson then relayed these orders by phone, since the founders carried the bulk of the physical inventory with them on the road. Intermittently, they stopped at local radio stations and asked for used record mailers in which the stations had received LPs. Packing their own albums in these mailers, they shipped them to purchasers from nearby post offices.[37]

Notwithstanding their relative success at festivals, the Rounders understood that they needed to place their albums in stores. The association with Jack's in San Francisco prompted momentary celebration, but it was plainly insufficient. Rounder required an ongoing relationship with at least one established distributor. Initially unable to secure such an affiliation, they began approaching retailers with the claim that Rounder was itself both a label and a distributor. In retrospect, this was a laughable, albeit an audacious, gambit. True distributors did not confine themselves to two records, particularly records that the so-called distributor had released itself. The founders, however, were completely serious, and they worked hard to turn this "distribution arm" into a genuine enterprise, one they eventually dubbed Rounder Distribution. They approached other small labels, offering to do the legwork needed to place albums with retailers, and their efforts gradually met with success.[38]

Rounder's first meaningful distribution triumph arose out of a relationship with a label that, quite by accident, had recorded a star. In 1969 acoustic guitarist Leo Kottke played a gig at the Scholar Coffeehouse in Minneapolis. Kottke is a celebrated virtuoso whose predominantly instrumental work blends elements of blues, jazz, and traditional folk. Oblivion Records, an aptly named label with no industry presence whatsoever, recorded the show, which it released as *12–String Blues*. That same year Kottke signed with Takoma Records, a small California independent. His Takoma release, *6 and 12 String Guitar*, found an audience. It was, in Irwin's words, "as steady a seller as there was in the roots market" of its day. In 1971 Kottke moved to Capitol Records, with which he subsequently recorded four albums. Despite Kottke's rising visibility, Oblivion could not secure New England distribution for its tiny and otherwise noncommercial catalog, and it welcomed a deal with the Rounders. Retailers wanted Oblivion's interesting, prefame Kottke record, affording Rounder a previously unavailable level of retail access for all of its relatively few offerings. Coming years before the breakthrough of George Thorogood, this experience illustrated the ability of a successful record to open doors.[39]

Kottke's other independent label, Takoma, provided Rounder the distributor with its first significant label catalog, as opposed to the single significant album that Oblivion offered. Acoustic guitarist John Fahey had cofounded Takoma in 1959, largely as a home for his own recordings, which traversed the same folk, blues, and jazz territory that Kottke later explored. By the late 1960s Fahey had found a wide following among a guitar-loving cognoscenti. In addition to Fahey's various albums, the Kottke LP, and numerous other bits of musical esoterica, Takoma was the home of Booker White, a Mississippi bluesman who had found a measure of renown as a folk boom "rediscovery." Riverboat Enterprises, a Boston company that had previously declined to distribute the fledgling Rounder Records, had been Takoma's New England distributor. However, after a falling-out with Riverboat, Takoma turned to Rounder. In the small label world of the early 1970s, Fahey's company was a major player, and this alliance suggests Rounder's growing favorable reputation. The Rounders then maximized their benefit by arranging to swap Takoma LPs with the disappointed Riverboat, which in turn provided Rounder Distribution with releases from Riverboat's more varied clients, including Arhoolie, County, and the Chicago blues label Delmark. This variety immeasurably enhanced Rounder's access to retail accounts.[40]

These early distribution efforts occurred against the backdrop of the formation of NAIRD, the National Association of Independent Record

Distributors. While the neophyte Rounders were particularly ignorant, even the owners of already established independent distributorships—those not affiliated with major labels—saw a need for better professional education and industry cooperation. In 1971 Riverboat's Steve Frappier began exploring the possibility of a national organization through which such distributorships could communicate with and learn from one another. Organizers scheduled an initial meeting in Chicago in February 1972, immediately preceding the respected University of Chicago Folk Festival. Most invitees distributed some type of roots music, so it was advantageous that Chicago was, in Irwin's words, "a strong blues and folk city, [so] many of those attending the meeting would be able to find places to stay with friends." A dozen people attended, including the three Rounders, and they represented nine entities. The organization's founders included distributors that serviced labels such as Delmark, Folkways, Arhoolie, and County. Bob Koester, Delmark's owner, and Bruce Iglauer, his associate who soon founded Alligator Records, also attended. Their presence sparked a brief controversy because they represented a label, not a distributorship, but they were allowed to stay. In its second year, NAIRD offered independent labels "associate" memberships. NAIRD, which later changed its name to the Association for Independent Music, survived for thirty-two years before industry consolidation contributed to its demise.[41]

In its formative years NAIRD shared Rounder's political objectives. Most early members, Irwin says, "were part of the counterculture and we felt that what we were doing was important both culturally and politically. We were helping to make available music and culture which were not being offered by the major labels." The Rounders took full advantage of the learning opportunities that NAIRD's annual conferences offered. Irwin recalls carrying a notebook from distributor to distributor, label to label, asking each the same questions. He sought the exchange of mundane paperwork, such as invoices and packing slips, so he could garner ideas. Conferences provided opportunities for Rounder Distribution to contract with new labels and for Rounder Records to form alliances with new distributors. Members shared information regarding who was trustworthy and which labels were easiest to sell. Labels contracted freely with multiple distributorships, and most distributors wanted agreements with as many labels as possible because, says Irwin, "there was so much good and valid music, which needed better exposure. . . . Distributors wanted to be known as a good source for all the music outside the mainstream, not just for selected labels."[42]

Recognizing the economic benefits of diverse offerings, Rounder sought distribution relationships beyond the narrow confines of the folk revival. It made an early inroad into the world of rhythm and blues with Detroit's minuscule Fortune Records. It distributed a small amount of jazz through Biograph and Delmark, which were predominantly blues labels. When New York City distributor Record People branched into New England in 1975, handling jazz as well as folk and blues, the Rounders—who understood the need to respond to competition—decided to increase their own jazz offerings. By the early 1980s they distributed Concord Jazz, Contemporary, and Muse, among others. They also handled El Saturn Records, a "label" limited to releasing the work of its owner, the eccentric avant-garde jazz master Sun Ra. Particularly in its early years, Rounder mixed its yearning for professionalism with a large dose of what I can only describe as "indie spirit." Glenn Jones, who began purchasing for the distribution company in the late seventies, recalls his periodic meetings with Sun Ra. Whenever Ra needed an infusion of funds he flew to Boston with a few hundred albums. Jones would meet him at the airport where he exchanged cash—Ra did not take checks—for records. Jones then had to place stickers on the record jackets in order to provide the titles and catalog numbers that retailers required.[43]

Building day-to-day professionalism proved a slow process. At times, inefficiency hurt feelings and severed professional relationships. Country Cooking, the innovative young bluegrass band from upstate New York, brought its third album to Rounder competitor Flying Fish because of the founders' perceived inattention, demonstrating that even hippie musicians wanted to earn a living. Banjoist Pete Wernick advised Rounder by letter that the band was switching labels, despite the fact that the musicians liked the founders personally and respected their politics. The band wanted better promotion and distribution and a record company that was more responsive to their questions. Urging the Rounders to accept his letter as constructive criticism, Wernick suggested that it was in their interests to change.[44]

Musician Robert A. "Tut" Taylor expressed related concerns in a letter he wrote to Rounder in the spring of 1974. Taylor, a virtuoso on the resonator guitar, was part of a circle of Nashville musicians working with multi-instrumentalist John Hartford. Predominantly an experimental bluegrass and old-time player, Hartford had the talent and good fortune to write "Gentle on My Mind," a smash hit for Glen Campbell in 1968. Armed with a Warner Brothers' recording contract, Hartford released *Aereo-Plain* in 1971, a landmark in hippie-flavored old-time music. His studio band included Taylor, guitarist Norman Blake, and fiddler Vassar Clements, who later billed himself as the progenitor of "hillbilly jazz." Though Hartford was then out of its reach, Rounder pursued his sidemen successfully, a coup for the young label. In 1972 Rounder released Taylor's *Friar Tut*, followed by separate releases from both Blake and Clements. Taylor coproduced Blake's effort and, also for Rounder, produced 1972's *Brother Oswald* by Beecher "Pete" Kirby, a veteran of the Grand Ole Opry. Blake, Clements, and Kirby also made guest appearances on *Will the Circle Be Unbroken*, the now legendary, Grammy-nominated old-time country album spearheaded by the rock world's Nitty Gritty Dirt Band in 1972. Through intense drive and hard work, the very young Rounder had placed itself in the thick of a burgeoning experimental old-time music scene, which it helped to foster and which stood on the edge of an unexpected commercial opportunity. It then, in Taylor's estimation, fumbled.

In his 1974 letter Taylor lambasted the company, claiming that it had handled manufacturing and distribution so poorly that all concerned had lost thousands of dollars. He then offered a sentiment that appeared to strike a chord with the young entrepreneurs. Although Rounder might be nonprofit, he wrote, if it chose to make records, it had an obligation to make them available to the public. Irwin's response blamed poor communication and pressing-plant difficulties. Though he maintained that the problems were not as bad as Taylor stated, he acknowledged deficiencies and stressed the founders' desire to learn and improve. "We are still open to suggestions for improvement," he wrote. "We are working hard to correct our shortcomings [and have made great progress] in the past few years." With respect to Rounder's nonprofit stance, he seemed almost defensive. "Lastly, on the non-profit question, we are not profit motivated, but that does not mean that we care any less about our work. In fact, we often work 14–16 hours a day without pay because we believe in what we are doing."[45]

Although the Rounders were young, inexperienced, and perhaps somewhat disorganized, many problems were almost certainly due to the fact that they stretched themselves so thinly. Their workload was enormous. In addition to tending to the needs of the distribution company, they were negotiating with artists, planning recording sessions, mixing records, and arranging for the manufacture of albums, which involved pressing the vinyl, creating cover art, and writing their often detailed liner notes. After graduating from Clark, Leighton pursued a master's in European history from

Northeastern University and, for a time, had an income-producing side job. From 1970 to 1982 Nowlin taught political science at Lowell Technological Institute, now subsumed within the University of Massachusetts system.

Running Rounder initially from their shared apartment, they rose early, gobbled some cereal, and worked—often, as Irwin said, for sixteen hours at a stretch. Holy Modal Rounder Peter Stampfel, who observed them in the label's early days, recalls with understatement, "It was their home, it was their work, it was what they did. And there was so much of it to do that they were pretty full-time." Food was merely fuel. Sleep, as Nowlin puts it, was "an interruption." The idea of a leisurely meal or an alternate activity was incomprehensible. After they retired for the evening, Irwin and Nowlin would frequently discuss plans from their respective bedrooms, which were actually doorless alcoves, shouting out ideas and schedules.[46]

Leighton grew irritated at times. She wanted occasionally to do something "frivolous," such as lie in bed and read a book. Of the three, she most desired a balanced life, and she has never possessed her partners' workaholic tendencies. Among the rural poor of her Maine hometown, she says, people did not live to work; they worked to live. Consequently, she views work as merely one aspect of a larger identity, not as something that defines her. In her mind, Irwin and Nowlin's all-encompassing work ethic is an outgrowth of their upbringing as middle-class males in families that had high professional expectations for their sons. She recalls the pleasure and validation that Irwin's father derived from seeing a Rounder release reviewed in the *New York Times*, and she contrasts that with her own parents' more generalized concern that their daughter's life was going well overall. Her parents were largely uninterested in the details of this strange thing that was Rounder Records. It was simply their daughter's work, and there were usually far more important things to talk about.[47]

The Rounders had assumed initially that their collective would grow, allowing for the distribution of the workload. It proved difficult, however, for someone to enter their world. A love of old-time music and a desire to enter the record business were not enough. A potential collectivist also had to share the Rounders' political ideals and be willing to live with and spend virtually all their time with his or her colleagues, working nonstop, for little money, in a single-minded devotion to the cause. More important, they had to find an emotional comfort zone within the shared history of the founders, a relationship that encompassed Leighton and Irwin's romance and its lengthy aftermath. They never found anyone who could manage this in the long term, and it is uncertain that they could ever have truly let someone in. Looking back, Nowlin concedes there was a "dynamic" among the original trio that "definitely excluded people." "It would," he adds, "have been a hard thing to penetrate."[48]

Only three made the attempt. Cornelius "Skip" Ferguson, a casual friend from the Boston area, tried his hand as a Rounder but departed quickly, dropping out of his colleagues' lives completely. Bruce Kaplan, a fellow old-time music enthusiast who met the founders at the Galax, Virginia, fiddling contest, was a Rounder from 1971 to 1974. He joined without relocating from his Chicago home. He may have lasted as long as he did because he was cut off from the stress of the founders' daily lives, but this separation also contributed to his departure. He left, however, with his enthusiasm for the roots music business intact. He founded Flying Fish Records, taking with him some of the Rounder artists with whom he was most involved. Flying Fish became a staple of the folk world until Kaplan's premature death in 1995, after which Rounder purchased its onetime competitor.

The final addition was Bill Kornrich, Nowlin's former roommate from Chicago who was a Rounder for two years beginning in the summer of 1974. When Kornrich joined Rounder, the collective had recently moved to a large house on Willow Avenue in Somerville, just outside Boston, which served as home, office, and warehouse. Kornrich moved in and began drawing the same minimal salary that the founders then received. Though memories vary, this amount lay somewhere between one hundred and four hundred dollars per month per person. The company was doing well financially. With the bulk of the money derived from distribution, Kornrich recalls gross revenue when he arrived of approximately thirty thousand dollars per month, which he believes had risen toward eighty thousand per month when he left in 1976.[49]

The collective was using most of this money to expand. In 1976 the company released 32 albums—an average of almost 3 per month—bringing its total to 124. It was distributing many more. Despite friendly times, Kornrich's tenure ended unhappily for him. He never grew truly close to Irwin and Leighton. In his mind they held strong views and generally presented a united front whenever disagreement arose. He believes that his friendship with Nowlin and the latter's closeness with the others presented a divide that none of them could bridge. Though he applauded the goal of releasing noncommercial, culturally distinctive music, he found Rounder's political trappings to be ridiculous as practiced. In his opinion, leftist rhetoric was merely a tool with which one faction or another tried to gain advantage when internal conflict arose.[50]

Kornrich's departure from the collective was entwined with the role of Danny Wilson, the younger brother of Rounder collaborator Mark Wilson. In the mid-1970s Danny tended the mail-order company, which had grown large enough to require full-time attention. He drew no salary, and he was not, by choice, a collective member. Working but not living at the Willow Avenue house, he purchased LPs from the distribution company, filled orders, and pocketed the markup. Kornrich insists with emotion that the founders, wanting the additional money, pushed Wilson out. The founders, with equal vehemence, deny any avaricious purge. Wilson remembers Kornrich with great affection, but recalls his departure as voluntary and devoid of any particular unpleasantness. Only Kornrich seems strongly affected by this now murky incident, which he characterizes as a betrayal of friendship.[51]

Kornrich's unhappy tenure at Rounder suggests at least two things. First, though the founders initially possessed a sincere utopian vision, they also possessed a group insularity and a desire for control that probably doomed any genuine collectivist impulse from the outset. Second, the desire to run their business successfully channeled them quickly into the existing commercial apparatus, one governed by the rules and the difficulties of capitalism. One early Rounder associate, whose involvement with the label overlapped that of Kornrich, offers oblique agreement with each of these propositions, noting sardonically that Kornrich only thought he was a member of the collective and that the Rounders did not so much transition to the capitalist system as come to recognize that they were part of it.[52]

In 1974 the Rounders incorporated, taking a large symbolic step into capitalism. Perhaps to deflect any personal unease, they approached this transition with characteristic humor and political rhetoric. Irwin became treasurer because his partners viewed him as a tightwad, and they named Leighton president to strike a blow for women's rights. Nowlin rounded out the corporate roster as secretary. As their functional roles evolved, Nowlin tended predominantly to business matters, Irwin focused on music, and Leighton, at least in the label's early years, handled publicity. These divisions were loose, however. For the most part, they shared management responsibilities and signing authority through consensus.

Leighton embraced her role as a woman in a male-dominated industry. Within the record business, publicity tended to be a woman's niche, but

Leighton never felt stereotyped. Instead, she hoped to shatter stereotypes by standing apart from the traditional designer-clad, "dress for success" image of the publicist. She felt a confidence that came from knowing that unlike most industry women, she was an owner, with a meaningful role in shaping her label's artistic identity. Though well versed in and respectful of the precepts of feminism, she was quite willing to foreground her gender when that proved helpful. She understood that some people were more relaxed with women than with men, believing that women were less likely to cheat them. A woman's smile, she knew, would "light up the room," whereas a man's smile might mean that he was mentally tabulating dollar signs. In her younger days, she realized that some of the older male blues and bluegrass artists saw her as a "cute little hippie girl," and she never felt demeaned by this. Music, she says, is "a sexy thing," and if her presence added "a charge" that made encounters among relative strangers more exciting, that was a plus.[53]

Each founder agrees that their initial conscious step away from collectivism was the mid-1970s hiring of their first salaried employee, and each credits Holy Modal Rounder Peter Stampfel with encouraging this transition. Stampfel saw how hard they were working and asked why they did not hire someone to help. They had resisted this step, which seemed in opposition to their desire for a company that had no bosses and shared all revenue. Stampfel, whom the Rounders respected, turned their rhetoric around, arguing that he would resent an ideology that denied him a job merely because he chose not to devote all aspects of his life to the enterprise. Some people, he pointed out, simply wanted interesting work. Whether it was due to Stampfel's influence, a desperate need for help, or changing attitudes about the wisdom of collectivism, the Rounders became employers, setting the stage for the union-organizing drive that stands as one of the more ironic episodes in the company's history.[54]

Early hires suggest that Stampfel anticipated correctly that music lovers, in particular, would happily accept employment with this young, hip record company. Scott Billington was a working musician when he joined the staff in 1976. He began as the company's first paid salesman, selling albums released by Rounder and its distributed labels to retailers as his swing band traveled between New England gigs. Eventually, he became Rounder's art director and then an accomplished record producer. Glenn Jones, also a musician, joined in the summer of 1977. He initially purchased LPs for Rounder's distribution arm, but he worked in shipping and receiving as well.

He realized quickly that there was little formal separation between employee responsibilities, and he liked the fact that the company was casual in tone and even a bit disorganized. Potential employees, he says, appreciated the passion evident within Rounder, and viewed the organization more as a calling than a job.[55]

Billington believes that as the founders shifted from self-identified collectivists to employers, they struggled with a figurative "schizophrenia that persisted for many years." On the positive side, he explains, this led to a workplace that empowered employees, encouraging them to take on added responsibilities voluntarily. On the negative side, employees who so extended themselves rarely received financial rewards, an omission that bred strong resentment. By 1979, now ensconced in a warehouse, the label employed roughly two dozen people, and George Thorogood's unexpected ascension to rock stardom compounded any preexisting problems.[56]

Before Thorogood the owners frequently worked alongside employees, performing functions as mundane as the physical shipment of LPs to stores. Afterward, the Thorogood phenomenon required them to address countless new business details. The owners became a more distant and—some employees assumed—a wealthier elite. Always hard workers, they could be tough taskmasters. Jones, whom the company fired in 2000, claims the owners would regularly accuse the workers of malingering, and he recalls one founder letting staffers know that they were completely expendable. With the company appearing to be successful, workers concluded, in Billington's words, that the time had come for "a better compensation package" and benefits such as health insurance and vacation time that were "more clearly defined." The founders, Billington adds, acted as if everybody's labor was in furtherance of an "altruistic vision." Despite admiring that vision, he believed that ownership imposed the obligation to balance vision with the need to provide "a little positive feedback and . . . some way to make it all make financial sense for the people that work for them."[57]

A group of employees, led in part by Jones, felt sufficiently aggrieved to approach Local 925 of the Service Employees International Union and, in 1979, initiate an ultimately successful organizing drive. The Rounders hired the Boston law firm of Hale and Dorr and resisted fiercely. Billington abstained from the vote, hoping that he might serve as some sort of conciliatory "third force." Not particularly political and somewhat of an idealist, he saw the issue less in terms of a clash between labor and capital and more as a human failure to communicate. "Sometimes," he says, "I feel if the Rounders had had better people skills, the union would not have happened." Upon losing, the founders were unforgiving. They closed ranks and stopped talking to organizers for almost a year. They were, Nowlin explains, "offended" that a "group of people had drawn a line in the sand and said, 'We're not in this together. It's us versus you.' And so we saw ourselves as under siege to some extent."[58]

Looking back at Rounder's response, Nowlin expresses no regret, though he concedes it is fair to ask how, given their initial vision, the Rounders found themselves opposing the organization of their workers. He offers a variety of explanations while acknowledging "some discomfort with hypocrisy." The founders, he says, worked inordinately hard themselves, in addition to reinvesting the bulk of their revenue in the company. They had "good motives" in dealing with their workers, though he concedes that poor management skills might have obscured their positive intentions. "If we can't manage to have a fourth or fifth member of the collective that's truly part of the collective," he says, "then it's not surprising that the same kind of distancing happened with [employees]." He says that research he conducted in 1979 demonstrated that Rounder's wages were consistent with those paid by similarly sized record companies. Working at Rounder, he notes, was hardly the equivalent of laboring in the Kentucky coal mines. Referencing the label's several recorded collections of union songs, he argues that a business need not be a union shop to explore and exalt labor's historic role.[59]

Those who adopt a prolabor stance may forever see Rounder's union history as a mark of rank hypocrisy driven by the desire for control and personal gain. Dave Marsh suggests as much when he arms his contemporary critiques of the label with snide references to the "good collectivists," insisting on a characterization that the Rounders abandoned long ago. Certainly, in instinctively taking "offense" at the organizing drive, the founders appear to have misunderstood the fundamental distinction between the position of owners—who may ultimately reap great rewards through their control of assets—and that of workers, who generally have fewer material resources and, absent protection, are always uneasily dependent on remaining in the owners' good graces. I believe subjectively that the founders feared that unionization could foster the demise of their company, at a time when Thorogood's success offered them a new level of cultural influence and profitability. Whether one sees them as most concerned by a perceived breach of faith by their employees, by the prospect of lost influence, or by the possibility of reduced profits depends largely on one's personal biases.

Mindful of uncertainties and varied perceptions, I have sketched the story of Rounder's union opposition not to condemn the company as antilabor nor to praise it for its involuntary status as a union shop, but because that story is an integral part of the company's history, helping to illustrate the often painful trade-offs faced by those who desire success in the marketplace.

The impact of Thorogood's commercial breakthrough reached beyond its contribution to Rounder's unionization. Artistically, as I discussed previously, it helped the founders conclude that their vision could encompass a far broader range of music than they once contemplated. Professionally, it thrust them into the marketplace to a degree previously unimagined. As they prepared Thorogood's debut for release, the Rounders pressed approximately seventeen hundred copies of the LP, plus an additional three hundred copies earmarked for promotion. They sent a routine, descriptive solicitation to their existing distributors, hoping it would produce orders. They also mailed promotional albums to selected radio stations, based on leads from their distributors and information gleaned from industry "tip sheets"—periodic mimeographed mailings containing airplay charts and brief reviews. The first station to play the record heavily was KTIM, a low-wattage outlet just north of San Francisco. Tony Berardini, the program director and a late-night DJ, loved the rawness of the album. He spread the word through tip sheets and, informally, among fellow DJs, with whom he gathered regularly to listen to new records.[60]

The founders began calling stations hoping to generate momentum. A young promoter working for another label offered to pitch the album to radio along with his own company's material, hoping to further his credibility by letting disc jockeys know that he cared about good music generally. Promoters employed by Rounder's distributors solicited airplay and sometimes helped advertise live appearances in their region. The founders cooperated eagerly and, in general, used the Thorogood momentum to enhance relationships with existing distributors, cultivate relationships with new distributors, and solidify relations with their pressing plant, which had to respond to an unexpected demand for LPs. With the release of Thorogood's second album, the cycle repeated with greater intensity. The founders arranged for Thorogood to perform at the annual conference of the National Association of Recording Merchandisers and for other industry groups. One or more of the founders accompanied him on tour almost constantly, including seventeen dates on which Thorogood opened for the Rolling Stones. While tending to an overwhelming amount of unfamiliar detail, they also had to address overtures from those offering to buy either Thorogood's contract or the entire label. Irwin, recalling the heady days when Thorogood became a star, says, "Each day was a challenge, each day was a learning experience. In a matter of a few months, we learned more about the real world of the record business than we had in the previous eight years."[61]

Thorogood introduced the Rounders to Duncan Browne, who for almost twenty years helped spearhead the company's expanding distribution efforts. Browne was a onetime Boston record store owner who had befriended Thorogood before the blues rocker signed with the label. He relocated to Los Angeles in 1975, where he worked for several record wholesalers and was a buyer for the Wherehouse record retail chain. He met Irwin and Leighton when they accompanied Thorogood to a Los Angeles filming of the television show *Midnight Special*. The Rounders, who were still juggling an extraordinary workload, offered Browne a management position. In a minor way, Browne's return to Massachusetts in the summer of 1979 helped fuel Rounder's union drive, as already unhappy employees voiced suspicion about this perceived industry operative who arrived from Los Angeles to run things. Analyzing the distribution company, Browne saw a relatively small operation centered mostly in New England. To distribute its own records outside that region, Rounder worked with a variety of independent distributors, drawing largely on contacts formed through NAIRD. Most of these distributors mixed Rounder albums with more commercial records, though a relative few focused with varying degrees of expertise on narrow niches such as bluegrass or blues. With the exception of deep-catalog stores such as the growing Tower chain, few retailers had much need for a wide range of Rounder offerings.[62]

Browne shared the founders' understanding that by representing more record companies Rounder Distribution could appeal to a wider range of retailers. Over the course of the 1980s the distribution company grew to encompass approximately five hundred labels, while also expanding its geographic reach. At various times in the eighties and early nineties, Rounder employed salespeople in Albany, Atlanta, Austin, Chicago, Denver, Nashville, New Orleans, Philadelphia, and Washington, D.C.[63] "Distributing other labels," says Leighton, "gave us the cash flow to be able to grow at a very rapid rate. That has allowed us the freedom to continue to do exactly what we want to do."[64] Moreover, by controlling distribution themselves, the Rounders could avoid the excessive reliance on others that sometimes led to disaster. Before Thorogood's appearance with the Rolling Stones at the New

Orleans Superdome in 1981, Rounder's local distributor had ordered only twenty-five copies of each of the artist's albums, presumably losing countless sales. A more serious situation arose in 1991 when St. Louis–based House Distribution, which distributed Rounder in much of the Midwest, faced bankruptcy. Rounder's response was to purchase the troubled firm. "Why go another 60 days," Browne said, "losing market share in that area? [There is] a need for effective distribution dealing with non-hit independent product. To really present those labels in an attractive way to retailers, one needs to have more of a presence in that [midwestern] marketplace." Thinking that a West Coast presence would also be helpful, the label entered negotiations for the purchase of Bayside Distribution, an established California operation. That effort did not bear fruit, but Rounder was clearly striving for its own national network.[65]

In seeking that national presence, Rounder was merely trying to stay abreast of its industry. By the early nineties, retail consolidation was beginning to devastate regional distribution networks. The increasingly dominant retail chains opted to work with national major-label distribution networks, which offered more money for promotion, a higher percentage of better-selling albums, and consistent practices with respect to product delivery, payment, and marketing. This trend worried many label executives, who feared catastrophic consequences if a single distributor developed a weak link somewhere within a national system.[66] Rounder hoped it could avoid pitfalls by becoming its own national distributor. In 1992 it joined forces with Seattle's Precision Distribution and with Rykodisc, another small Massachusetts record company, to form REP, which aspired to distribute the "top-twenty indie labels," including Rounder Records, on a national basis. The founders retained sole ownership of Rounder Distribution, which continued to service several hundred other labels. They renamed it Distribution North America (DNA), and, in 1994, that firm formed a partnership with southern California's Valley Media. Nowlin saw the resulting distributorship—which operated under the DNA name—as one that combined national and regional capabilities. "We have the national distribution capability," he said. "But we are happy to do regional distribution" where that was more appropriate for smaller labels or targeted releases.[67]

Rounder sought simultaneously to improve its marketing. To this end, Susan Piver joined the company in October 1992, moving from tiny Antone's Records, an Austin, Texas, blues label. Antone's released perhaps five records per year. In 1992 Rounder released approximately ninety albums. For Piver, it was a large step up. No one offered her a precise job description. The Rounders wanted to sell more records, and they hoped that she could help. She discovered a twenty-two-year-old company that, in her opinion, lacked any coherent marketing philosophy. She endeavored to create a systematic approach, hoping that it would both sell albums and survive the end of her tenure. Her predecessor had worked alone and from what she could determine did little but place print ads in relevant media. The company was awash in lists—lists of retail outlets, lists of radio stations, lists of print media. No one had coordinated these lists so that, for example, those charged with radio promotion could determine if a receptive broadcast market also contained a store that sold, or might sell, Rounder's records. Piver initiated such co-ordination, as she sought to maximize Rounder's strengths. In a company strong on genre diversity she was the first to engage in genre promotion in a meaningful way. She created separate "genre catalogs" for retailers, so they could more easily delve into the company's myriad offerings. To help stores that wanted to augment their blues line, or their old-time offerings, but did not know how to begin, she supplied in-house "best-seller" lists in distinct musical categories. She initiated genre-specific promotions in which she might, for example, participate in IBMA's "bluegrass month" by providing relevant discounts to distributors. Her goal was to awaken both distributors and retailers to the potential within the vast, somewhat confusing Rounder offerings.[68]

Piver also established Rounder's first formal release schedules. The company had generally released albums when they were completed, with little regard for the number and nature of other albums coming out at the same time. She attempted to group releases in a manner that made marketing sense, while encouraging the creation of meaningful marketing priorities. She tried to attend to those priorities for a reasonable time, to give an album a fair opportunity to succeed. At times the founders chafed at these systems. They sometimes competed with one another, with each urging greater attention to a favored release. They could also display short attention spans. Rounder has always released a great many albums annually, and the founders were often eager to shift their efforts to newer projects without regard to whether a prior release still warranted attention. As part of her efforts, Piver established sales projections for each new release. Rounder had never done this systematically before, but once the system was in place the founders often asked if sales matched expectations. Although Piver never saw the founders as overly encouraging of her efforts, she accepted that encouragement was simply not their style. They indicated their acceptance by allowing her to proceed, by making sporadic efforts to rein in their own occasionally pronounced disorganization, and by authorizing the marketing expansion that she desired. Over the course of her four years at Rounder, Piver built a department of thirteen people, which she supervised as the newly designated vice president of sales and marketing.[69]

While Piver struggled with marketing, Rounder's attempts to expand its distribution network foundered. In 1994, after a partnership of barely two years, Rykodisc purchased Rounder's interest in REP under contentious circumstances. DNA took over the distribution of Rounder's own albums. In 1997, however, DNA also fractured, and Valley Media acquired Rounder's one-half share of that enterprise. After roughly a quarter century, Rounder was no longer in the distribution business. In the short term DNA—now owned by Rounder's ex-partner—continued to distribute Rounder's own releases. Long-term distribution arrangements remained unsettled. Leighton—hinting at Rounder's earlier difficulties with both cocollectivists and employees—observes that whereas the Rounders have been successful as partners with one another, formal relationships with third parties have been far more difficult. She maintains, however, that the biggest single factor in the demise of Rounder's role as a distributor was the ongoing retail crisis of the 1990s, which devastated so many of Rounder's retail clients.[70]

In addition to its impact on distribution, retail contraction significantly increased the number of returns received from stores. By industry practice, if an album fails to sell within a negotiated period of time, stores have the right to return it without payment. In the early nineties, as stores competed for the deepest catalog imaginable, Piver had found an ideal environment in which to pursue her tactic of aggressive genre promotion. Everyone, she recalls, wanted a bluegrass section or a blues or a folk section or all three. With two decades of eclecticism behind it, Rounder was well positioned to satisfy retailers who were interested in more than the hits. As the stores consumed one another, things changed dramatically. *Billboard* reported in 1996 that "returns are coming back to manufacturers so heavily now that their warehouses can't keep up with the flow."[71] Rounder had historically seen returns that hovered in the range of 10 percent of records shipped. In 1996 returns topped 30 percent, and they remained unacceptably high for several years. Gross revenue declined dramatically, requiring the company to reduce staff and alter release plans. It weathered the downturn in the short term because the early nineties had been strong, helped by the breakthrough success of Alison Krauss. In 1995 the young fiddler and singer, who merged bluegrass with contemporary country and pop flavorings, became the first Rounder act to sell more than one million albums, providing Rounder with a huge infusion of cash. The label's long-term prospects, however, were uncertain.[72]

The cumulative turmoil of the nineties forced the Rounders to confront the future with clearheaded realism if they hoped to continue releasing large numbers of diverse records. For more than two decades, Leighton says, the founders had tended to run the company "from the gut." They had been "remarkably successful," she adds, "at being able to have a company grow by our instincts, as opposed to having to pay attention to the laws [that govern] how companies grow." Now, they realized, they needed to pay greater attention to those laws. Their historical retail base was declining dramatically. Emerging corporate retail outlets offered less shelf space, drove tougher bargains, and wanted to deal with fewer distributorships. For Rounder to maintain a presence in what Leighton calls the "transitional" and "challenging" industry of the late 1990s, it needed to either adapt or settle for a reputation as a small boutique. It chose to adapt.[73]

John Virant, a youthful Harvard-educated lawyer, played a large role in Rounder's transition. Virant joined the company as an unpaid intern in the early 1990s. The founders soon offered him a salaried position as Rounder's first general counsel. In this role he took on much of the negotiating that Nowlin had handled previously. Leighton cites Virant's successful effort to secure the lucrative Raffi catalog for the label's Rounder Kids imprint as one of several projects that impressed the founders. "There are a lot of things like that that John helped bring about—things that people like [Ken, Bill, and I] might have lost patience with." In 1997 the previously insular threesome named Virant the label's president and chief executive officer, thus delegating an unprecedented level of authority to a relative outsider. Virant was a typically idiosyncratic choice. He had been a lawyer for only five years, and his work at Rounder constituted the totality of his professional experience in both law and the record industry. He had proved himself to the founders, however, which was all that mattered. "We think his ideas for Rounder and its future are compatible with ours," Leighton said at the time. "We all feel that the way the record business is right now, John's skills and background are a good complement to ours. It is nice to have somebody help shoulder some of those responsibilities." Hinting at a new approach, Virant added,

"For the last 27 years, everything has fallen on Ken, Bill and Marian. I think the idea is to rely on me more and move the company forward."[74]

In noting that everything had "fallen on" the founders, Virant suggests that there were personal as well as business reasons for his promotion. Leighton appears to confirm this with her reference to the founders' diminishing patience and her expression of pleasure at the arrival of someone who could help "shoulder" responsibilities. Leighton had particularly pressing personal needs in the 1990s, which stemmed from that eternal gender issue—motherhood. In the eighties she had married blues musician and record producer Ron Levy, and she gave birth to a son in 1988. By the early 1990s, with her marriage effectively over, she was raising her child alone. Nowlin's own son was born in 1991, but he had a wife who could help shoulder parental responsibility. Leighton was determined to be a conscientious mother, but she was unwilling to surrender the perquisites of Rounder ownership. In her view, she had done her part over roughly twenty years, and she now required a completely appropriate accommodation. In practical terms, this boiled down to her need for reduced involvement in label operations despite full compensation. Her requirements, combined with the stress occasioned by the changing retail environment and the failures of REP and DNA, tested the founders' partnership to a greater extent in the 1990s than ever before. Leighton had always viewed Irwin and Nowlin as extremely progressive with respect to gender equality, but she believes that their commitment faltered, momentarily, when confronted with this highly personal test. In the end, however, she got what she needed.[75]

Leighton may have succeeded because each of the partners desired the increased personal freedom that Virant's ascension allowed. Nowlin, for his part, felt "great relief" when the new CEO began handling the often contentious union-contract negotiations.[76] An avid baseball historian, he has published several books on the sport since Virant took the company reins. Irwin had spent part of the nineties caring for an ill girlfriend, who eventually passed away due to ovarian cancer. In 1997 he married for the first time. Virant's rise offered Irwin—always more comfortable with music than business—the opportunity to spend more time working with artists and to enjoy married life. As her son grew older, Leighton took additional advantage of her enhanced freedom, and began working toward her second master's degree, in American literature and language through the Harvard Extension School. With each of the founders assuming significant outside responsibilities, it had been many years since they could comfortably devote sixteen hours per day to the label. Although they had able assistance, they bore the weight of all major decisions, and it is not surprising that they desired a respite. Trusting Virant, they gave him the room he needed to make a difference.

As one of his first tasks Virant had to bring order to Rounder's unsettled distribution arrangements amid the relatively new corporate retail environment. This was the context in which he helped negotiate the distribution agreement with Mercury/Polygram that had so concerned *Sing Out!*'s Mark Moss. He also began to reshape the company's staff. One arguably predictable casualty of Virant's promotion was Duncan Browne, then holding the title of general manager. Browne was there when Virant joined Rounder and had urged his appointment as counsel. Now after eighteen years, during which Browne developed more authority and autonomy than anyone other than the founders, he watched the newcomer rise to the top. He left within a year in the summer of 1998, assuming that to the founders he represented the past. Virant hired Polygram executive Paul Foley—a man with more than two decades of industry experience—to fill the marketing position that Piver once held. Foley recruited Sheri Sands, a onetime Polygram coworker with whom he was personally involved. Sands, who joined the company in June 1999, also had more than twenty years of industry experience. Foley was then promoted to general manager, and Sands—only eight months after she arrived—assumed the vice presidency of sales and marketing. Speaking in 2001, Virant discussed his determination to reshape the company through these and other hires. "It's a balancing act," he said. "In building the strongest team at the label, I wanted a good mix between new hires and long-term employees. . . . There have been music enthusiasts involved from the start, but the company needed more business-savvy employees to move to the next level."[77]

To the consternation of some employees, Virant's influence extended to Rounder's music. Within a year of taking charge, he created Zoe Records, a wholly owned Rounder imprint dedicated to "exciting and innovative acts in independent rock." Zoe owes its existence to the value the founders placed on Virant. Worried that he might leave to work at a major label, they augmented his promotion with an offer to create an imprint designed specifically to appeal to his musical interests. "We knew," says Nowlin, that there was other music "that he liked that wasn't just our kind of music. So it was a very conscious creation to accommodate other musical tastes."

Virant named Zoe after his young daughter, and as his flagship artist he signed Juliana Hatfield. In the late eighties Hatfield had sung and written for the Blake Babies, which had modest success in collegiate rock circles. In the nineties she was a soloist with a cult following who, in the words of the *All-Music Guide*, "married her ringing hooks to sweet, lovelorn pop and startlingly honest confessional songs." Briefly, she seemed "primed to become a crossover success in the wake of the commercialization of alternative rock." That success never came, and Hatfield remains a minor rock star with a vaguely alternative image. As Nowlin acknowledges readily, her music has absolutely nothing to do with Rounder's historical mission. Of her signing, he says simply, "That's one of John's things."[78]

In the space of less than two years Rounder had placed a lawyer in charge, entered a distribution alliance with a major label, augmented its management team with former major-label executives, and begun a rock imprint. Collectively, these changes fostered a period of internal turmoil that reflected the seemingly eternal divide between the sensibilities of art and commerce. Singer-songwriter Jennifer Truesdale Brogan, who resigned her position as national marketing coordinator in 2000 after nine years at the label, said, "What you're in danger of having is a group of business people, not music people. That's my main fear. You can't sell indigenous Chinese classical music," she added, "the way you sell mainstream pop." Brad San Martin, an avowed bluegrass fanatic, Berklee School of Music graduate, and Rounder intern, met Virant in 1999 while successfully seeking a paid position on the company's promotion staff. During the job interview, Virant sought the young applicant's assistance in understanding the distinction between bluegrass and old-time music. It's a fairly common area of confusion, but San Martin was nonetheless puzzled to find that it bedeviled the CEO of the storied Rounder Records.[79]

Paul Foley became, in the words of the *Boston Phoenix*, "a lightning rod" for criticism. Shay Quillen, who worked in promotion for six years before leaving in 1999, describes him as a "suit," using the old stereotype applied to soulless financiers. "He wanted to break someone big," says Quillen, who clearly believed that in Foley's hands this would mean the loss of Rounder's soul. One unhappy employee who wished to remain anonymous told the *Phoenix* derisively, "We call it Foley Records." San Martin saw staffers "seething" about the personal relationship between Foley and Sands, which suggested favoritism to some. He ultimately concluded that the resentment was unfair and counterproductive. Foley, he says, is "a resourceful individual" with deep industry experience who "understands the relationships necessary to market a successful release." Touching on the stereotypical divide between commerce and art, or between head and heart, he adds, Foley "holds his cards close to his chest, while we wear our hearts on our sleeves. It's a personality clash as much as anything. If you meet him halfway, he's a good guy." The resentment was especially unfair to Sands, San Martin says. In addition to her "thorough background in retail and distribution," she is, he maintains, a likable person and "a big music fan. She is passionate and devoted to it. She isn't . . . hungry for every eccentric tidbit, but she loves the stuff. We've had long conversations about cool, off-kilter releases"—not old-time fiddle records, but not stereotypical major-label pap either.[80]

The *Phoenix* reported plunging morale in an April 2000 article that asked if Rounder was "going corporate" and claimed that between seven and ten longtime label employees had resigned in the preceding several months. Promotion chief Brad Paul, speaking in 2004, confirmed the staff upheaval. "There was a lot of turnover three to four years ago, when it seemed like every time I turned around, another face was leaving. Some left on their own, some didn't."[81] Resentment reached a peak in March 2000 when Foley fired Glenn Jones, the twenty-three-year employee who served as union shop steward and had negotiated every one of Rounder's union contracts. At the time of his termination, Jones was using company e-mail to circulate a draft letter objecting to the recent promotion of Sands. Foley learned of the draft, and within six days Jones received three separate warnings of poor performance or violation of company rules—sufficient grounds for dismissal under the union contract.

After consultation among Virant and the founders, Jones was fired. Noting the context within which he received his sudden cluster of warnings, Jones argued that his termination was obviously in retaliation for protected union activity and was an attempt to frighten activists and break the union. The founders maintained that not only were the stated grounds valid but Jones had also been an unduly disruptive influence for years, beyond the requirements of his union role. Jones initiated a formal grievance procedure in an effort to win reinstatement. While the matter was pending, however, the parties agreed that Jones would cease all efforts to return in exchange for a confidential monetary settlement. The dispute caught the attention of *Billboard*, which saw in this "contorted tale" confirmation that "though some ignored it until recently, Rounder is very much in the record business, and that business sometimes entails some unpleasant realities and tactics."[82]

To the founders, the Jones affair unfairly tarred the public image of a new management team they consider highly qualified and essential to survival. Eventually, the internal disarray calmed down. The staff stabilized with a mixture of old and new employees, and everyone, Brad Paul insists, is "on the same page."[83] In 2006, a majority of qualified employees signed a union decertification petition, and Rounder's status as a union shop came to an end. In the minds of union opponents, this reflects the contentment of Rounder's employees, who no longer find organized labor relevant to their needs. For others, this is the sad and inevitable result of a conscious management effort to cull union supporters from the payroll. The truth may lie somewhere in between, but behind the union's demise lies the continued existence of cultural divisions at Rounder, which likely mirror broader divisions beyond the label's walls.

Terry Kitchen was one of Rounder's last union shop stewards, and he was a vocal proponent of continued union representation. A songwriter, performer, and recording artist who has worked at Rounder since 1988, Kitchen exemplifies the type of socially aware artist that one would expect to find making common cause with the label's original progressive and collectivist impulses. In voicing support for the union, he did not speak of personal benefits. Instead, he emphasized the value of a common purpose among workers. With a union, he stressed, even the lowest-paid employees know that others are watchful of their interests. Without prompting, he speaks of the salutary role that unions have played in American life, and he expresses dismay that a record label that has exalted labor through art would reject its own connection to the union movement.[84]

Whereas some coworkers characterized Glenn Jones as a divisive figure, Kitchen exudes calm and humility. He concedes that Rounder's management undoubtedly favored union decertification, but he makes no claim that the company purged union supporters inappropriately. Indeed, he accepts some personal responsibility for the union's demise, and it saddens him that he was not able to present a more persuasive case on labor's behalf. Speculating on why Rounder employees discarded their union, he cites a variety of factors. The country is becoming less conscious of social-justice issues, he says, and so are the young people coming to work at Rounder. Certain label fringe benefits have become so institutionalized that newer, younger employees are ignorant of the union's role in securing such advantages. Given changes in Rounder's distribution system, the percentage of warehouse workers at the label is declining while that of office workers is growing. Thus, while the union's more labor-friendly blue-collar base shrinks, an increasing percentage of white-collar staffers is identifying with management, with whom they work side by side within the company offices.[85]

In contrast to Kitchen, the two young antiunion employees who spearheaded the decertification drive appear devoid of either communal impulses or any sense of history. The sole factor that drove their union opposition, they maintain, was their personal aversion to the payment of union dues. Each states that they received no benefit from the union and preferred to divert dues money into their personal retirement accounts. One stresses that since the union's demise he continued to receive health and dental insurance, apparently ignorant of the fact that past union advocacy prompted such benefits in the first place. That same individual expresses dismay that dues were not, in his view, used for any meaningful purpose. In his own comments on dues, Kitchen expresses pride that, in part, they funded English-language classes and computer instruction for immigrant union members who were not necessarily Rounder employees. Seemingly, such activities are of little consequence to those who evaluate dues solely by determining the percentage of money that flows, directly, back into their pockets.[86]

Kitchen allows that his social views have no direct impact on the sale of records, and he acknowledges that Rounder may do a better job of selling records today than it did a dozen years ago. Moreover, this exceedingly brief snapshot of union supporters and opponents cannot reflect fully the undoubtedly complex viewpoints of the varied men and women that the company employs. Yet there remains value in understanding the distinction between these self-appointed union proponents and opponents. If Rounder holds a special place in American cultural history, beyond the selling of records, it is because it once chose to articulate a progressive vision that reflects the American spirit at its most generous. Almost forty years after the company began, Kitchen continues to exemplify that vision. If his views are replaced entirely by the self-interested stance expressed by the union foes, then Rounder has changed in truly fundamental ways, quite apart from any change reflected by the musical genres it represents or the nature of its commercial alliances. Even absent a union, Rounder can choose, in its treatment of employees, to exemplify American progressivism at its best.

The distribution arrangement that Virant structured in 1998 has survived through the Universal Music Group, Polygram's corporate successor. It gives Universal a stake in the success of selected albums that have the potential to appeal to a reasonably sized niche audience of the type that favors, for example, the relatively mainstream sounds of Nanci Griffith or Alison Krauss. The distributor employs a professional promotion staff that works with both Rounder and retailers. It also handles the physical manufacture of the discs, ships them, provides store play copies, and replenishes depleted stock. In 2004 Rounder's top retail accounts were all national chains—Barnes and Noble, Borders, Best Buy, and Wal-Mart, with Internet pioneer Amazon rounding out the top five. The label could not market to these retailers, says Nowlin, by taking the approach it had used with the "old Tower," which was staffed by music devotees eager to stock at least one of everything. These contemporary merchandisers, for good or ill, work more effectively with an entity such as Universal. Nowlin praises Sands—whom he calls a "brilliant" music promoter—and Foley for their ability to serve as crucial "translators" between Rounder's historical culture and the contemporary record industry.[87]

Rounder generally seeks Universal distribution for only those albums that are projected to sell at least seventy-five hundred copies, making an occasional exception for a touring artist with the potential to build an audience. The label does not want to strain the relationship by pushing obviously poor sellers through the major-label distribution system. Although seventy-five hundred units is an extraordinarily low threshold where the majors are concerned, it is historically higher than the sales enjoyed by much of Rounder's inventory. Albums expected to sell below this threshold are distributed through several respected independents. These smaller firms continue to survive, but they have neither the financial wherewithal of Universal nor the leverage afforded by the larger firm's major-label catalogs. Much of the music that once formed Rounder's heart goes through such independent distribution. This includes most Cajun and zydeco music, old-time musicians such as Dirk Powell, and all of Mark Wilson's output. Although these smaller sellers receive little or no promotional money, Rounder continues to release them, and Nowlin argues that placing a niche album with a willing distributor geared toward such product affords it far better treatment than placement with an uninterested Universal.[88]

Zoe Records, the middle-of-the-road rock imprint Virant began in 1998, seems tailor-made for a major-label distributor that wants—with relatively little risk—to embrace contemporary pop and rock that appeals to those suddenly sought-after consumers over the age of twenty-five. Better-known signings include the Cowboy Junkies, a critics' favorite that emerged in the eighties with an ethereal, vaguely country-tinged sound, and Lisa Loeb, a pop songwriter who had previously placed tunes on the soundtracks to main-stream films such as *Reality Bites* and *Legally Blonde*. In 2003, Zoe's release of *Failer* by the young Canadian Kathleen Edwards prompted an outpouring of critical praise, much of which compared her to rocker Sheryl Crow and country/folk favorite Lucinda Williams. Critic Michael D. Clark offered a fairly typical observation in noting that Edwards mixed "arena guitars and lap steel with country twang and punkish moans." Zoe has also entered the DVD market, releasing among other things a disc featuring contemporary concert footage of seventies star Boz Scaggs singing his greatest hits. Among the imprint's odder releases is *Rush in Rio*, a DVD of the once popular hard-rock trio whose lyrics display a penchant for science fiction and fantasy themes. A classic rock band for the trailing edge of the baby boom, Rush was Virant's favorite group when he was growing up. Although it prompted a good deal of discussion, skeptical founders deferred to their CEO's passion. "No way," says Nowlin, when asked if any of the founders would have conceived of such a project, adding that he "couldn't name a single song on the thing." Mainstream rock, however, has its advantages. The label budgeted *Rush in Rio* to break even if thirty-five thousand units sold. By late 2004 sales had exceeded two hundred thousand, making it among Rounder's most successful offerings.[89]

Whether or not one enjoys Zoe's artistic direction, it is clear that the imprint's music bears little relation to that which made its parent label unique. In the long run, it remains to be seen whether the Zoe aesthetic is a harbinger of an entirely new direction for Rounder or something that supplements, and financially assists, a continued focus on vernacular sounds in a tough retail climate. Mark Moss feared in 1998 that the Polygram—now the Universal—arrangement could spell the end of the small-selling traditional records that Rounder has historically championed. The virtually simultaneous creation of Zoe underscored that concern. Though Rounder's overall output reflects a growing percentage of Zoe music, recent history suggests that the label is hewing to its original mission to a considerable degree. In part it is accomplishing this through the extensive use of anthologies that repackage music that the label had released previously. In the wake of *O Brother*'s success, for example, Rounder released a string of bluegrass and old-time music anthologies—ten in 2002 alone—each containing previously issued material. These include collections devoted to, among other things, gospel bluegrass, bluegrass versions of well-known pop and rock songs, bluegrass performed by women, and bluegrass paeans to motherhood.

Repackaging is nothing new in the record industry, and Rounder has repackaged its own material for some time, particularly since the mideighties arrival of the CD. Compilation albums are particularly desirable in the case of a label with Rounder's unique heritage. Due to the founders' eclecticism, their aggressive release schedule, and their heavy focus on active performers, Rounder's back catalog is one of the preeminent sites of recorded vernacular music created by musicians active in the final third of the twentieth century. In an increasingly restrictive retail environment, anthologies constitute one way to keep such older material in stores. Crowded retail outlets are quick to jettison discs, especially if an artist is no longer active or was never a commercial success. A well-packaged compilation offering an appealing theme, contemporary artwork, and updated liner notes is more likely to attract the attention of both retailers and music journalists than the straight reissue of an old album. Few retailers, for example, would stock separate CD reissues of Rounder's original LPs by the Fuzzy Mountain String Band. However, a single disc compilation with historical notes and new artwork found a place on store shelves in 1995, bringing new attention to this influential group.[90]

The continued availability of Rounder's cultural treasure trove is important, but the test of whether the label remains a vital presenter of vernacular expression depends on the extent to which it releases new music by active musicians. By the year 2000 its early models, Folkways and Arhoolie, had, in comparative terms, turned into musical museums, largely content to reissue older material on CD. Rounder, by contrast, has never stopped issuing current material, though market realities have compelled it to alter its commercial standards. In the beginning it issued what the founders liked, ignoring commercial considerations entirely. Later, the founders would consider releasing an album if they anticipated that it would break even. However, speaking at the 1998 Folk Alliance conference, Irwin explained that breaking even is no longer sufficient unless the project is "folklorically important," such as the collected works of folklorist Alan Lomax or the repertoire of fiddler Ed Haley.[91]

Given contemporary market forces, Irwin often evaluates more than music when he considers signing an artist. He wants to know whether a performer has the business sense needed to succeed in a competitive professional environment or the commitment to learn. He considers whether the artist is willing to tour, to work with an agent, to meet with the press, and to handle these functions in a responsible manner. In considering the wealth of material that hopeful musicians submit to Rounder, he evaluates everything from the packaging of their homemade audition CDs to the quality of their press packets. Though this material is all likely to change if an artist is signed, he nonetheless notices whether artists strive to present themselves from the outset in a professional manner. Such considerations would never have allowed for the release of George Pegram's Rounder debut, but Irwin believes that they are necessary if music is to gain a hearing in the crowded, competitive contemporary marketplace.[92]

Despite Irwin's conscious winnowing process, Rounder, to its credit, continues to release music by idiosyncratic vernacular artists, many of whom are unlikely to become polished self-promoters. In some cases, it appears, the nature and quality of the music prevail over any commercial consideration. In 2003 Mark Wilson, Rounder's longtime advocate of deep tradition, produced an album by fiddler and singer Donald MacLellan that Wilson, ever the purist, hopes will help cut through the "balderdash [that] has been promoted under the heading of 'Celtic music.'"[93] In the economically fickle field of Cajun music, the hard-touring Steve Riley and the Mamou Playboys have continued to record for Rounder, as has Charivari, a traditionally based acoustic quintet that released its second Rounder CD in 2005. In the first years of the twenty-first century a random and decidedly partial selection of other Rounder releases included albums from acoustic bluesman Corey Harris, conjunto master Mingo Saldivar, and Cape Breton fiddler Natalie MacMaster, a major draw on the festival circuit. Rounder stalwart Jimmy Sturr, a Grammy-winning star of the polka circuit, has released an album each year between 1994 and 2004.

Since the year 2000, Rounder's country music offerings—broadly defined—have included albums by the young bluegrass traditionalists Open Road, as well as additional bluegrass releases from the well-established Doyle Lawson and Quicksilver and the widely heralded singer James King, whom the label brought to roots music prominence in the 1990s. Contemporary old-time performances came from Dirk Powell, Bruce Molsky, the married duo of Ginny Hawker and Tracy Schwarz, and the youthful, all-female Uncle Earl. In 2006 Rounder released the nationally distributed debut of hard-country honky-tonker James Hand, who had been performing away from the media's eye for more than thirty years. Fifty-three years old at the time of the release, Hand was only six years younger than George Pegram was in 1970, when the old-time banjo master seemed so ancient to the young Rounder founders. His style, reminiscent of that which Hank Williams and Lefty Frizzell pioneered in the 1950s, is more distant in time from its commercial heyday than Pegram's old-time sound was at the time of his Rounder debut, illustrating the long-standing truism that "folk music" is often the pop music of an earlier era.

Commentators who imply that Rounder was a relatively static cottage industry for twenty-five or thirty years before suddenly "going corporate" simply do not understand the label's history. Rounder began as an idealized romantic hobby, but its founders realized quickly that they needed to master business fundamentals if they wanted people to hear their records. To a considerable degree it was artists—northern hippies and southern authentics alike—who prompted this change. These artists embraced the medium of records to reach the public and, in many cases, to earn a living, and they expected their record company to help them achieve these goals.

Every forward step the Rounders have taken has been in furtherance of their continued desire to sell an eclectic array of music. Viewed in this light, the sales tables at festivals, the initial distribution efforts, the embrace of professional marketing strategies, the installation of a new generation of management, the alliance with Universal, and the creation of Zoe Records have all been of a piece. Each has helped foster the creation and dissemination of a diverse selection of vernacular music unlike anything that anyone else has produced. Folkways never embraced commercial reality to the same degree. It withered on the vine until the Smithsonian purchased it in 1987 and rejuvenated it, though largely as an archive. Elektra went pop and stopped producing tradition-based music. Arhoolie has produced a stunning array of vernacular music but has only rarely managed to significantly support the financial aspirations of working performers. Postboom folk labels have been content to occupy tiny niches. Alligator, founded in 1971, confines itself to the blues. Red House, begun in the mid-1980s, specializes in contemporary singer-songwriters. Sugar Hill, now owned by the Welk Music Group, has emphasized contemporary bluegrass and its offshoots. Only Rounder, with more than three thousand releases, embraces the music of the world, the amateur as well as the professional.

Rounder is a labor of love that would not have existed but for the romantic yearnings of Irwin, Nowlin, and Leighton, who desired passionately to touch worlds other than their own. John Virant and his management team now tend to grand business strategies and mundane details. They act, however, in the context of the art that the founders choose to embrace. Once a week the founders join Billington, Virant, and a few other staffers to make decisions regarding Rounder's artists—current and potential—and their albums. They discuss who to sign and what to release. The founders show great deference to Virant, whom they clearly admire and respect. They claim, however, that they maintain the final say about the company's overall artistic balance.[94] Their historical involvement in creativity is a primary reason that Rounder has attained a position of unique importance in American culture. With respect to the label's enormous existing catalog, that position is secure. The unanswered question about the legacy of Rounder Records is whether the label will continue to be uniquely important once its founders leave the scene.

CONCLUSION

Gone to the Internet, Everyone

When she arrived in Malibu in 1989 to help midwife the birth of the Folk Alliance, Phyllis Barney was a government fishery expert who, in her spare time, ran a pioneering electronic bulletin board that helped folk fans keep abreast of performances and other community developments. With the encouragement of Alliance cofounder Clark Weissman, himself an early Internet user, Barney began presenting computer workshops at Alliance conferences, beginning with the second meeting in Philadelphia. The organization had been presenting such workshops for several years when the use of the Internet and the World Wide Web became pervasive, allowing people everywhere to communicate with one another instantaneously and en masse. Revivalists, like people involved in virtually every interest group imaginable, now communicate incessantly through a broad array of Listservs and Web-based bulletin boards.[1]

Whereas the Alliance conferences have been instrumental in diminishing revival factionalism, the Internet has also played a salutary role in that regard. Within online discussion groups, advice, information, and philosophical debate flow freely. Appalachian fiddle fans have conversations with singer-songwriters and Kingston Trio buffs, and the result is a new level of communication and understanding. Meaningful differences surface, of course, but—notwithstanding the inevitable presence of a few incessant quarrelers—debate usually fades after a few rounds of vigorous discussion. Since everyone has an opportunity to find a cyberaffinity group and to publicize his or her point of view, there is less sustained resentment.

Technology has also revolutionized the accessibility of recorded music. With so much music available on the Web, no one needs to feel aggrieved by the perceived dominance of one niche or another. The Rounder founders began their label in part because, just a few years after the boom, they could not locate recordings of the music they most enjoyed. In the 1990s, as consolidation tightened its stranglehold on the music industry, only the strongest small labels could endure. Those artist-oriented companies that released just a few commercially offbeat albums per year, and lacked a historical presence within the nonmainstream music industry, had little chance. No start-up label could have flourished by following the relatively loose-knit strategies that had worked for Rounder a quarter century earlier.

Fortunately—perhaps amazingly—just as one set of business conditions threatened folk music's commercial viability, a new set of conditions arose to offer the possibility of commercial rejuvenation. Readily accessible and easy-to-use digital software has revolutionized do-it-yourself recording. Musicians no longer need commercial studios and extraordinarily expensive equipment to make professional-sounding compact discs. The resulting profusion of self-made CDs has inundated the independent marketplace. Although virtually none of these recordings has any broad commercial impact, they may help an individual artist get gigs, and they invigorate the egalitarian spirit that folkies have always loved. Some of these CDs draw reviews from niche magazines such as *Sing Out!* and the *Old-Time Herald*, and folk radio has embraced the phenomenon. Discussion on FOLKDJ-L reveals many disc jockeys who take pride in cultivating those talented artists who seem the most independent, by virtue of their complete lack of affiliation with established labels or distribution streams.[2]

Acknowledging the profusion of self-made CDs, Rounder's Nowlin says that some artists make a reasonable choice in deciding to forego contracts with established labels such as his own. Those who don't wish to tour heavily, or who do not want to enmesh themselves in highly organized promotional efforts, may be better off, he says, selling CDs at shows and on the Web. That same choice would benefit artists whose sales expectations cannot justify foregoing the percentage of revenue retained by labels, distributors, and retailers. Not surprisingly, a sympathetic entrepreneur has devised an artist-friendly, for-profit sales and marketing system for these independent releases.

Derek Sivers, the creator and owner of CD Baby, is a "Rounder founder" for the twenty-first century. As an unknown musician in the midnineties, Sivers sold approximately fifteen hundred copies of his own self-manufactured CD, primarily through direct contact with fans at performances. He could not, however, obtain commercial distribution. Frustrated, he established his own online store in 1997 after asking a few musician friends if he could sell their recordings along with his own.[3]

In public Sivers is a personable and low-key self-promoter, and artists have embraced his business model. He serves musicians working in any genre provided they are "independent," which he defines—in typical art-versus-commerce fashion—as "not having sold one's life, career, and creative works over to a corporation." He will stock as few as five CDs from a single artist in return for a onetime charge, which was thirty-five dollars in the summer of 2007. Artists establish their own retail prices. Sivers charges a flat-fee per CD sold and guarantees that the artist will be paid within one week of every sale, even if that requires payment for only a single disc. Every day on which CD Baby sells a CD it sends an e-mail to the artist that provides, absent consumer objection, the name and address of the purchaser. For no additional fee his "store" offers an advertising page containing artist-created text, a link to the artist's Web site, and sound samples.

As of mid-2007 Sivers, now assisted by a paid staff, reported sales of 3.4 million physical CDs for 190,000 "independent" artists. Judging from extensive discussion on FOLKDJ-L and FOLKBIZ, musicians love CD Baby, which has maintained a reputation for integrity. One company feature that attracts artists and consumers alike is the organization of the "store," where Sivers demonstrates a good understanding of the practical subdivisions of the various genres offered. The "Folk" section has a "traditional" subcategory, along with other subdivisions bearing titles such as "Gentle" or "Angry" or "Political" or—revealing a keen sense of revival history—"like Joni."

Ultimately, digital technology may alter permanently the manner in which artists and entrepreneurs deliver recorded music to consumers, perhaps leading to the complete disappearance of physical CDs. At the start of the new millennium, sales of CDs have been trending downward, while digital sales of individual songs have been rising. In 2005 alone, digital downloads increased by approximately 150 percent over the prior year. In the final week of 2005, the sale of digital tracks increased threefold over such sales one year earlier. Moreover, by 2005's end, the sale of digital playback systems began to outstrip that of traditional systems that play only physical

CDs. Some industry executives are hesitant to concede that these numbers forecast a permanent trend. Indeed, in the second quarter of 2006 download sales showed signs of leveling off. Other observers, however, see this latest development as nothing more than a momentary market fluctuation. Downloading, they insist, will dominate the music industry's still-evolving future, offering new opportunities for eclectic, independent music makers in all genres.[4]

This technological and commercial revolution should help assuage Mark Moss's onetime fear regarding the continued availability of the niche music he loves. With the ability to forego not only the mass manufacture of discs, but also brick-and-mortar retail and traditional distribution networks, an optimistic John Janick, cofounder of the independent label Fueled by Ramen, notes that music lovers, more than ever before, now "have everything at their fingertips. They can go find something that's cool and different. They can tell people about it and it starts spreading." Visitors to the "honkingduck" Web site, for example, can listen, without charge, to more than seven hundred recordings made from the 1920s to the 1940s, encompassing "early country music, string bands, dance calls, sacred harp, skits, ballads, popular songs, etc." The Web is filled with "playlists" compiled by fans who group songs by artist, genre, age, or country of origin, alerting like-minded aficionados to the music's existence and its cyberspace location. The resulting "democratization of music," in the words of writer Jeff Leeds, stands on the cusp of "shifting the industry's balance of power" away from entertainment conglomerates and toward artists and fans.[5]

Countless legal downloading services have made commercially available the catalogs of thousands of small labels from around the world. In 2005 Smithsonian Folkways Recordings launched Smithsonian Global Sound, which sells digital versions of almost the entire Folkways catalog, as well as the archival holdings of the International Library of African Music, in Grahamstown, South Africa, plus recorded music from the Archive and Research Centre for Ethnomusicology, in New Delhi, India. On a slightly more popular front, celebrated jazz label Verve has initiated the Verve Vault, through which it makes digitally available thousands of previously out-of-print recordings that form a significant part of the story of American jazz. CD Baby has embraced this new digital world, and it now offers artists the option of selling tracks through partnerships with more than fifty legal downloading services. These varied digital entrepreneurs all hope to profit not by "the standard industry strategy" of selling millions of copies of relatively few albums but by selling mere hundreds of copies of thousands of albums.[6]

Rounder has also seen downloading's commercial and cultural potential. In 2005 the label inaugurated "The Rounder Archive," which offers digitized albums, old and new, that the company can no longer market economically in physical form. Consumers can download both music and liner notes. Those who wish to order a custom-made physical CD can do that as well. With each disc burned to order, manufacturing costs are virtually nonexistent, and there is no need for warehousing. Still avid preservationists, the founders are excited about the possibility of being able to reissue some of the more esoteric parts of their collection. "We always felt bad," Nowlin says, "about . . . albums that we really loved but can't figure out a way to possibly sell right now. Maybe," he adds, "[digital downloading] is a way." Discussing the project, Irwin voices a fan's distress about the recording industry's more confining economic realities. "When we started out," he says, "we resented the major labels who owned the Charlie Poole, Gid Tanner, Monroe Brothers, etc., masters and wouldn't put out the material." Now, he adds, "we find that we've been doing the same and of course we have a better understanding of why they didn't do so back then." Downloading, he hopes, will offer "a way in which we can make material available in a cost effective way but still with quality intact."[7]

As an inevitable outgrowth of the never-ending revival, the "idea of the folk" continues to make periodic incursions into mass culture. In 2003 the film *A Mighty Wind* offered a humorous but fond look back at the days of the great boom. Presented as a mock documentary, this cinematic roman à clef pokes gentle fun at some of the more whitewashed commercial performers who were successful back when ersatz folk music dominated popular entertainment. The film ignores virtually every element of the boom in its focus on high-energy Kingston Trio clones and overly romanticized pseudoballadry. It presents neither serious folk song scholarship nor old-time music, bluegrass, or blues. It contains nary a hint of left-wing politics. In short, it highlights the quintessentially one-dimensional view of the folk phenomenon that staunch revivalists have always loathed.

Folk fans, however, seemed to love it. At the least, a clear majority of vocal folk fans who posted comments on various Internet discussion lists loved it. Dissenting voices generally complained that it was simply not funny enough. In part, this acceptance stems from revivalists' desire to avoid the public image of dour solemnity that the film gently mocks. Folk fans understand that their long insistence on playing music "right," along with popular caricatures of stern "protest singers," has led to a perception that they are a particularly humorless crowd. In their generally positive response to *A Mighty Wind*, revivalists have shown that they can laugh at themselves.

Judging by the same discussion lists, revivalists have also demonstrated a willingness to embrace their own history in full. It has been decades since the Kingston Trio "threatened" an idealized folk heritage, and the passage of time has helped place the trio's role in perspective. In the sixties they appeared to be a dominant force, pushing aside "worthier" efforts. Decades later, it's apparent that this perceived dominance lasted for just a brief moment within an ongoing movement that has endured for more than 150 years. In context, the trio was important but hardly preeminent. Revivalists have also arrived at a greater acceptance of the valuable role that commerce and popularization can play in the preservation and dissemination of traditional heritage. No less a personage than Bob Dylan has acknowledged, "I liked The Kingston Trio. Even though their style was polished and collegiate, I liked most of their stuff anyway."[8]

Whereas many revivalists still treasure their outsider status, others revel in those moments when "their" music bubbles into the mainstream. One of the most celebrated such moments occurred in 2006, when rock legend Bruce Springsteen released *We Shall Overcome: The Seeger Sessions*, an album of traditional tunes, civil rights anthems, and antiwar songs drawn from Pete Seeger's recorded repertoire. Accompanied by roughly a dozen musicians, Springsteen utterly transforms Seeger's simple guitar and banjo arrangements, as he imbues the tunes with elements of gospel, Dixieland jazz, western swing, Irish reels, rock and roll, and a variety of other sonic flourishes. The album begins with the star's raucous, laughing countdown to the traditional "Old Dan Tucker," signifying that this is, for the most part, a party record. Describing the project, Springsteen confirms that he wanted "a wild sound . . . a whiskey drinking sound."[9]

Springsteen goes on to complain that people—presumably, himself included—too often forget the greatness of America's traditional folk song repertoire. Acknowledging implicitly the value of earlier innovators such as the Highwoods String Band or Louisiana's Beau Jocque, he says that this is music that has gotten lost "by the fact that it hasn't been recontextualized" for a new era. "If you recontextualize the stuff a little bit," he explains, "it comes to life again." Thus, by his own recontextualization, Springsteen manages to pay homage to revival legend Seeger while simultaneously distancing himself from stiffer notions of authenticity that have too often situated the revival as something apart from popular culture—something overly precious or harshly didactic.[10]

Beyond affirming the inherent beauty and vibrancy of the songs, Springsteen reminds us of revivalism's eternal verities—the continuing value of homemade music, of vernacular art, of social activism, and of our ongoing concern about the potential pitfalls of technological change. He claims, for example, that the album was recorded live, at his home, by an unrehearsed band that functioned largely as a jam session. He speaks of the need to appreciate the diverse geographic "locales that music gets made in," observing that in "big places . . . you get all the things that come with modern life, but you lose some of the grit." He discusses the value of "true folk instruments . . . that didn't have to be plugged in," because they were "made for travel" and were thus suitable for "bars and union halls" as well as for homes. He talks about the difference between music that is "made," by which he appears to refer to that which is crafted carefully for mass consumption, and music that is "played," or created in the moment by artists following nothing but their creative instincts.[11] His words are overly romantic, perhaps. Still, Springsteen helps expose one more new audience—in a never-ending chain of new audiences—to these issues, which constitute an integral part of folk music revivalism's ongoing quest for meaning.

Springsteen's fame and his major record label ensured a large audience for *The Seeger Sessions*. With the music industry in a state of extraordinary flux, the extent to which new recording and distribution technologies will offer unknown musicians their own artistic and commercial opportunities remains to be seen. Some industry participants believe that traditional business structures will necessarily survive, if only to serve those artists who seek mass popularity. If you want "to sell millions of records worldwide," says Rob Wells of Universal Music, "you'll need the infrastructure a major record deal will give you, because it's expensive."[12]

To most in the folk world, however, such grandiose needs are irrelevant. Tom Neff, a onetime Folk Alliance board president, embraces the digital revolution, which he predicts will prompt a "renaissance" in the "personal music making" that constitutes the essence of folk. Neff runs Grassy Hill Radio, a free service that streams folk music of every imaginable type over the Internet twenty-four hours per day, seven days per week. He welcomes submissions from unknown artists who can, "with nothing more than the Internet, a sound card, a CD-R and a printer . . . produce and distribute high fidelity music, press it, print it, and stream it to the world." Neff anticipates decades of warfare involving intellectual property rights and technological freedom. In the end, however, he foresees "the piecemeal destruction of a commercial house of cards" that is now struggling to retain control of the recording and distribution of music. "People can take their ideas straight to MP3 and the world," he says, "and you and I can hear them, and that, my friends, will revive [the] folk process." In the meantime, Neff emphasizes, those who advocate art that is idiosyncratic, daring, and community based must remember that, in the end, "folk wins. Folk will win. Music will win."[13]

Notes

INTRODUCTION: WHERE HAVE ALL THE FOLKIES GONE?

1. *Program Book: 16th Annual International Folk Alliance Conference* (San Diego, Calif., 2004), 2.

2. Jeff Eilenberg, "What's Happening," *Sing Out!* February–April 1993, 5.

3. "Folk Frenzy," *Time*, July 11, 1960, 81; "It's Folksy . . . It's Delightful, It's a Craze," *Newsweek*, June 6, 1960, 112.

4. Neil V. Rosenberg, introduction to *Transforming Tradition: Folk Music Revivals Examined*, edited by Rosenberg (Urbana: University of Illinois Press, 1993), 1–2; Ralph Rinzler in "The Folksong Revival: A Symposium," *New York Folklore Quarterly* 19 (1963): 83, 129.

5. On earlier uses of folk culture, see Jane S. Becker, *Selling Tradition: Appalachia and the Construction of an American Folk, 1930–1940* (Chapel Hill: University of North Carolina Press, 1998); Robbie Lieberman, *My Song Is My Weapon: People's Songs, American Communism, and the Politics of Culture, 1930–1950* (Urbana: University of Illinois Press, 1989); and David E. Whisnant, *All That Is Native and Fine: The Politics of Culture in an American Region* (Chapel Hill: University of North Carolina Press, 1983).

6. Archie Green, "The Campus Folksong Club: A Glimpse at the Past," in *Transforming Tradition*, edited by Rosenberg, 61, 66.

7. Marc Eliot, *Death of a Rebel: A Biography of Phil Ochs* (1979; reprint, New York: Franklin Watts, 1989); Michael Schumacher, *There but for Fortune: The Life of Phil Ochs* (New York: Hyperion, 1996).

8. For a discussion of the different performing styles of revival singers, see Robert S. Whitman and Sheldon S. Kagen, "The Performance of Folksongs on Recordings," in *The American Folk Scene: Dimensions of the Folksong Revival*, ed. David A. De Turk and A. Poulin Jr. (New York: Dell Publishing, 1967), 72.

9. I. Sheldon Posen, "On Folk Festivals and Kitchens: Questions of Authenticity in the Folksong Revival," in *Transforming Tradition*, edited by Rosenberg, 127.

10. Ibid., 133–14.

11. Ibid., 136.

12. *Program Book: 5th Annual International Folk Alliance Conference* (Tucson, 1993), 6.

13. For a concise survey of early country music duet singing, see Charles Wolfe, "Close Harmony," chap. 2 of *In Close Harmony: The Story of the Louvin Brothers* (Jackson: University Press of Mississippi, 1996).

14. Kate Brislin and Katy Moffatt, *Sleepless Nights*, Rounder Records CD 0374. Randy Pitts' liner notes tell the story of the all-night Tucson singing session.

15. For attendance figures, see "Tucson '93: How Can I Keep from Singing?" *Folk Alliance Newsletter* (Summer 1993): 1; "Folk Alliance Conference in Boston Surpasses All Records," *Folk Alliance Newsletter* (Summer 1994): 1.

16. Bruce Jackson, "The Folksong Revival," *New York Folklore* 11 (1985): 195, 201 (reprinted with modifications in *Transforming Tradition*, edited by Rosenberg, 73).

17. Gene Bluestein, *Poplore: Folk and Pop in American Culture* (Amherst: University of Massachusetts Press, 1994); Robert Cantwell, *When We Were Good: The Folk Revival* (Cambridge: Harvard University Press, 1996); Ronald D. Cohen, *Rainbow Quest: The Folk Music Revival and American Society, 1940–1970* (Amherst: University of Massachusetts Press, 2002); Ronald D. Cohen, ed., *Wasn't That a Time! Firsthand Accounts of the Folk Music Revival* (Metchuen, N.J.: Scarecrow Press, 1995); Ron Eyerman and Andrew Jamison, *Music and Social Movements: Mobilizing Traditions in the Twentieth Century* (Cambridge: Cambridge University Press, 1998); Rosenberg, *Transforming Tradition*. Published later is Dick Weissman, *Which Side Are You On? An Inside History of the Folk Music Revival in America* (New York: Continuum, 2005).

18. "Folk entrepreneur" is from R. Serge Denisoff, "The Proletarian Renascence: The Folkness of the Ideological Folk," *Journal of American Folklore* 82 (January 1969): 51. In 1996 Randy Pitts moved to Nashville and became an artists' booking agent.

19. Balfa quotation from "Dirk Powell and Christine Balfa of Balfa Toujours," interview by Hadley Castille, http://www.whatbayou.com/balfatoujours.html.

20. Dirk Powell, interview.

21. Dana Jennings, "A Regular Gig on the Far Side of Celebrity," *New York Times*, January 11, 1998, AR1, 42.

22. Jeff Davis, "Traditional," *Folk Alliance Newsletter*, July–October 2003, 17, 18.

23. See Scott Alarik, *Deep Community: Adventures in the Modern Folk Underground* (Cambridge, Mass.: Black Wolf Press, 2003).

CHAPTER 1: FOLKLORE, FAKELORE, AND POPLORE:

FROM THE CREATION OF THE FOLK TO THE GREAT BOOM

AND BEYOND

1. Frank Page quoted in Teddy Allen, "All Shook Up: Elvis Took Local Fans for an Unforgettable (Hay)ride," *Shreveport Times*, August 16, 2002, A1.

2. "Folk Music, What's That? *Sing Out!* Asks Pete Seeger," *Sing Out!* 2, no. 3 (1980): 2, 3.

3. "Hip-Hop as Folk Culture," *Program Book: 13th Annual International Folk Alliance Conference* (Vancouver, B.C., 2001), 83. The program characterized early hip-hop as "the shared expression of a distinct community."

4. Information regarding the World Wide Web location of all the electronic discussion groups mentioned in this book appears in the "Note on Citations."

5. Post by BillK RB12, "Jewel, Can She Be Defined as a Folk or Pop Singer?" rec.music.folk, June 7, 1997.

6. Mark D. Moss, "The First Words," *Sing Out!* August–October 1994, 2.

7. Mark Moss, interview.

8. Andrew L. Yarrow, "Resurgent Sing-alongs Mix Banjos with Environmental-

ism," *New York Times*, October 13, 1992, B4; Don McLeese, "Don't Let the 'Folk' Fool You: Bash Is Fun," *Austin American-Statesman*, July 23, 1995, B1; Amy Phillips, "Folk the Pain Away," *Village Voice*, January 24, 2003; Jon Pareles, "Madonna's Real Art: Getting Attention," *New York Times*, April 18, 2003, E1.

9. Tom Lanham, "Rhapsody in Blue," *Pulse*, February 2001, 32.

10. Daniel Gewertz, "Clueless: Mainstream Media Gets Folk Wrong, Over and Over," *Boston Herald*, December 20, 2002, S23.

11. *Funk and Wagnalls Standard Dictionary of Folklore, Mythology, and Legend*, 1949 ed., s.v. "Folklore."

12. Jan Harold Brunvand, "New Directions for the Study of American Folklore," reprinted in *Readings in American Folklore*, edited by Brunvand (New York: W. W. Norton, 1979), 416, 417 (published originally in the journal *Folklore* [1971]); Brunvand, ed., *American Folklore: An Encyclopedia* (New York: Garland Publishing, 1996), s.v. "Folklore."

13. The four paragraph-closing quotations come, respectively, from Ilana Harlow, "Introduction," *Journal of American Folklore* 111 (1998): 231; Roger Abrahams, "The Public, the Folklorist, and the Public Folklorist," in *Public Folklore*, edited by Robert Baron and Nicholas Spitzer (Washington, D.C.: Smithsonian Institution Press, 1992), 17, 19; Ian McKay, *The Quest of the Folk: Antimodernism and Cultural Selection in Twentieth-Century Nova Scotia* (Montreal: McGill-Queen's University Press, 1994), 3; and Jackson Lears, "Packaging the Folk: Tradition and Amnesia in American Advertising, 1880–1940," in *Folk Roots, New Roots: Folklore in American Life*, edited by Jane S. Becker and Barbara Franco (Lexington, Mass.: Museum of Our National Heritage, 1988), 103.

14. Regina Bendix, *In Search of Authenticity: The Formation of Folklore Studies* (Madison: University of Wisconsin Press, 1997), 21. Bendix asked these questions with respect to the construct of "authenticity."

15. Bluestein, *Poplore*, 101 (see introduction, n. 17).

16. For disciplinary histories, see Simon J. Bronner, *American Folklore Studies: An Intellectual History* (Lawrence: University Press of Kansas, 1986); and Rosemary Levy Zumwalt, *American Folklore Scholarship: A Dialogue of Dissent* (Bloomington: Indiana University Press, 1984).

17. William Thoms, "Folklore," in *The Study of Folklore*, edited by Alan Dundes (Englewood Cliffs, N.J.: Prentice-Hall, 1965), 4–6 (Thoms published originally in 1846). See also Duncan Emrich, "'Folklore': William John Thoms," *California Folklore Quarterly* 5 (1946): 355–74 and, for the concluding Thoms quote, 360.

18. "On the Field and Work of a Journal of American Folk-lore," *Journal of American Folk-lore* 1 (1888): 3–7.

19. Dillon Bustin, "New England Prologue," in *Folk Roots*, edited by Becker and Franco, 3.

20. Richard M. Dorson, *Folklore and Fakelore: Essays toward a Discipline of Folk Studies* (Cambridge: Harvard University Press, 1976), 33–34.

21. Kay L. Cothran, "Participation in Tradition," in *Readings in American Folklore*, edited by Brunvand, 444, 445 (see chap. 1, n. 12).

22. Becker, *Selling Tradition*, 19 (see introduction, n. 5).

23. Edward Tylor, writing in 1871, quoted in Simon J. Bronner, *Following Tradition: Folklore in the Discourse of American Culture* (Logan: Utah State University Press, 1998), 16.

24. Archie Green, *Only a Miner: Studies in Recorded Coal-Mining Songs* (Urbana: University of Illinois Press, 1972), 5.

25. Henry Glassie, "Tradition," *Journal of American Folklore* 108 (1995): 395.

26. Bendix, *In Search of Authenticity*, 6, 68–76.

27. For discussions of authenticity in the context of contemporary music, see Joli Jensen, *The Nashville Sound: Authenticity, Commercialization, and Country Music* (Nashville: Country Music Foundation Press and Vanderbilt University Press, 1998); and David Grazian, *Blue Chicago: The Search for Authenticity in Urban Blues Clubs* (Chicago: University of Chicago Press, 2003).

28. Benjamin Filene, *Romancing the Folk: Public Memory and American Roots Music* (Chapel Hill: University of North Carolina Press, 2000), 12, 13, 15; Scott Alarik, "Child's Garden of Verses: The Life Work of Francis James Child," *Sing Out!* Winter 2003, 64; "Sybil with Guitar," *Time*, November 23, 1962, 54.

29. Filene, *Romancing the Folk*, 23.

30. John A. Lomax, comp., "Collector's Note," in *Cowboy Songs and Other Frontier Ballads* (New York: Macmillan, 1910), n.p.

31. Ibid.; Nolan Porterfield, *Last Cavalier: The Life and Times of John A. Lomax, 1867–1948* (Urbana: University of Illinois Press, 1996), 153–55, and, with respect to the original publication of "Home on the Range," 528n66. Regarding Child's editing, see Filene, *Romancing the Folk*, 14–15.

32. Bill C. Malone, *Country Music, U.S.A.*, rev. ed. (Austin: University of Texas Press, 1985), 38.

33. I draw my discussion of the early country music industry from ibid., 1–75; Archie Green, "Hillbilly Music: Source and Symbol," reprinted in *Torching the Fink Books, and Other Essays on Vernacular Culture*, by Green (Chapel Hill: University of North Carolina Press, 2001), 17 (article first published in 1965); Richard A. Peterson, *Creating Country Music: Fabricating Authenticity* (Chicago: University of Chicago Press, 1997).

34. Peterson, *Creating Country*, 14–15, 35; Green, "Hillbilly Music," 19. Throughout the literature, the phrase "old time" and the variant "old timey" are sometimes hyphenated and sometimes not. Except when quoting others, I use the hyphenated phrase "old-time," following the approach of the *Old-Time Herald*, the contemporary magazine devoted to the genre.

35. Wiggins is quoted in Peterson, *Creating Country*, 34; Malone, *Country Music, U.S.A.*, 45. My discussion of the commercialization of rural southern music draws from the latter, 1–75.

36. Peterson, *Creating Country*, 35.

37. Lieberman, *My Song Is My Weapon*, 35 (see introduction, n. 5); Richard A. Reuss, "American Folksong and Left-Wing Politics, 1935–56," *Journal of the Folklore Institute* 12 (1975): 94–95.

38. For a survey of published folk song collections in the first half of the twentieth century, see Debora Kodish, *Good Friends and Bad Enemies: Robert Winslow Gordon and the Study of American Folksong* (Urbana: University of Illinois Press, 1986), 1–12.

39. B. A. Botkin, ed., *A Treasury of American Folklore: Stories, Ballads, and Traditions of the People* (New York: Crown Publishers, 1944), 258–61 (Abe Lincoln), 230–40 (John Henry), 122 (Stackalee).

40. Ibid., xxi.

41. Richard M. Dorson, "Folklore and Fake Lore," *American Mercury*, March 1950, 335, 338–40.

42. Richard M. Dorson, "A Theory for American Folklore," in *American Folklore and the Historian*, by Dorson (Chicago: University of Chicago Press, 1971), 26–27 (chapter published originally in 1959).

43. Botkin, *Treasury of American Folklore*, xxiii; Dorson, *American Folklore and the Historian*, 45–47.

44. Tony Scherman, "This Man Captured the True Sounds of the Whole World," *Smithsonian*, August 1987, 110.

45. Nat Hentoff, "A Record Becomes Elektra: On the Birth of a Label," *Rogue*, July 1959, 21; Dave Van Ronk (writing as Blind Rafferty), "The Elektra Catalog: A Sarcophagus," *Caravan*, August 1957. Van Ronk confesses authorship in his memoir, *The Mayor of MacDougal Street*, by Van Ronk with Elijah Wald (Cambridge, Mass.: Da Capo Press, 2005), 64–65.

46. Happy Traum, interview.

47. "Like from the Halls of Ivy," *Time*, July 11, 1960, 56.

48. On "Tom Dooley's" success, see Cantwell, *When We Were Good*, 2 (see introduction, n. 17); Dave Van Ronk, interview.

49. Ron Radosh, "Commercialism and the Folk Song Revival," *Sing Out!* Spring 1959, 27; Stephen Fiott, "In Defense of Commercial Folk Singers," *Sing Out!* December 1962–January 1963, 43–45.

50. Sandy Paton, "Horton Barker: An Appreciation," *Sing Out!* April–May 1963, 5–6. For a similar treatment, see Frank Warner, "Frank Proffitt," *Sing Out!* October–November 1963, 6–9.

51. "Pickin' Scruggs," *Time*, June 30, 1961, 53; "The Milk Drinkers," *Newsweek*, August 12, 1963, 80.

52. "The Fourth Rose," *Time*, January 29, 1965, 68. See also "Wild about Harry," *Time*, July 1, 1957, 66; "Like from the Halls of Ivy," 56; "Pickin' Scruggs"; "The Faculty," *Time*, June 16, 1961, 56; "Reality in Academia," *Time*, October 16, 1961, 61; "Pop Records," *Time*, December 22, 1961, 40; "The Folk Girls," *Time*, June 1, 1962, 39; "It's Folksy," 112 (see introduction, n. 3); "Doubling His Talent," *Newsweek*, February 24, 1958, 63; "Strange Saga of a Song," *Newsweek*, November 24, 1958, 70; "Just Folks," *Newsweek*, October 1, 1962, 50; and "On the Road," *Newsweek*, September 28, 1964, 92.

53. "Folk Frenzy," *Time*, July 11, 1960, 81 (New Lost City Ramblers); "Folk Singers: Solitary Indian," *Time*, December 10, 1965, 62 (Buffy St. Marie); "The Fourth Rose" (Biff Rose); "Reality in Academia" (Highwaymen).

54. Traum, interview.

55. "Just Playin' Folks," *Saturday Evening Post*, May 30, 1964, 25 (Carolyn Hester); Cheryl Anne Brauner, "A Study of the Newport Folk Festival and the Newport Folk Foundation" (master's thesis, Memorial University of Newfoundland, 1983), 248; Judy Collins quoted in Jac Holzman and Gavin Daws, *Follow the Music: The Life and High Times of Elektra Records in the Great Years of American Pop Culture* (Santa Monica, Calif.: First Media Books, 1998), 140.

56. Robert Shelton, "Folk Music Festival," *Nation*, August 1, 1959, 59.

57. Robert Shelton, "5-Day Folk Fete Attracts 70,000," *New York Times*, July 29, 1968, sec. 1, p. 26; Ellen Willis, "Newport: You Can't Go Down Home Again," *New Yorker*, August 17, 1968, 86, 88, 90.

58. John S. Wilson, "Folk Fete Shines without Superstars," *New York Times*, July 22, 1969, sec. 1, p. 32.

59. Brauner, "Study of the Newport Folk Festival," 155; Wilson, "Folk Fete Shines."

60. Ted Drozdowski, "Folk Explosion," *Boston Phoenix*, July 12, 2001; Eric Von Schmidt and Jim Rooney, *Baby Let Me Follow You Down: The Illustrated Story of the Cambridge Folk Years*, 2d ed. (Amherst: University of Massachusetts Press, 1994), 301–2.

61. Von Schmidt and Rooney, *Baby Let Me*, 301–2, 304.

62. Roger Abrahams, "Folklore in Culture: Notes toward an Analytic Method," reprinted in *Readings in American Folklore*, edited by Brunvand, 390, 392.

63. Alan Dundes, *Essays on Folkloristics* (Meerut, India: Folklore Institute, 1978), 6–9 (emphasis in original).

64. Alan Dundes, *Folklore Matters* (Knoxville: University of Tennessee Press, 1989), 41–44, 53.

65. Dan Ben-Amos, "Toward a Definition of Folklore in Context," in *Toward New Perspectives in Folklore*, edited by Americo Paredes and Richard Bauman, 3–15 (Austin: University of Texas Press, 1972).

66. Ibid.

67. Bluestein, *Poplore*, 1–11; Green, *Only a Miner*, 3, 14.

68. Bluestein, *Poplore*, 101–2. Seeger's remarks appear in a back-cover blurb to the first paperback edition of ibid.

69. Archie Green, "Vernacular Music: A Naming Compass," *Musical Quarterly* 77 (1993): 35, 36, 43.

70. Neil Rossi, interview.

71. Happy Traum, "The Swan Song of Folk Music," *Rolling Stone*, May 17, 1969, insert, pp. 7–8.

72. David S. Rotenstein, "The Folk Festival Folks," *Philadelphia Inquirer*, August 23, 1992.

73. "What's Happening/Festivals/Fox Hollow," *Sing Out!* October–November 1967, 2.

74. Julie McCullough, "FSGW History" (1999), http://www.fsgw.org/history .htm. The examples of society activities are from *Folklore Society of Greater Wash-*

ington Newsletter, December 1999, 4–6. On Seamus Ennis, see Kristen Baggelaar and Donald Milton, *Folk Music: More than a Song* (New York: Thomas Y. Crowell, 1979), 121.

75. Larry Kelp, "Just Folk," *East Bay Express,* June 18, 1993, 1. For further information on the Freight and Salvage, see Philip Elwood, "25 Years of Roots and Hoots," *San Francisco Examiner,* June 4, 1993, D17; Sam McManis, "Just Plain Folk," *San Francisco Chronicle,* February 23, 2001; and Derk Richardson, "Half a Century High," *San Francisco Bay Guardian,* June 9, 1993.

76. Kelp, "Just Folk."

77. Andrew C. Revkin, "A Village Pied Piper for the Spirit of Folk," *New York Times,* national ed., January 4, 1999, B1, B5.

78. Jack Hardy, liner notes to the audio recording *Fast Folk: A Community of Singers and Songwriters,* Smithsonian Folkways Recordings, SFW CD 40135.

79. Noel Coppage, "Cornelia Street Songwriters Exchange: Does the Folkie Revival Start Here?" *Stereo Review,* December 1980, 85, 86 (emphasis in original); Rod MacDonald, "Hear Ye! Hear Ye! NYC: The Musician's Cooperative," *Sing Out!* July–September 1983, 24, 28.

80. Revkin, "Village Pied Piper."

81. MacDonald, "Hear Ye!"

82. From 1982 through the suspension of publication in 1997, *Fast Folk* released 105 issues, each consisting of a magazine and album. In 1999 the Smithsonian Institution acquired the series, along with the cooperative's archives. Smithsonian Folkways Recordings sells made-to-order CDs of any given *Fast Folk* recording. See Jeff Place, "The Songs, the Writers, and the Performers," in the liner notes to the audio recording *Fast Folk: A Community of Singers and Songwriters.*

83. All information regarding Clark Weissman's activities is from his interview with the author.

84. Information on the 2005 CTMS festival is from the organization's Web site, http://www.ctmsfolkmusic.org.

85. Dick Spottswood, "A 25th Anniversary Retrospect," *Bluegrass Unlimited,* July 1991, 22.

86. Evan Hatch, *"Living Blues:* Ever Living, Ever Growing," *Southern Register: The Newsletter of the Center for the Study of Southern Culture,* Fall 2000, 1, 3.

CHAPTER 2: FROM CLUB 47 TO UNION GROVE: THE BIRTH
OF ROUNDER RECORDS

1. Paul Grein, "Toto Is the Big Story at the 25th Annual Grammy Awards," *Billboard,* March 5, 1983, 3, 66.

2. Mark A. Humphrey, "Bright Lights, Big City: Urban Blues," in *Nothing but the Blues: The Music and the Musicians,* ed. Lawrence Cohn (New York: Abbeville Press, 1993), 175.

3. Scott Billington, interview; "uncomfortable concept" from Billington, e-mail to author, January 25, 2005. Billington coproduced *Alright Again!* with Brown's manager, Jim Bateman.

4. Howard Mandel, "Clarence 'Gatemouth' Brown: The Real Thing," *Down Beat*, September 1983, 23–25.

5. Michele Chihara, "Reeling at Rounder: Is Cambridge's Pet Indie Label Going Corporate?" *Boston Phoenix*, April 27, 2000.

6. Pete Welding, "George Thorogood and the Destroyers," *Down Beat*, July 13, 1978, 34.

7. Ken Irwin (B), interview; Irwin, e-mails to author, August 2, 2002.

8. Theodore Irwin, *Strange Passage* (New York: Harrison Smith and Robert Haas, 1935), 12, 179, 315.

9. Irwin (B), interview; Irwin, e-mail to author, August 2, 2002.

10. Christine Stansell, *American Moderns: Bohemian New York and the Creation of a New Century* (New York: Henry Holt, 2000), 240–41; Rita Irwin and Clementina Paolone, M.D., *Practical Birth Control: A Guide to Medically Approved Methods for the Married* (New York: Robert M. McBride, 1937), xii, xiii, 64 (emphasis in original).

11. Irwin, e-mails to author, October 4, 2002, May 6, 2004, March 31, 2006 (quote); Irwin (D), interview.

12. Quotations in this and the following paragraph are from Irwin (D), interview. Other material from Irwin (A), interview.

13. Irwin's first bluegrass album was *The Greenbriar Boys*, Vanguard Records VRS-9104 (1960). Details on the band are from Neil V. Rosenberg, *Bluegrass: A History* (Urbana: University of Illinois Press), 146–48, 158.

14. Nowlin (D), interview.

15. Nowlin (A), interview.

16. Nowlin (D), interview.

17. Ibid.

18. Irwin, e-mail to Lara Pellegrinelli, April 17, 1996.

19. Nowlin (A), interview.

20. David Haney, "Hillbilly at Harvard," *Bluegrass Unlimited*, April 1988, 58.

21. Nowlin (D), interview; Nowlin (A), interview (on cliquishness).

22. Nowlin (A), interview.

23. Nowlin (D), interview.

24. Nowlin (A), interview. See also Tony Trischka, "Ken Irwin and Rounder Records: 25 Years of Bluegrass," *Bluegrass Unlimited*, July 1996, 16, 17.

25. Regarding the Lillys and Hillbilly Ranch, see Sam Charters, "The Lilly Brothers of Hillbilly Ranch," *Sing Out!* July 1965, 19–22; Sam Charters, liner notes to the audio recording the Lilly Brothers and Don Stover, *The Prestige/Folklore Years, Volume Five: Have a Feast Here Tonight*, Prestige/Folklore Records PRCD-9919-2 (reissued in 1999 by Fantasy, Inc.); and Fred Pement, "Background/Recording Session," liner notes to the audio recording the Lilly Brothers and Don Stover, *Live at Hillbilly Ranch*, Hay Holler Records HH-CD-1333.

26. Pement, "Background/Recording Session"; Irwin (D), interview.

27. Irwin, e-mail to Pellegrinelli, April 2, 1996; Trischka, "Ken Irwin," 16, 17.

28. Marshall Wyatt, "Every County Has Its Own Personality: An Interview with Dave Freeman," *Old-Time Herald*, Winter 1999–2000, 12.

29. Irwin, e-mail to Pellegrinelli, April 2, 1996.

30. Irwin, e-mail to author, August 26, 2002.

31. Pat J. Ahrens, *Union Grove: The First Fifty Years* (published privately by Pat J. Ahrens, 1975). On fiddling conventions generally, see Audrey A. Kaiman, "The Southern Fiddling Convention: A Study," *Tennessee Folklore Society Bulletin*, March 1965, 7–16.

32. Ken Irwin, "Union Grove Long and Peripheral," BGRASS-L, December 29, 2001. Irwin and Nowlin were uncertain about whether they first attended Union Grove in 1965, 1966, or 1967. After a lengthy three-way e-mail exchange, with reference to contest registrants in various years, I settled on 1966 as the likeliest year for that first trip.

33. Nowlin (A), interview; Irwin quotations from Trischka, "Ken Irwin," 17–18. On Pegram's career, see Steven Stolder, "George Pegram," in *Music Hound/Folk: The Essential Album Guide*, edited by Neil Walters and Brian Mansfield (Detroit: Visible Ink Press, 1998), 622–23; and Bob Carlin, liner notes to the audio recording *George Pegram*, Rounder Records CD 0001 (CD reissue of the original album, with additional material).

34. Trischka, "Ken Irwin," 18; Charles Wolfe, "Rounder Is 25! The Early Days of Rounder, Vol. 1," *Old-Time Herald*, Fall 1995, 35, 36. Kessinger details are from Baggelaar and Milton, *Folk Music*, 211 (see chap. 1, n. 74). On Kessinger at Union Grove, see Ahrens, *Union Grove*, 37.

35. Alan Jabbour, interview.

36. Ibid.

37. Nowlin (B), interview.

38. Ibid.

39. Ibid.

40. Ibid.

41. Ibid.; William Chapman, "55,000 Rally against War; GI's Repel Pentagon Charge," *Washington Post*, October 22, 1967, A1; Jimmy Breslin, "Quiet Rally Turns Vicious," *Washington Post*, October 22, 1967, A1.

42. Nowlin (B), interview.

43. Ibid.; Nowlin, e-mail to author, August 26, 2002.

44. Irwin (D), interview. During her marriage and for some time thereafter, Leighton used the name Marian Leighton Levy. She asked me to refer to her as Marian Leighton in this book.

45. Leighton (C), interview, for quotations, and (A), interview.

46. Leighton (A) and (C), interview.

47. Leighton, e-mail to author, September 3, 2002.

48. Leighton (B) and (C), interview; Leighton, e-mail to author, September 3, 2002.

49. Leighton (B), interview.

50. Leighton (C), interview.

51. Ibid.

52. Ibid.

53. Leighton (D), interview.

54. Ibid.

55. Leighton (A), interview.

56. Ibid.

57. Nowlin (D), interview.

58. Leighton (B), interview.

59. Irwin, e-mail to author, August 2, 2002.

60. Irwin (B), interview; Leighton (B), interview.

61. Leighton, e-mail to author, September 4, 2002; David Welsh, "The Passa-maquoddy Indians," *Ramparts*, March 1967, 40, 42; Warren Hinckle, "The Social History of the Hippies," *Ramparts*, March 1967, 5, 9.

62. Quotations from William G. Nowlin Jr., "The Political Thought of Alexander Berkman" (Ph.D. diss., Tufts University, 1980), 50, 72; Nowlin (B), interview; Leighton (B), interview.

63. Leighton (C), interview.

64. Leighton (A), interview.

65. Nowlin (A), interview.

66. Wolfe, "Rounder Is 25!" 36.

67. Robert Carlin, "The Small Specialty Record Company in the United States," *Pickin'*, August 1977, 16, 22. This article provides a comprehensive list of folk-oriented independent labels in the United States in the mid-1970s.

68. Irwin (D), interview.

CHAPTER 3: SURREALISTIC BANJOS AND ZYDECO RHYTHMS: ROUNDER'S BROAD AESTHETIC

1. I. Sheldon Posen, introduction to "On Folk Festivals and Kitchens: Questions of Authenticity in the Folksong Revival," in *Transforming Tradition*, edited by Rosenberg, 127, 129 (see introduction, n. 4).

2. Glassie, "Tradition," 395 (see chap. 1, n. 25).

3. Irwin (A), interview, explaining the three-pronged basis of the label name; Wolfe, "Rounder Is 25!" 35, 36 (see chap. 2, n. 34).

4. "Rising Sun Blues," trad., arr. and adapted C. Ashley–Smithsonian Folkways Pub., BMI. Released originally on the audio recording *Old Time Music at Clarence Ashley's*, vol. 2, Folkways LP FA 2359. Rereleased on CD as *The Original Folkways Recordings of Doc Watson and Clarence Ashley, 1960–1962*, Smithsonian Folkways Recordings SF40029/30.

5. Peter Stampfel, interview.

6. Nick Tosches, "Records," *Rolling Stone*, June 10, 1971, 43.

7. Stampfel, liner notes to the 1963 audio recording *The Holy Modal Rounders*, Prestige/Folklore Records 14031, reprinted as notes to the CD *The Holy Modal Rounders, 1 and 2*, Fantasy Records FCD-24711-2.

8. Stampfel quoted in Larry Kelp, liner notes to *The Holy Modal Rounders, 1 and 2*.

9. Van Ronk quoted in ibid.; Stampfel's remarks from the audio recording *Holy Modal Rounders: Live in 1965*, privately produced and released as HMR-1.

10. Irwin (B), interview; Trischka, "Ken Irwin," 16, 18 (see chap. 2, n. 24); Bob Carlin, liner notes to the audio recording *George Pegram*, Rounder Records CD 0001 (CD reissue of the original album, with additional material).

11. Arthur Palmer Hudson, "The Carolina Folk Festival," *Southern Folklore Quarterly* 12 (1948): 177, 178.

12. Nowlin (A), interview.

13. Carson Taylor, "We Had a Sure Feeling We Had Seen the Champ," *Franklin County Times* (Rocky Mount, Va.), May 29, 1969, quoted in Ahrens, *Union Grove*, 119 (see chap. 2, n. 31).

14. Nowlin (A), interview; contract between Rounder and Pegram in Rounder file folder marked 0001, photocopy in author's possession.

15. Rossi, interview.

16. Ibid.; "Fiddler's Town," *Newsweek*, April 29, 1968, 96.

17. Rossi, interview.

18. Ibid.

19. Nowlin (A), interview.

20. Richard K. Spottswood, "Record Reviews," *Bluegrass Unlimited*, March 1971, 14. On Spottswood, see Alan J. Steiner, "Dick Spottswood's Homegrown Music Hour," *Bluegrass Unlimited*, August 1990, 57.

21. "Jimi Hendrix, 1945–1970," *Rolling Stone*, October 15, 1970; "Janis Joplin, 1943–1970," *Rolling Stone*, October 29, 1970; "Singing Songs for Woody Guthrie," *Rolling Stone* October 15, 1970, 10.

22. Dennis Wilen, "Philly Folkies' Community Vibes," *Rolling Stone*, October 15, 1970, 20.

23. Paul W. Soelberg, "Modern Country Radio: Friend or Foe?" *Billboard*, October 17, 1970, CM-44.

24. See Pat J. Ahrens, *A History of the Musical Careers of DeWitt "Snuffy" Jenkins, Banjoist, and Homer "Pappy" Sherrill, Fiddler* (Columbia, S.C.: published privately by Pat J. Ahrens, 1970).

25. Ahrens, interview; Ahrens, *"Snuffy" Jenkins and "Pappy" Sherrill: The Hired Hands* (Columbia, S.C.: published privately by Pat J. Ahrens, 2002).

26. L. Mayne Smith, "An Introduction to Bluegrass," *Journal of American Folklore* 78 (1965): 245, reprinted in *The Bluegrass Reader*, ed. Thomas Goldsmith (Urbana: University of Illinois Press, 2004), 77–79.

27. Stephen L. Betts, "Joe Val and the New England Bluegrass Boys," in *Music Hound Country: The Essential Album Guide*, edited by Brian Mansfield and Gary Graff (Detroit: Visible Ink Press, 1997), 450–52.

28. Liner notes to the audio recording Joe Val and the New England Bluegrass Boys, *One Morning in May*, Rounder Records 0003.

29. Walter V. Saunders, "Record Reviews," *Bluegrass Unlimited*, January 1972, 10.

30. Nowlin (B), interview; mission statement text from the liner notes to the audio recording *Mountain Moving Day*, Rounder Records 4001, p. 15.

31. Pete Wernick, interview.

32. Tony Trischka, interview by Brian L. Knight, "Getting the Bends with Tony Trischka," *Vermont Review*, http://members.tripod.com/vermontreview/Interviews/trischka.htm.

33. Wernick, interview.

34. George B. McCeney, "Record Reviews," *Bluegrass Unlimited*, March 1972, 10; Wernick, interview.

35. Wernick, interview; George B. McCeney, "Record Reviews," *Bluegrass Unlimited*, January 1975, 20.

36. Wernick, interview; Russ Barenberg, e-mail to Irwin, December 10, 2004, forwarded to author. Miller (in an interview with the author) recalls Monroe saying, "Keep playing those new notes." Wernick, Joan Leonard, and others later recorded a third album billed as Country Cooking with the Fiction Brothers. Throughout Country Cooking's history, album personnel shifted. Moreover, there was never a complete personnel match between the recording and live performance bands, prompting ongoing audience confusion about the identity of the band members and the band's style and repertoire.

37. Tony Trischka, "New Acoustic Music," *Bluegrass Unlimited*, November 1985, 12, 14–15, 20.

38. Ibid., 14.

39. Nowlin (B), interview.

40. Ibid.; Naomi Weisstein, interview.

41. Weisstein, interview.

42. Ibid.; "Mountain Moving Day," music: Naomi Weisstein, words: Yosano Akiko, Naomi Weisstein; "Papa Don't Lay That Shit on Me," music: traditional, words: Virginia Blaisdell, Naomi Weisstein. In 2005 Rounder reissued the album on CD with expanded notes and additional music, under the title *Papa Don't Lay That Shit on Me*, Rounder Records CD 4001.

43. Happy Traum, liner notes to the audio recording *Mud Acres: Music among Friends*, Rounder Records 3001.

44. Ibid.

45. Nowlin (B), interview.

46. "Smooth, pretty style" is from Leighton (A), interview, used in reference to Mary McCaslin.

47. Irwin (A), interview.

48. I draw the parody of Thorogood's articulation from Greil Marcus, "Reviews," *Rolling Stone*, March 23, 1978, 67.

49. Nowlin (A), interview; liner notes to the audio recording George Thorogood and the Destroyers, *Move It on Over*, Rounder Records 3024.

50. Nowlin (A), interview.

51. Fred Schruers, "George Thorogood and the Destroyers: The Other End, New York City, February 24, 1978," *Rolling Stone*, April 20, 1978, 84; Welding, "George Thorogood," 34 (see chap. 2, n. 6); 34; Dan Oppenheimer, "George Thorogood Passes Through," *Village Voice*, July 10, 1978, 47.

52. Liner notes to *Move It on Over*.

53. Sales figures from "George Thorogood Legal Battle Shifts to Massachusetts Courts," *Variety*, July 11, 1979, 73.

54. Billington, interview.

55. Billington, e-mail to Irwin, January 25, 2005, forwarded to author.

56. Billington, interview.

57. Ibid.

58. Christopher Blagg, "Spilling the (Snap) Beans on Zydeco: An Ardoin Family Perspective," *Offbeat*, September 2001, 60, 63.

59. Billington, interview.

CHAPTER 4: TOWARD AN AUTHENTICITY OF SELF: OLD-TIME
MUSIC IN A MODERN WORLD

1. For an excellent discussion of one particular old-time music scene, that of Bloomington, Indiana, beginning in the 1970s, see John Bealle, *Old-Time Music and Dance: Community and Folk Revival* (Bloomington: Quarry Books, 2005). Bealle offers a detailed description and analysis of this scene and its connections to the larger folk revival.

2. Mark Wilson, interview. Regarding Wilson generally, see Kerry Blech, "In the Field: An Interview with Mark Wilson," *Old-Time Herald*, Winter 2000–2001, 12.

3. Wilson, "The North American Traditions Series: Its Rationale," from the Rounder Records Web site, http://www.rounder.com/series/nat/nat_rat1.html.

4. Wilson, interview.

5. Ibid.

6. Wilson, introduction to the liner notes to the audio recording *Kentucky Old-Time Banjo*, Rounder Records CD 0394.

7. "Autobiographical Sketch of Buddy Thomas," liner notes to the audio recording by Thomas titled *Kitty Puss: Old-Time Fiddle Music from Kentucky*, Rounder Records CD 0032 (released originally on LP in 1976).

8. Wilson, "North American Traditions Series."

9. Wilson, interview.

10. Philip F. Gura, "Some Thoughts on the Revival: Alan Jabbour and Old-Time Music," *Old-Time Herald*, Summer 1991, 24.

11. Bill Hicks, "Where'd They Come From? Where'd They Go? A Brief History of the Fuzzy Mountain Stringband," *Old-Time Herald*, Spring 1995, 20, 21; Thomas Carter, "Looking for Henry Reed: Confessions of a Revivalist," in *Sounds of the South*, edited by Daniel Patterson (Chapel Hill: Southern Folklife Collection, 1991), 71, 85.

12. Richard Spottswood, "Record Reviews," *Bluegrass Unlimited*, October 1972, 11.

13. Jabbour's field notes and his original recordings of Reed are in the Library of Congress. Listeners can hear 184 of these recordings at http://memory.loc.gov/ammem/hrhtml/hrhome.html.

14. Carter, "Looking for Henry Reed," 81–82; Hicks, "Where'd They Come From?" 21.

15. Ben-Amos, "Toward a Definition," 3 (see chap. 1, n. 65); Bealle, *Old-Time Music*, 60; Burt Feintuch, "Musical Revival as Musical Transformation," in *Transforming Tradition*, edited by Rosenberg, 187 (see introduction, n. 4).

16. Philip F. Gura, "Roots and Branches: Forty Years of the New Lost City Ramblers, Part 2," *Old-Time Herald*, Spring 2000, 18, 23.

17. Alice Gerrard, "Colby Street to New York and Points South: The Highwoods Stringband," *Old-Time Herald*, Summer 1992, 26, 27.

18. Ibid., 27, 28.

19. Mike Greenstein, "New York Stringbands: The Highwoods and Cranberry Lake," *Bluegrass Unlimited*, February 1979, 36, 38; Seeger quoted in Gerrard, "Colby Street," 30.

20. Dick Kimmel and Nancy Kimmel, "The Highwoods Stringband," *People into Music/Pickin'*, August 1978, 62, 63.

21. Kerry Blech, liner notes to the audio recording Highwoods String Band, *Feed Your Babies Onions*, Rounder Records CD 11569. This CD compiles selected tracks from the Highwoods' three Rounder LPs from the 1970s. "Record Reviews," *Bluegrass Unlimited*, June 1976, 44–45; "Record Reviews," *Bluegrass Unlimited*, July 1978, 30 (the quotation comes from this review).

22. Blech, liner notes; Seeger quoted in Gerrard, "Colby Street," 30; Brad Leftwich, liner notes to *Feed Your Babies Onions*.

23. Alan Jabbour, interview; Jabbour, "Issues in Old-Time Music," *Old-Time Herald*, November 1993–January 1994, 24, 25.

24. Jabbour, interview; Joe Wilson, "Confessions of a Folklorist," *Old-Time Herald*, Spring 1990, 25, 27.

25. Greenstein, "New York Stringbands," 37.

26. Mac Benford, "Folklorists and Us: An Account of Our Curious and Changing Relationship," *Old-Time Herald*, Spring 1989, 25.

27. J. Wilson, "Confessions of a Folklorist," 27.

28. J. Wilson, interview.

29. J. Wilson, "Confessions of a Folklorist," 27.

30. J. Wilson, interview.

31. Hicks (letter to the editor), "Issues in Old-Time Music," *Old-Time Herald*, Summer 1990, 18; Nat Clark (letter to the editor), "Issues in Old-Time Music," *Old-Time Herald*, Fall 1990, 20.

32. John Coffey (letter to the editor), "Issues in Old-Time Music," *Old-Time Herald*, Summer 1990, 19; Tracy Schwarz (letter to the editor), "Issues in Old-Time Music," *Old-Time Herald*, Winter 1989–1990, 27.

33. Hicks (letter to the editor); J. Wilson, "Confessions of a Folklorist," 31.

34. Jabbour, interview.

35. Ibid. See also Gura, "Some Thoughts on the Revival."

36. Jabbour, interview.

37. Carter, "Looking for Henry Reed," 86.

38. J. Wilson, "Confessions of a Folklorist," 25; J. Wilson, interview.

39. Bruce Molsky, interview.

40. Ibid.

41. Ibid. The referenced performance took place at Austin's Cactus Cafe on October 12, 2000.

42. Ibid. Haley quoted in Mark Wilson and Guthrie T. Meade, liner notes to the audio recording *Parkersburg Landing*, Rounder Records 1010.

43. Molsky, interview; M. Wilson quoted in Bruce Miller, "Not to Be Fiddled With," *Pittsburgh City Paper*, July 3, 2003, http://www.pittsburghcitypaper.ws/scripts/printIt.cfm?ref=189.

44. Molsky, interview.

45. Michael F. Brown, *Who Owns Native Culture?* (Cambridge: Harvard University Press, 2003), 251–52.

CHAPTER 5: LIKE POLITICS IN CHICAGO: THE FOLK ALLIANCE
STRIVES FOR UNITY

1. Bob Woodcock, "Letters/Regional Organization," *Sing Out!* 26, no. 3 (1977): 53.

2. Michael Cooney, "Roads Scholar," *Sing Out!* April–June 1985, 43, 45; Cooney, "Roads Scholar," *Sing Out!* October–December 1985, 53; Cooney, "Roads Scholar," *Sing Out!* Fall 1986, 63.

3. Mimi Bluestone, "What's Happening/Pay the Fiddler," *Sing Out!* 28, no. 1 (1980): 34, 36.

4. Richard Carlin, "Folk Forum: Folk Musicians, Folk Clubs, and Dollars," *Sing Out!* 26, no. 3 (1977): 34.

5. Mimi Bluestone, "What's Happening/Report from the Rendezvous: Hey Rube!" *Sing Out!* 28, no. 3 (1980): 40, 41–42. See also Bluestone, "What's Happening/Rendezvous 1980: Paying the Fiddler," *Sing Out!* 28, no. 2 (1980): 40, 42; and Michael Cooney, "Roads Scholar," *Sing Out!* October–December 1984, 59, 60–61.

6. Scott Alarik, "Stephen Baird and the Folk Arts Network," *Sing Out!* Summer 1990, 10.

7. See Augusta Heritage Center of Davis and Elkins College, *2000 Catalog.*

8. Margo Blevin, interview.

9. Sonny Thomas, interview.

10. "Important Announcement," *Sing Out!* Summer 1988, 86. Margo Blevin, in a letter to the author dated January 10, 2005, recalls that Weissman placed similar notices in the *Old-Time Herald.* Blevin saw these additional advertisements as attempts to reach beyond urban folk fans and communicate with "traditional musicians, who had fewer avenues at that time, and non-musicians such as folklorists and music scholars."

11. Clark Weissman, addressing the General Session of the International Conference of the North American Folk Music and Dance Alliance, Boston, February 18, 1994. Tape recording in possession of author, prepared by Chesapeake Audio/Video Communications, Inc. (Elkridge, Md.), in cooperation with the Folk Alliance.

12. Blevin, interview.

13. Sandy Paton, interview.

14. "Proceedings of Folk Alliance Meeting no. 1," Malibu, California, January 19–22, 1989, provided to author by former Folk Alliance executive director Phyllis Barney.

15. Blevin, interview.

16. Blevin, letter to author, January 10, 2005.

17. Ibid.; George Balderose, interview.

18. Anne Blaine, interview; Thomas, interview.

19. Juel Ulven, interview.

20. Shelly Romalis, interview. Romalis, whose personal sympathies leaned toward the backyard players, was paraphrasing a sentiment directed against her and her like-minded colleagues.

21. Jim Hirsch, interview.

22. Ulven, interview; Thomas, interview.

23. Blaine, interview; Dianne Tankle, interview.

24. Hirsch, interview.

25. Ulven, interview.

26. "Proceedings of Meeting no. 1," 10–11.

27. Thomas, interview.

28. Ulven, interview.

29. Scott Alarik, "The Continuing Tradition of Folk-Legacy Records," *Sing Out!* Spring 1991, 26, 28.

30. Ibid., passim.

31. Dianne Tankle and Robert Cohen, interview. "I know it when I hear it" are the author's words. "Folkie sound" and "the whole gestalt" are Cohen's.

32. Lisa Grayson, *Biography of a Hunch: The History of Chicago's Legendary Old Town School of Folk Music* (Chicago: private publication by Old Town School of Folk Music, 1992), passim (Hamilton quote on p. 7).

33. Ibid., 32–34.

34. Ibid., 35–39.

35. Hirsch, interview; Ulven, interview.

36. "*Sing Out!* Survival Threatened," *Sing Out!* 28, no. 4 (July–August 1980): inside front cover.

37. Mark Moss, "Friends of *Sing Out!*" *Sing Out!* 28, no. 5 (September–October 1980): 31; "And Lots of Thanks . . . ," *Sing Out!* 28, no. 5 (September–October 1980): inside front cover; *Sing Out!* (April–June 1983) was the first issue that designated Moss as editor.

38. Jack Bernhardt, "Art Menius: Working to Make Bluegrass Grow," *Bluegrass Unlimited*, November 1987, 54.

39. Ibid., passim.

40. Ibid., 55–56.

41. Mark Fenster, "Commercial (and/or?) Folk: The Bluegrass Industry and Bluegrass Traditions," in *Reading Country Music: Steel Guitars, Opry Stars, and Honky-Tonk Bars*, edited by Cecelia Tichi (Durham: Duke University Press, 1998), 74, 75.

42. Menius, e-mail to author, December 27, 1999.

43. Menius, e-mail to author, January 14, 2000.

44. Balderose, interview.

45. Moss, interview. In postinterview communication, Moss explains that he and other committee members understood that *traditional* and *contemporary* were not mutually exclusive terms. The drafters, he says, used the phrase *contemporary folk* as a term of art to describe music that people characterize as "folk," though it is not traditional in a strict sense. In his words, it was "a genre used interchangeably with, say 'singer-songwriter' . . . conceptually music made within our broader folk community that doesn't draw (directly) from tradition" (e-mail to author, October 17, 2005 [ellipsis and parentheses in original]).

46. A letter from the Folk Alliance Steering Committee to the Malibu conference attendees, November 30, 1989, included a copy of the proposed bylaws (documents in possession of the author).

47. Menius, e-mail to author, December 27, 1999.

48. Menius, e-mail to author, January 5, 2000.

49. Romalis, interview.

50. Ulven, interview.

51. Mike Agranoff, "At the Microphone," *Folk Alliance Newsletter*, Winter 1993, 20. Pitts first made his joke about "songs of personal indulgence" in an informal conversation with the author. I attribute it here with his permission. "Those Festivals" © Peter Siegel (BMI).

52. Mitch Ritter, "Linen Shorts," *Dirty Linen*, August–September 1999, 83; "Map of My Heart" (1998) by Lynn Miles (SOCAN and ASCAP), on the audio recording Lynn Miles, *Night in a Strange Town*, Philo Records 11671-1215-2.

53. Jody Stecher, interview. Stecher is married to singer Kate Brislin, whose duet performance with Katy Moffatt so impressed me at the Tucson Folk Alliance conference.

54. Sandy and Caroline Paton, interview.

55. Scott Alarik, "Solitude vs. Solicitude: The Music of Gordon Bok," *Sing Out!* February–April 1992, 2, passim.

56. Menius, e-mail to author, December 27, 1999.

57. All songs by Tish Hinojosa, 1992 Manazo Music (ASCAP), appearing on the audio recording Tish Hinojosa, *Culture Swing*, Rounder Records 3122.

58. "Ghost in the Music" by Nanci Griffith and Eric Taylor, 1986 Griffmill Music (ASCAP); "Year Down in New Orleans" by Nanci Griffith, 1986 Griffmill Music (ASCAP), from the audio recording *Once in a Very Blue Moon*, Philo Records CD 1096.

59. Ulven, interview; Charlie Pilzer, interview.

60. Philip Van Vleck, "Dar Williams: Travels in Two Worlds," *Dirty Linen*, June–July 2001, 47, 50.

61. Irwin Stambler and Lyndon Stambler, *Folk and Blues: The Encyclopedia* (New York: St. Martin's Press, 2001), s.v. "Williams, Dar."

62. Menius, e-mail to author, December 27, 1999; Blevin, interview.

63. Ian Robb, "The British-North America Act," *Sing Out!* August–October 1994, 50–51.

64. Moss, "The First Words," 2 (see chap. 1, n. 6).

65. Phyllis Barney, "The Alliance Strikes Back" (letter to the editor), in "The Last Words," *Sing Out!* November 1994–January 1995, 195.

66. Menius, e-mail to author, December 27, 1999.

67. I attended this session, and the description and quotations come from my handwritten notes, taken during the meeting.

68. *Program Book: 11th Annual International Folk Alliance Conference* (Albuquerque, 1999), passim.

69. John McCutcheon, interview.

70. Blevin, interview.

71. Under Barney's stewardship, the Alliance fostered a series of regional conferences, an initiative that members have greeted with enthusiasm. Four such conferences occur annually throughout the United States. Smaller than the international conference, they provide a more intimate atmosphere within which members can conduct business.

72. Louis Jay Meyers, interview.

73. Letter from Leslie Berman, president of the Folk Alliance Board of Directors, to Meyers, November 6, 2006, electronic copy in possession of author.

74. Menius, e-mails to author, March 1, 2006, July 21, 2007.

75. Barney, e-mails to author, May 10, 2006, July 27, 2007.

CHAPTER 6: CONSOLIDATION BLUES: FOLK MUSIC
IN CONTEMPORARY MARKETS

1. Don Henley, "Killing the Music," *Washington Post*, February 17, 2004, A19.

2. Irwin (D), interview.

3. "Old-Time Music Is Very Much Alive," liner notes to the audio recording *O Brother, Where Art Thou?* Mercury Records 088 170-069-2; Michelle Nikolai, "Way Out of Tune," *Nashville Scene*, June 14, 2001.

4. Neil Strauss, "The Country Music Country Radio Ignores," *New York Times*, national ed., March 24, 2001, AR1, 31; Nikolai, "Way Out of Tune"; Soelberg, "Modern Country Radio" (see chap. 3, n. 23).

5. The radio station survey appears in "Sing Out! Radio Partners," *Sing Out!* Summer 2004, 219; Samuel G. Freedman, "An Island of Idiosyncrasy on the AM Dial," *New York Times*, national ed., August 12, 2001, AR28. See also Paul Farhi, "Mega Hurts: Clear Channel's Big Radio Ways Are Getting a Lot of Static These Days," *Washington Post*, May 29, 2002, CO1.

6. "Clear Channel Cluster Makes It Lightning Rod," *Hollywood Reporter*, February 18, 2003, online at lexis-nexis.com (accession no. 3727155).

7. Damian Cave, "Inside Clear Channel," *Rolling Stone*, August 13, 2004, http://www.rollingstone.com/news/story/_/id/6432174.

8. Farhi, "Mega Hurts."

9. Roy Bragg, "Smaller Radio Rivals Blast San Antonio–Based Clear Channel," *Knight-Ridder Tribune Business News,* February 5, 2003, online at lexis-nexis.com (accession no. 3694552).

10. Mark Moss, "FCC, Media Mergers, and Mike," FOLKDJ-L, May 22, 2003.

11. Samuel G. Freedman, "Public Radio's Private Guru," *New York Times,* November 11, 2001, AR1.

12. Valerie Block, "Let the Music End Sour Notes: Critics Say Record Executives Blame Game Is Smoke Screen for Dearth of Quality Releases," *Crain's New York Business,* January 20, 2003, online at lexis-nexis.com (accession no. 3670096); "Major Label," in the *Free Dictionary,* at http://encyclopedia.thefreedictionary.com/Major%2olabel.

13. "Annual Airplay Summaries: 2005 Top Labels Report," http://www.folkradio.org. Rounder held the first position, and its subsidiary, Philo, held the sixth. Total airplays include repeat plays of the same song.

14. Quotations are from John McLaughlin, "Pitching against the Majors," *Sing Out!* Winter 2003, 16. See also McLaughlin, "Better Get It While You Can," FOLK-DJ-L, July 5, 2003.

15. The discussion thread titled "Better Get It While You Can," FOLKDJ-L, July 4 and 5, 2003.

16. Burt Helm, "Invasion of the Robo-DJs," *Business Week Online,* April 8, 2005, http://www.businessweek.com/bwdaily/dnflash/apr2005/nf2005048_4639_db042.htm.

17. Art Menius posted the Clear Channel press release on the IBMA Listserv under the heading "Clear Channel, Americana and Bluegrass," March 31, 2006. For format description, see "What Is Americana Music?" on the home page of radio station WTCR at http://www.wtcramericana.com/.

18. Chris Morris, "Music Biz Must Face Urgent Problem: Reaching Potential Over-25 Audience," *Billboard,* January 12, 2002, 1; Russell Shorto, "The Industry Standard," *New York Times Magazine,* October 3, 2004, 50.

19. Ed Christman and Geoff Mayfield, "Tower Aims to Sharpen Competitive Edge," *Billboard,* November 2, 1991, 47.

20. Chad Rubell, "Music Retailers in Battle," *Marketing News,* December 5, 1994, 2.

21. Don Jeffrey, "Lowball Pricing Divides Retailers, Labels," *Billboard,* December 24, 1994, 63.

22. Zac Crain, "Accidental Death Wars between the Electronics Giants Are Killing Dallas' Independent Music Stores," *Dallas Observer,* July 11, 1996, online at lexis-nexis.com.

23. Warren Cohen, "Wal-Mart Wants $10 CDs," *Rolling Stone,* October 12, 2004, http://www.rollingstone.com/news/story/_/id/6558540; Brian Garrity, "Another Tough Year for the Biz," *Billboard,* December 27, 2003, 5, YE10.

24. W. Cohen, "Wal-Mart Wants $10 CDs"; Dreese quoted in David Segal, "Requiem for the Record Store," *Washington Post,* February 7, 2004, A1.

25. Irwin (A), interview.

26. Alice Gerrard, "Old-Time Music, CDs, and E-mail," *Old-Time Herald*, Spring 1993, 24.

27. Steve Morse, "Godsmack on Rounder?" *Boston Globe*, December 5, 2004, N10. The Listserv comments all appear in a thread titled "Godsmack on Rounder Records? (Boston Globe)," BLUES-L, December 6 and 7, 2004.

28. D. M. [Dave Marsh], "Size Doesn't Matter," *Rock and Rap Confidential*, August–September 1999, 3; D. M. [Dave Marsh], "Home to Roost," *Rock and Rap Confidential*, April 2000, 1.

29. Mark D. Moss, "The First Words: Why Size Matters," *Sing Out!* Fall 1998, 2.

30. Ed Christman, "Rounder, Mercury Ink P&D Deal," *Billboard*, July 4, 1998, 6.

31. Moss, "First Words" (1998).

32. Nowlin (A), interview; Irwin (A), interview; Irwin, e-mail to author, August 16, 2004.

33. Nowlin (A), interview.

34. Steve Morse, "Godsmack on Rounder?" reporting fifty million dollars in gross revenue, in contrast to 1997's total of twenty-four million dollars reported in Christman, "Rounder, Mercury."

35. Nowlin (A), interview.

36. Each of the Rounders discussed these early road trips in interviews with the author. The reference to "hippie radicals" and "young hustlers" is from Irwin (A), interview. Irwin recalls Bob Koester, the owner of Delmark Records, using these words to describe the founders' professional development.

37. Nowlin (A), interview.

38. Ibid.

39. Irwin (C), interview. The quote is from Irwin, e-mail to author, February 5, 2005.

40. Irwin (C), interview. On Takoma's history, see http://www.fantasyjazz.com/html/anniversary_takoma.html. Record label personnel and promoters marketed Booker White as "Bukka" White, a name the artist reportedly loathed.

41. Irwin, e-mail to author, September 29, 2004.

42. Ibid.

43. Irwin, e-mail to author, February 7, 2005; Sun Ra story from Glenn Jones, interview.

44. Pete Wernick, letter to Rounder dated "Sept. 5," located in a Rounder file folder marked "Country Cooking," copy in possession of author. Flying Fish released the third Country Cooking album in 1976, suggesting that Wernick wrote his letter in September 1975.

45. Letter of June 3, 1974, signed "Tut" and an undated letter to Tut Taylor signed "Ken for Rounder," from a Rounder folder maintained in connection with the audio recording Tut Taylor, *Friar Tut*, Rounder Records 0011. Copies are in the author's possession.

46. Irwin, Nowlin, and Leighton, all interviews; Stampfel, interview.

47. Leighton (D), interview.

48. Nowlin (C), interview.

49. Bill Kornrich, interview.

50. Ibid.

51. Ibid.; Nowlin (C), interview; Dan Wilson, e-mails to author, October 25, 27, November 8, 2004.

52. The unidentified Rounder associate made these remarks in an e-mail to the author dated September 26, 2002, but did not wish to discuss the company for attribution.

53. Leighton (D), interview.

54. Stampfel, interview. Each of the Rounders remembered his advice and its significance to them.

55. Billington, interview; Jones, interview.

56. Billington, interview.

57. Billington, interview; Jones, interview.

58. Billington, interview; Nowlin (C), interview.

59. Ibid.

60. Irwin, e-mail to author, February 4, 2005, quoting a remark that Berardini e-mailed to Irwin.

61. Irwin, e-mail to author, February 4, 2005; unsigned internal Rounder memorandum, addressed to "k" and dated "12-30-77," copy provided to author by Irwin.

62. Duncan Browne, interview.

63. Nathan Cobb, "Easy Rounder," *Boston Globe Magazine*, August 20, 1989, 22; Deborah Russell, "Rounder, Rykodisc Merging Their Indie Distrib Firms," *Billboard*, May 9, 1992, 10, 95.

64. Gary Susman, "Silver and Gold," photocopy of an otherwise unidentified article in the author's possession, contained within a Rounder corporate promotion packet, prepared in conjunction with the label's twenty-fifth anniversary in 1995.

65. Irwin (C), interview, discussing the New Orleans distributor; Browne quoted in Deborah Russell, "Grass Route: Rounder Still Looking to Close House Deal," July 27, 1991, 36; Deborah Russell, "Grass Route," *Billboard*, December 7, 1991, 49.

66. Deborah Russell, "Independent Distributors Building National Networks," *Billboard*, February 22, 1992, 1, passim.

67. Nowlin (C), interview, explaining Rounder's varied distribution companies. The closing Nowlin quotation is from Ed Christman, "Valley, Rounder Form Unusual Partnership," *Billboard*, May 21, 1994, 48.

68. Susan Piver, interview.

69. Ibid.

70. Nowlin (C), interview; Leighton (B), interview. Through an entity called Rounder Kids, Rounder still distributes children's music. Valley Media filed for bankruptcy in 2001.

71. Piver, interview; Ed Christman, "Worsening Retail Conditions Finally Arrive at Label's Door," *Billboard*, February 10, 1996, 58.

72. Nowlin (C), interview. Krauss's 1995 hit was titled *Now That I've Found You: A Collection*, Rounder Records 0325. It eventually sold more than two million copies. Krauss has remained Rounder's largest-selling act, and as of 2007 she has won more Grammy Awards than any other female artist.

73. Leighton (B), interview.

74. Leighton and Virant quoted in Chris Morris, "Rounder Taps Virant as 1st President/CEO," *Billboard*, November 1, 1997, 65.

75. Leighton (D), interview.

76. Nowlin (C), interview.

77. Browne, interview; Rounder's personnel changes summarized in Chihara, "Reeling at Rounder" (see chap. 2, n. 5); Virant quoted in Richard Henderson, "30 Years of Loving Music: A Label Based on Traditional Values," *Billboard*, February 10, 2001, 18, 26.

78. The Zoe description is from Rounder's Web site, http://www.rounder.com; Nowlin (C), interview; regarding Hatfield, see the *All-Music Guide*, http://www.allmusic.com.

79. Jennifer Truesdale Brogan quoted in Chihara, "Reeling at Rounder"; Brad San Martin, e-mail to author, October 13, 2002.

80. Chihara, "Reeling at Rounder"; Shay Quillen, interview; San Martin, e-mail to author, October 13, 2002.

81. Chihara, "Reeling at Rounder"; Brad Paul quoted in Morse, "Godsmack on Rounder?"

82. Jones, interview; Nowlin (C), interview; Irwin (C), interview; Chihara, "Reeling at Rounder"; Chris Morris, "Dismissal at Rounder Records Turns into an Employee/Management Issue," *Billboard*, May 13, 2000, 127.

83. Chihara, "Reeling at Rounder"; Paul quoted in Morse, "Godsmack on Rounder?"

84. Terry Kitchen, interview.

85. Ibid.

86. Kitchen, interview. I spoke to one of the two antiunion advocates in a brief, unrecorded phone call on August 13, 2006. Thereafter, each of these employees explained their position in separate e-mails to me, dated August 14, 2006. In the absence of a contrary agreement, I neither quote these employees nor identify them.

87. Nowlin (C), interview.

88. Irwin (C), interview; Nowlin (C), interview.

89. Nowlin (C), interview; Michael D. Clark, "Beginner's Pluck: Kathleen Edwards Breaks New Ground with Debut Album," *Houston Chronicle*, January 17, 2003, http://www.chron.com/cs/CDA/ssistory.mpl/ae/music/albums/1739779.

90. Hicks, "Where'd They Come From?" 20 (see chap. 4, n. 11).

91. Irwin, speaking at "Record Labels," February 11, 1998, a panel discussion at the tenth annual International Folk Alliance Conference, Memphis. A tape recording of the discussion is in the author's possession.

92. Ibid.

93. Web site notes to the audio recording Donald MacLellan, *The Dusky Meadow*, Rounder Records CD 7044, online at http://www.rounder.com/index.php?id=album .php&catalog_id=6456.

94. Nowlin (C), interview.

CONCLUSION: GONE TO THE INTERNET, EVERYONE

1. Phyllis Barney, interview.

2. Discussion threads titled "Artists on Labels vs. Truly Indie Artists," FOLKDJ-L, February 2, 2005; and "Labels and Such," FOLKDJ-L, February 2, 2005.

3. Nowlin (C), interview; CD Baby is found on the Internet at http://www.cdbaby .com. My discussion of the company in this and the following paragraphs draws from this Web site and from Sivers' remarks at a panel discussion titled "Changing Face of Distribution" at the 2004 Folk Alliance conference.

4. "Legitimate Music Downloading Enjoys Dream Week," *CNET News.com*, January 8, 2006, http://news.com.com/2102-1027_3-6023769.html; Jeff Leeds, "The Net Is a Boon for Indie Labels," *New York Times*, December 27, 2005, E1; Frank Green, "Digital Downloads Slowing," *San Diego Union-Tribune*, June 24, 2006, C1.

5. honkingduck.com; Leeds, "Net Is a Boon."

6. Robert Levine, "Buying Music from Anywhere and Selling It for Play on the Internet," *New York Times*, January 9, 2006, C1; Yuki Noguchi, "With Online Music, It's a Buyer's Market," *Washington Post*, June 24, 2006, A1.

7. Nowlin (C), interview; Irwin, "More Positive Ideas for Record Labels," IB-MA-L, June 23, 2004.

8. Bob Dylan, *Chronicles: Volume One* (New York: Simon Schuster, 2004), 32–33.

9. Springsteen quoted from the DVD *We Shall Overcome: The Seeger Sessions*, Columbia 82876 82867 2.

10. Ibid.

11. Ibid.

12. Mike Collett-White, "Rock Wannabes Turning to the Web, but Going Tough," *Reuters*, January 23, 2006, http://www.tiscali.co.uk/music/news/060123_rock_wannabes_turning _to_web.html.

13. Tom Neff, "Intellectual Property Wars," FOLKDJ-L, February 17, 2000.

Note on Citations

INTERVIEWS

Unless otherwise specified, all references to "interview" in the notes refer to unpublished interviews that I conducted personally. I list all of these interviews below, plus additional interviews that I did not incorporate, expressly, into the book. These all enhanced my understanding. I conducted all interviews via telephone unless the list specifies a location. In such cases the interview took place in person at that location. I possess tape recordings of all interviews, except as noted.

I interviewed Ken Irwin, Bill Nowlin, and Marian Leighton—the founders of Rounder Records—over the course of several meetings and phone conversations. I am indebted to Lara Pellegrinelli who, as a Harvard University graduate student, also interviewed Irwin, Nowlin, and Leighton. Dr. Pellegrinelli provided me with copies of her transcripts and allowed me to quote from them. I do not possess tape recordings of her interviews. In the notes, I distinguish among multiple interviews with the same person by parenthetical alphabetic notations, as shown below.

Ahrens, Pat. August 30, 2002.
Balderose, George. December 8, 1999.
Barney, Phyllis. May 8, 2000. Washington, D.C.
Billington, Scott. October 15, 1999. Cambridge, Mass.
Blaine, Anne. January 21, 2000.
Blevin, Margo. February 16, 2000.
Broderick, Bing. October 14, 1999. Cambridge, Mass.
Browne, Duncan. October 8, 2000.
Cohen, Robert. December 6, 1999.
Connell, Dudley. May 9, 2000. Alexandria, Va.
Daigrepont, Bruce. July 10, 2001.
Diamant, Tom. June 5, 2006.
Dickens, Hazel. May 11, 2000. Washington, D.C.
Doucet, Michael. January 6, 2005.
Dunford, Michael. July 31, 2000.
Fawver, Susan. June 15, 2001.
Foster, Dan. April 18, 2000. Austin, Texas.
Hickerson, Joe. November 17, 1999. Austin, Texas.
Hirsch, Jim. December 15, 1999.
Hood, John. July 23, 2000. Austin, Texas.
Irwin, Ken (all in Cambridge, Mass., except the telephone interview):
   (A) June 9, 1999.

(B) October 13 and 14, 1999.

(C) October 29, 2004 (by telephone).

(D) November 10, 1995, by Lara Pellegrinelli.

Jabbour, Alan. June 9, 2000.

Jones, Glenn. June 8, 2000.

Kissil, Don. March 1, 2000.

Kitchen, Terry. August 14 and 15, 2006 (not recorded).

Kornrich, Bill. September 13, 2002.

Ledgin, Stephanie. November 10, 1999.

Leighton, Marian (all in Cambridge, Mass., except the telephone interview):

(A) June 8 and 10, 1999.

(B) October 12 and 13, 1999.

(C) November 10, 1995, by Lara Pellegrinelli.

(D) May 15, 2006 (by telephone).

Levine, Marlene and Dick (interviewed jointly). May 27, 2000. Austin, Texas.

Lilly, John. February 16, 2001. Vancouver, B.C.

McCutcheon, John. September 6, 2000.

Menius, Art (by e-mail).

Meyers, Louis Jay. February 17, 2006. Austin, Texas (not recorded).

Miller, John. July 20, 2006 (not recorded).

Molsky, Bruce. October 13, 2000. Austin, Texas.

Moss, Mark:

(A) December 6, 1999.

(B) February 22, 2006 (not recorded).

Musselman, Jim. May 2, 2006.

Nowlin, Bill (all in Cambridge, Mass., except the telephone interview):

(A) June 8, 9 and 10, 1999.

(B) October 13 and 14, 1999.

(C) July 19 and 23, 2004 (by telephone).

(D) December 7, 1995, by Lara Pellegrinelli.

Olivier, Barry. January 20, 1994. Berkeley, Calif.

Paton, Caroline and Sandy (interviewed jointly). December 1, 1999.

Paul, Brad. October 14, 1999. Cambridge, Mass.

Pilzer, Charlie. November 4, 1999.

Pitts, Randy. March 20, 2000. Austin, Texas.

Piver, Susan. October 8, 2000.

Powell, Dirk. August 21, 2000.

Quillen, Shay. October 31, 2002.

Romalis, Shelly. December 1, 1999.

Rossi, Neil. June 10, 2001.

Sandomirsky, Sharon. March 7, 2000. Austin, Texas.

San Martin, Brad (by e-mail).

Schwarz, Peter. June 14, 2001. Austin, Texas.

Spottswood, Richard. May 9, 2000. Silver Spring, Md.

Stampfel, Peter. October 5, 2000.

Stecher, Jody. February 15, 2001. Vancouver, B.C.

Tankle, Dianne. December 6, 1999.

Thomas, Sonny. February 10, 2000. Cleveland, Ohio.

Traum, Happy. March 23, 1992. Woodstock, N.Y.

Trischka, Tony. August 22, 2000.

Ulven, Juel. February 3, 2000.

Van Ronk, Dave. Spring 1993. Berkeley, Calif.

Weissman, Clark. December 28, 2001 (not recorded).

Weissman, Elaine. February 17, 2001. Vancouver, B.C. (not recorded).

Weisstein, Naomi. July 10, 2001.

Wernick, Pete. August 17 and 18, 2000.

Whitstein, Charles. September 3, 2000.

Wilson, Dan (by e-mail).

Wilson, Joe. May 10, 2000. Washington, D.C.

Wilson, Mark. October 1, 1999.

LISTSERVS AND ELECTRONIC DISCUSSION GROUPS

Throughout the book I refer to various electronic Listservs and bulletin boards, sometimes with reference to specific messages. In referencing a message I cite, in this order, the name (or screen name) of the individual posting the message, the title of the relevant discussion thread, the name of the Listserv or bulletin board, and the date of the posting. In the following list I provide the URL to the archive or home page of the specified resource, from which readers can find specific messages.

BGRASS-L (bluegrass music discussion). http://lsv.uky.edu/archives/bgrass-l.html.

BLUES-L (blues music discussion). http://lists.netspace.org/archives/blues-l.html.

FOLKBIZ (folk musician business discussion). http://lists.psu.edu/archives/folkbiz.html.

FOLKDJ-L (for and about folk and bluegrass DJs). http://lists.psu.edu/archives/folkdj-l.html.

FOLKMUSIC (new American singer-songwriters discussion). http://www.escribe.com/music/folkmusic/.

IBMA-L (International Bluegrass Music Association). http://lsv.uky.edu/archives/ibma-l.html.

MUDCAT CAFE (wide-ranging folk music discussion). http://mudcat.org. Readers can access the discussion forum by clicking on "Lyrics & Knowledge." By using the search function, they can locate thread names, a poster's name, or keywords of their choosing.

REC.MUSIC.FOLK (wide-ranging folk music discussion). http://groups-beta.google.com/group/rec.music.folk/about.

Index

Jackson, Bruce, 14, 17
Jackson, Mahalia, 145
Jack's Record Cellar, 181–82
Jagger, Mick, 104
Janick, John, 214
Jarrell, Tommy, 124, 127–28
Jenkins, DeWitt "Snuffy," 96–97, 114
Jewel, 23, 25
Jimi Hendrix Experience, 82, 100
Jim Kweskin Jug Band, 105
Jocque, Beau, 111–13, 216
Joffrey Ballet, 97
"John Henry," 92
Johnston, Annie, 51
Jones, Glenn, 185, 190–91, 202–3
Jones, Norah, 174–75
Joplin, Janis, 95
Journal of American Folklore, 26, 28

Kanawha Records, 73, 91, 119
Kaplan, Bruce, 188
Kaplansky, Lucy, 54
Keith, Bill, 105–6
Kerrville Folk Festival, 24
Kessinger, Clark, 73
Kettle of Fish, 7
King, Chris Thomas, 168
King, James, 208
"King of the Road," 79
The Kingston Trio: and Bill Nowlin, 65; and commercialism, 4, 6, 38–39, 115; as influence, 4, 39, 93, 100, 121–22, 144, 211, 215–16; and Newport Folk Festival, 42
Kirby, Beecher "Pete," 186
Kitchen, Terry, 203–4
Koester, Bob, 184, 238n36
Koken, Walt, 85, 121–23
Kornrich, Bill, 76, 188–89
Korson, George, 23
Kottke, Leo, 183
Krauss, Alison, 168, 198, 205, 240n72
Kronos Quartet, 175
KTIM, 193
Kweskin, Jim, 105

LaBeef, Sleepy, 107
Lampell, Millard, 95
Lavin, Christine, 107
Lawson, Doyle, and Quicksilver, 208
Lead Belly, 89, 106, 115

Led Zeppelin, 108
Leeds, Jeff, 214
Leftwich, Brad, 123
Legally Blonde, 206
Lehigh Valley (Pennsylvania) Folksong Society, 146
Lehrer, Tom, 63
Leighton, Marian (aka Marian Leighton Levy): and Bill Nowlin, 82, 84, 99; childhood of, 77–81; and concert production, 85–86; and feminism, 80–81, 83, 189–90, 199; and fiddling conventions, 73; and higher education, 80–81, 186–87, 199; initial exposure to folk music, 81–82; on John Virant, 198; and Ken Irwin, 73, 77, 81–85, 187–88, 199; marriage and motherhood, 199; parents of, 77–79, 81, 83–84, 187; and politics, 79–80, 82–84, 99; and pop and rock music, 78–79, 82–83; as reader, 79–80, 84–85, 187; and religion, 78–80, 83; and roles within Rounder, 189–90; 209–10; on Rounder's distribution efforts, 194; on Rounder and industry changes, 198. *See also* Irwin, Ken; Nowlin, Bill; Rounder Records
Leonard, Joan "Nondi," 100–101, 230n36
LeRoy, Lance, 148
Levy, Marian Leighton. *See* Leighton, Marian
Levy, Ron, 199
Liberty Flyer, 148
Library of Congress, 14, 35, 103, 182
Lilith Fair, 158
Lilly Brothers, 68–70, 86–87, 98
The Limeliters, 6
Linardos, Byron, 44
Linear Productions, 147
listservs. *See* Internet
"Little Darlin'," 63
Little Richard, 65, 82–83, 92
Living Blues, 57
Local 1000 (American Federation of Musicians), 161
Loeb, Lisa, 205
Lomax, Alan, 7, 23, 36, 104, 207
Lomax, John, 7, 23, 31–33, 36, 155
Louisiana Hayride, 21
Louvin Brothers, 12
Lowell Technological Institute, 187
Lower Telegraph Avenue Freedom Fighters String Band, 90

MICHAEL F. SCULLY holds a Ph.D. in American studies and is also an attorney. He resides in Austin, Texas, with his wife and two children.

Music in American Life

Opera on the Road: Traveling Opera Troupes in the United States, 1825–60
  Katherine K. Preston
The Stonemans: An Appalachian Family and the Music That Shaped Their Lives
  Ivan M. Tribe
Transforming Tradition: Folk Music Revivals Examined   *Edited by*
  Neil V. Rosenberg
The Crooked Stovepipe: Athapaskan Fiddle Music and Square Dancing in
  Northeast Alaska and Northwest Canada   *Craig Mishler*
Traveling the High Way Home: Ralph Stanley and the World of Traditional
  Bluegrass Music   *John Wright*
Carl Ruggles: Composer, Painter, and Storyteller   *Marilyn Ziffrin*
Never without a Song: The Years and Songs of Jennie Devlin, 1865–1952
  Katharine D. Newman
The Hank Snow Story   *Hank Snow, with Jack Ownbey and Bob Burris*
Milton Brown and the Founding of Western Swing   *Cary Ginell, with special*
  assistance from Roy Lee Brown
Santiago de Murcia's "Códice Saldívar No. 4": A Treasury of Secular Guitar
  Music from Baroque Mexico   *Craig H. Russell*
The Sound of the Dove: Singing in Appalachian Primitive Baptist Churches
  Beverly Bush Patterson
Heartland Excursions: Ethnomusicological Reflections on Schools of Music
  Bruno Nettl
Doowop: The Chicago Scene   *Robert Pruter*
Blue Rhythms: Six Lives in Rhythm and Blues   *Chip Deffaa*
Shoshone Ghost Dance Religion: Poetry Songs and Great Basin Context
  Judith Vander
Go Cat Go! Rockabilly Music and Its Makers   *Craig Morrison*
'Twas Only an Irishman's Dream: The Image of Ireland and the Irish in American
  Popular Song Lyrics, 1800–1920   *William H. A. Williams*
Democracy at the Opera: Music, Theater, and Culture in New York City,
  1815–60   *Karen Ahlquist*
Fred Waring and the Pennsylvanians   *Virginia Waring*
Woody, Cisco, and Me: Seamen Three in the Merchant Marine   *Jim Longhi*
Behind the Burnt Cork Mask: Early Blackface Minstrelsy and Antebellum
  American Popular Culture   *William J. Mahar*
Going to Cincinnati: A History of the Blues in the Queen City   *Steven C. Tracy*
Pistol Packin' Mama: Aunt Molly Jackson and the Politics of Folksong
  Shelly Romalis
Sixties Rock: Garage, Psychedelic, and Other Satisfactions   *Michael Hicks*
The Late Great Johnny Ace and the Transition from R&B to Rock 'n' Roll
  James M. Salem
Tito Puente and the Making of Latin Music   *Steven Loza*

Juilliard: A History   *Andrea Olmstead*

Understanding Charles Seeger, Pioneer in American Musicology   *Edited by Bell Yung and Helen Rees*

Mountains of Music: West Virginia Traditional Music from *Goldenseal*   *Edited by John Lilly*

Alice Tully: An Intimate Portrait   *Albert Fuller*

A Blues Life   *Henry Townsend, as told to Bill Greensmith*

Long Steel Rail: The Railroad in American Folksong (2d ed.)   *Norm Cohen*

The Golden Age of Gospel   *Text by Horace Clarence Boyer; photography by Lloyd Yearwood*

Aaron Copland: The Life and Work of an Uncommon Man   *Howard Pollack*

Louis Moreau Gottschalk   *S. Frederick Starr*

Race, Rock, and Elvis   *Michael T. Bertrand*

Theremin: Ether Music and Espionage   *Albert Glinsky*

Poetry and Violence: The Ballad Tradition of Mexico's Costa Chica   *John H. McDowell*

The Bill Monroe Reader   *Edited by Tom Ewing*

Music in Lubavitcher Life   *Ellen Koskoff*

Zarzuela: Spanish Operetta, American Stage   *Janet L. Sturman*

Bluegrass Odyssey: A Documentary in Pictures and Words, 1966–86   *Carl Fleischhauer and Neil V. Rosenberg*

That Old-Time Rock & Roll: A Chronicle of an Era, 1954–63   *Richard Aquila*

Labor's Troubadour   *Joe Glazer*

American Opera   *Elise K. Kirk*

Don't Get above Your Raisin': Country Music and the Southern Working Class   *Bill C. Malone*

John Alden Carpenter: A Chicago Composer   *Howard Pollack*

Heartbeat of the People: Music and Dance of the Northern Pow-wow   *Tara Browner*

My Lord, What a Morning: An Autobiography   *Marian Anderson*

Marian Anderson: A Singer's Journey   *Allan Keiler*

Charles Ives Remembered: An Oral History   *Vivian Perlis*

Henry Cowell, Bohemian   *Michael Hicks*

Rap Music and Street Consciousness   *Cheryl L. Keyes*

Louis Prima   *Garry Boulard*

Marian McPartland's Jazz World: All in Good Time   *Marian McPartland*

Robert Johnson: Lost and Found   *Barry Lee Pearson and Bill McCulloch*

Bound for America: Three British Composers   *Nicholas Temperley*

Lost Sounds: Blacks and the Birth of the Recording Industry, 1890–1919   *Tim Brooks*

Burn, Baby! BURN! The Autobiography of Magnificent Montague   *Magnificent Montague with Bob Baker*

The University of Illinois Press
is a founding member of the
Association of American University Presses.

Composed in 10/13.5 Janson Text
with Electra display
by Barbara Evans
at the University of Illinois Press
Manufactured by Thomson-Shore, Inc.

University of Illinois Press
1325 South Oak Street
Champaign, IL 61820-6903
www.press.uillinois.edu